LEGAL REASONING AND
POLITICAL CONFLICT

Cass R. Sunstein

LEGAL
REASONING
AND
POLITICAL
CONFLICT

OXFORD UNIVERSITY PRESS
New York   Oxford

Oxford University Press

Oxford   New York
Athens   Auckland   Bangkok   Bogotá   Bombay
Buenos Aires   Calcutta   Cape Town   Dar es Salaam
Delhi   Florence   Hong Kong   Istanbul   Karachi
Kuala Lumpur   Madras   Madrid   Melbourne
Mexico City   Nairobi   Paris   Singapore
Taipei   Tokyo   Toronto   Warsaw

and associated companies in
Berlin   Ibadan

Copyright © 1996 by Oxford University Press, Inc.

First published by Oxford University Press, Inc., 1996

First issued as an Oxford University Press paperback, 1998

Oxford is a registered trademark of Oxford University Press

Library of Congress Cataloging-in-Publication Data
Sunstein, Cass R.
Legal reasoning and political conflict / Cass R. Sunstein.
p.   cm.   Includes bibliographical references and index.
ISBN 0-19-510082-4
ISBN 0-19-511804-9 (Pbk.)
1. Law—Methodology.   2. Law and politics.   3. Law—United States—Methodology.
4. Law—Political aspects—United States.   I. Title.
K213.S86   1996   340'.11—dc20   95-25265

2 4 6 8 10 9 7 5 3 1

Printed in the United States of America
on acid-free paper

For Ellen

Preface

What is "legal reasoning"? The question is important not only for law-yers and law students, but also for ordinary citizens thinking about the place of law, and courts of law, in society. In nearly every nation, legal reasoning can seem impenetrable, mysterious, baroque. Sometimes it does not seem to be a form of reasoning at all. In this book I try to reduce some of the mystery. As we will see, legal reasoning is far easier to understand if we attend to the basic methods and goals of lawyers and judges: thinking with analogies; creating, using, and modifying rules; adopting particular practices of interpretation; and allocating authority to certain people and certain institutions. Much of this book is designed to attend to these methods and goals, and to explain how they produce legal outcomes. In law, as in families, schools, workplaces, and elsewhere, people reason in ways that grow out of the particular social role in which they find themselves.

In describing legal reasoning, I aim to focus attention on the most distinctive characteristic of the judge's job: to decide concrete controver-sies involving particular people and particular facts. To decide cases, a good judge is likely to want to know about the particular facts. The judge is not likely to express broad views on the great issues of the day, at least if those views do not contribute to the particular outcome. The judge's intense focus on concrete controversies leads participants in law toward a special approach, one that is especially well-adapted to a situation of fundamental social disagreement: considerable distrust of ambitious, large-scale theories. Ordinary courts are reluctant to traffic in abstractions. Judges often proceed on a case-by-case basis; they are practitioners of the old, much-reviled, and indispensable art of *casuistry*.

This point is a clue to a mystery: how the enterprise of law is possible in a heterogeneous society composed of people who sharply disagree about fundamental values. When legal reasoning operates at its best, participants in law are attuned to the fact that people legitimately disagree on basic principles. They try to resolve cases without taking sides on large-scale social controversies. They produce *incompletely theorized agreements on particular outcomes*, a central feature of legal reasoning and a topic that receives considerable attention in this book. Good judges recognize that fundamental decisions are best made democratically, not judicially.

For similar reasons, judges—and here we can speak too of others who design legal requirements, including legislators, administrators, and ordinary citizens—have a complex and ambivalent attitude toward rules. Certainly they do not oppose rules as a general matter. Of course people engaged in legal reasoning have no rule against rules. Judges understand that rules help people to plan their affairs. They understand that rules can constrain official arbitrariness, discrimination, and caprice. But rules may misfire, precisely because they are too rigid and because they are laid down in advance; they can go badly wrong when applied to concrete cases not anticipated when the rule was set down. Does a 60 mile-per-hour speed limit ban an ambulance from rushing to the hospital, or a police officer from driving as fast as he must to apprehend a fleeing suspect? In some cases, the general rule may be far too general to work well; and there may lie, in this example and in this possibility, a pervasive concern about using rules to order diverse human affairs. Much of legal reasoning reflects this concern.

A good deal of my discussion is descriptive, but I attempt as well to offer some arguments of my own about the limits of both theories and rules. These arguments will go against the grain, at least in the United States, and probably more generally. Many Americans, and not a few non-Americans, have been greatly stirred by the opinions of the Warren Court, especially in the area of race relations, where the Court is often thought to have revolutionized American society. Many people think that the Supreme Court of the United States is the major "forum of principle" in American government. Many people think that the Court's basic job is to describe and elaborate the best and most abstract national commitments, including the defining ideals of liberty and equality. American thought in this vein has had a large international influence, not least in Eastern Europe in the aftermath of Communism. We are also in the midst of a period of enormous enthusiasm for rule-bound justice. The rule of law is often thought to require firm rules laid down in advance, and enthusiasm for the rule of law, understood in terms of rule-bound justice, has enjoyed an enormous revival in post-Communist societies.

There is much truth in these conventional views. An important place should be found for high-level, abstract thinking in democratic deliberation; consider the work of James Madison, Abraham Lincoln, Franklin Roosevelt, or Martin Luther King, Jr. Some of the most riveting and even glorious moments in any nation's legal system come when a high court recognizes an abstract principle involving, for example, human liberty or equality. Consider the American Supreme Court's invalidation of racial segregation, or its announcement that sex discrimination is usually unacceptable in a nation committed to the equal protection of the laws. Certainly rules deserve a large and honored place in any system of law. But I do mean to suggest that those engaged in legal reasoning are aware that rules are sometimes not feasible or desirable, and also that the most important political judgments come not from courts, but instead from democratic arenas. Even more, I mean to insist on the important virtues of the law's distinctive approach to the problem of social heterogeneity and disagreement: agreements on results and on low-level principles amid confusion or dissensus on large-scale theories.

With these claims I hope, of course, to make a contribution to debates about the nature of law and about the possibility and character of legal reasoning. In the process I hope to describe how people who disagree on basic principle might find a way to live together harmoniously and with mutual respect. I am aiming also to offer a general introduction to the study of law and legal thinking. The introduction is designed especially for people who want to know what the enterprise of law is all about, whether or not they are actually embarking on the formal study of law. To this end I have avoided technical terms and assumed no prior knowledge of law. As we will see, the distinctive concerns and tools of the law are by no means limited to law.

This book grows out of the 1994 Tanner Lectures in Human Values, delivered at Harvard University in November 1994. I am especially grateful to my audiences at Harvard for their extraordinary graciousness and for their probing comments and questions. Of the many people who offered help on that occasion, I single out for special thanks my commentators Jean Hampton and Jeremy Waldron, and also Joshua Cohen, Christine Korsgaard, Martha Minow, Martha Nussbaum, John Rawls, Tim Scanlon, and Amartya Sen. I also drew on some material here for the 1995 Wesson Lectures on Democracy at Stanford University, where I received many helpful suggestions. Susan Moller Okin, Kathleen Sullivan, and John Ferejohn offered especially valuable thoughts and criticisms in connection with the lectures.

For extremely helpful comments on the manuscript, I am grateful to Bruce Ackerman, Alexander Blankenagel, Daniel Brudney, Ruth Chang, Joshua Cohen, Robert Cooter, Richard Craswell, Einer Elhague, Jon Elster, Charles Fried, Amy Gutmann, Don Herzog, Stephen Holmes, Bonnie Honig, Elena Kagan, Dan Kahan, Oliver Lepsius, Larry Lessig, Saul Levmore, William Meadow, Martha Minow, Carl Nichols, Martha Nussbaum, Susan Moller Okin, Wiktor Osistynski, Richard Pildes, Richard Posner, Joseph Raz, Lisa Ruddick, Frederick Schauer, Stephen Schulhofer, Keith Sharfman, Anne-Marie Slaughter, David Strauss, Mark Tushnet, Candace Vogler, Lloyd Weinreb, and Leon Wieseltier; Ackerman, Elster, Holmes, Posner, and Strauss deserve particular thanks, for each has provided over a decade of relevant discussion and also several rounds of comments. I am grateful also to participants in a work-in-progress lunch at the University of Chicago; to members of legal theory workshops at Oxford University and the University of California, Berkeley; to my editor, Helen McInnis, for her encouragement and valuable suggestions; to Sophie Clark for extremely helpful thoughts and for research assistance; and to Marlene Vellinga for secretarial help. Some parts of this book have appeared, though in much different form, in three essays: On Analogical Reasoning, 106 Harvard Law Review 741 (1993); Incompletely Theorized Agreements, 108 Harvard Law Review 1733 (1995); and Problems with Rules, 86 California Law Review 953 (1995). I am grateful to the Harvard and California Law Reviews for permission to include some previously published material here. For financial support I thank the John M. Olin Foundation Fund and the Russell Baker Scholars Fund.

As I look over this long list of names and institutions, I see very clearly that this book is a product of many voices and many hands; and I am more grateful than I can say to my friends and colleagues for their help and support.

Chicago   C.R.S.
October 1995

Contents

LEGAL REASONING AND POLITICAL CONFLICT

We think utility, or happiness, much too complex and indefinite
an end to be sought except through the medium of various sec-
ondary ends, concerning which there may be, and often is,
agreement among persons who differ in their ultimate standard;
and about which there does in fact prevail a much greater una-
nimity among thinking persons, than might be supposed from
their diametrical divergence on the great questions of moral
metaphysics. As mankind are more nearly of one nature, than of
one opinion about their own nature, they are more easily
brought to agree in their intermediate principles . . . than in
their first principles. . . .

John Stuart Mill, Bentham

One other capital imperfection [of the Common Law
is] . . . the *unaccommodatingness* of its rules. . . . Hence the hardness of heart which is a sort of endemical disease of lawyers. . . . Mischief being almost their incessant occupation, and
the greatest merits they can attain being the firmness with
which they persevere in the task of doing partial evil for the
sake of that universal good which consists in steady adherence
to established rules, a judge thus circumstanced is obliged to di-
vest himself of that anxious sensibility, which is one of the most
useful as well as amiable qualities of the legislator.

Jeremy Bentham, Of Laws in General

Introduction: Law Amid Diversity

The Problem and a Solution

There is a familiar image of justice. She is a single figure. She is a goddess, emphatically not a human being. She is blindfolded. She holds a scale.

In the real world, the law cannot be represented by a single figure. Legal institutions consist of many people. Courts are run by human beings, not by a god or goddess. Judges need not be blindfolded; what they should be blind *to* is perhaps the key question for law. And judges have no scale. Far from having a scale, they must operate in the face of a particular kind of social heterogeneity: sharp and often intractable disagreements on matters of basic principle.

Some of these disagreements are explicitly religious in character. What is the role of religion in schools? Some of them involve conflicts among religion, agnosticism, and atheism. Should sexual practices be regulated on religious grounds? Other disagreements are fundamental in the sense that they involve people's deepest and most defining commitments. What is the appropriate conception of liberty and equality? How should people educate their children? Is there such a thing as free will? Should government punish people on the basis of deterrence only, or should it consider retribution as well? Is the free speech principle about democracy or instead autonomy? Just how fundamental is the right to private property? What is the appropriate conception of gender relations?

3

There is much dispute about whether well-functioning democracies try to resolve such disagreements, and about how they should do so if they do try. Perhaps government should seek what John Rawls describes as an "overlapping consensus"[1] among diverse reasonable people, thus allowing agreements to be made among Kantians, utilitarians, Aristotelians, Christians, and others. Perhaps diverse people in America, England, South Africa, or Russia might commit themselves in a founding document to certain political rights: freedom of speech, religious liberty, political participation, racial equality, and others. Thus a sympathetic observer refers to the "hope that we can achieve social unity in a democracy through shared commitment to abstract principles."[2]

This is certainly possible. But an investigation of actual democracies, and especially of law in actual democracies, raises many questions. Democracies, and law in democracies, must deal with people who distrust abstractions altogether. Participants in law are no exception. Judges are certainly not ordinary citizens. But neither are they philosophers. More particularly, judges have to decide a lot of cases, and they have to decide them quickly. Many decisions must be made rapidly in the face of apparently intractable social disagreements on a wide range of basic principles. These disagreements will be reflected within the judiciary and other adjudicative institutions as well as within the citizenry at large. At least this is so if adjudicative institutions include, as they should, some of the range of views reflected in society generally.

In addition to facing the pressures of time, these diverse people must find a way to live with one another. They should also show each other a high degree of mutual respect or reciprocity. Mutual respect may well entail a reluctance to attack one another's most basic or defining commitments, at least if it is not necessary to do so in order to decide particular controversies. Participants in law, as well as in democratic debate generally, do well to follow this counsel.

My largest suggestion in this book is that well-functioning legal systems tend to adopt a special strategy for producing stability and agreement in the midst of social disagreement and pluralism: Arbiters of legal controversies try to produce *incompletely theorized agreements*. Sometimes these agreements do involve abstractions, accepted amid severe disagreements on particular cases; thus people who disagree on pornography and hate speech can accept a general free speech principle, and those who argue about homosexuality and disability can accept an abstract anti-discrimination principle. But sometimes incompletely theorized agreements involve concrete outcomes rather than abstractions, and because of the special importance of this phenomenon in law, this is what I will be emphasizing here.

When people disagree on an abstraction—Is equality more important than liberty? Does free will exist?—they often move to a level of greater particularity. This practice has an especially notable feature: It enlists silence, on certain basic questions, as a device for producing convergence despite disagreement, uncertainty, limits of time and capacity, and heterogeneity. Incompletely theorized agreements are a key to legal reasoning. They are an important source of social stability and an important way for people to demonstrate mutual respect, in law especially but also in liberal democracy as a whole.

Consider some examples. People may believe that it is worthwhile to protect endangered species, while having quite diverse theories about why this is so. Some people may stress what they see as human obligations to species or nature as such; others may point to the role of endangered species in producing ecological stability; still others may emphasize that obscure species can provide valuable medicines for human beings. Similarly, people may invoke many different grounds for their shared belief that the law should protect labor unions against certain kinds of employer coercion. Some people emphasize the democratic functions of unions; others think that unions are necessary for industrial peace; others believe that unions protect basic rights. So too people may favor a rule of strict liability for certain torts from multiple diverse starting-points—with some people rooting their judgments in economic efficiency, others in distributive goals, still others in conceptions of basic rights.

Of course people often disagree about these issues. What I am emphasizing here is that much of the time, the agreements that we obtain are a result of incompletely theorized judgments. Examples of this kind are exceptionally common. They are the day-to-day stuff of law.

The agreement on particulars is incompletely theorized in the sense that the relevant participants are clear on the result without agreeing on the most general theory that accounts for it. Often they can agree on an opinion or a rationale, usually offering low-level or mid-level principles. They may agree that a rule—reducing water pollution, allowing workers to unionize—makes sense without entirely agreeing on the foundations of their belief. They may accept an outcome—reaffirming the right to have an abortion, protecting sexually explicit art—without understanding or converging on an ultimate ground for that acceptance. What accounts for the opinion, in terms of a full-scale theory of the right or the good, is left unexplained.

Incompletely theorized results have obvious disadvantages; but in a legal system, they have crucial virtues as well. Those virtues are connected with the limited place of courts of law in a democratic society, where fundamental principles are best discussed and announced in democratic arenas.

My emphasis on incompletely theorized agreements is intended partly as descriptive. These agreements are a pervasive phenomenon in Anglo-American law—my emphasis here—and they can be found in many other legal systems as well. They are also a clue to the enterprise of adjudication and the common law in general and to the particular practice of analogical reasoning. Such agreements play an important role in any well-functioning legal regime. Their persistence offers a challenge to people who think that areas of law actually reflect some general theory, involving (for example) utilitarian or Kantian understandings.[3]

But my goal is not simply descriptive. Any account of a subject as complex as legal reasoning will inevitably be selective, and hence it will have evaluative dimensions. In any case I seek to make a series of claims about the appropriate nature of law. There are special virtues to avoiding large-scale theoretical conflicts. There are special virtues to incompletely theorized judgments in law. Incompletely theorized agreements can operate as foundations for both rules and analogies, and such agreements are especially well-suited to the institutional limits of the judiciary. Courts consist of highly diverse people, who have a weak democratic pedigree and limited fact-finding capacity, and who must render many decisions, live together, avoid error to the extent possible, and show respect to each other, to the people who come before them, and to those affected by their decisions. Incompletely theorized agreements are an appropriate response to this situation.

In social life, people reason in ways that grow out of the particular role in which they find themselves. They know what actions are permissible, and what actions are off-limits, only because of their role. If the point is not often noticed, it is only because it is so self-evident. People take their roles for granted and live accordingly. Consider the close relationship between reasoning and role for such diverse figures as parents, students, waiters, doctors, employees, consumers, and automobile drivers. Any particular role is accompanied by a set of relevant and irrelevant considerations. What I am urging here is that the particular social role of judges fits well with incompletely theorized agreements.

Of course it would be wrong to say that there is no place in society or law for ambitious theories. Such theories are an important part of academic life, which can influence political institutions; certainly such theories are legitimately a part of democratic deliberation. Indeed, many of the most important moments in American politics—the Civil War, the New Deal, the founding itself—have involved large theories, and in many cases the nation has converged on some such theory. Even judges might accept a general theory if it can be shown to be a good one and if they can be persuaded to agree to it. But most participants in law are, and should be, very cautious before taking this step. In American government and in all well-functioning constitutional democracies, the real forum of high principle is politics, not the judiciary—and the most fundamental principles are developed democratically, not in courtrooms.

How People Converge

It seems clear that people may agree on a *correct* outcome even though they do not have a theory to account for their judgments. Jones may know that dropped objects fall, that bee stings hurt, that hot air rises, and that snow melts, without knowing exactly why these facts are true. The same is true for morality. Johnson may know that slavery is wrong, that government may not stop political protests, that every person should have just one vote, and that it is bad for government to take property unless it pays for it, without knowing exactly or entirely why these things are so. Moral judgments may be right or true even if they are reached by people who lack a full account of those judgments.

The same is true for law. Judge Wilson may know that under the American Constitution discrimination against the handicapped is generally permitted, whereas discrimination against women is generally banned, without having a full account of why the Constitution is so understood. Judge Thompson may know that if you steal someone's property, you must return it, without having a full account of why this principle has been enacted into law. We may thus offer an epistemological point: People can know *that* x is true without entirely knowing *why* x is true. Very often this is so for particular conclusions about law.

There is a political point as well. Sometimes people can agree on individual judgments even if they disagree on general theory. Diverse judges may agree that *Roe v. Wade*,[4] protecting the right to choose abortion, should not be overruled, though the reasons that lead each of them to that conclusion sharply diverge. Some people think that the Court should respect its own precedents; others think that *Roe* was rightly decided as a way of protecting women's equality; others think that the case was rightly decided as a way of protecting privacy; others think that the decision reflects an appropriate judgment about the social role of religion; still others think that restrictions on abortion are unlikely to protect fetuses in the world, and so the decision is good for pragmatic reasons. We can find incompletely theorized political agreements on particular outcomes in many areas of law and politics—on both sides of racial discrimination controversies, both sides of disputes over criminal justice, both sides of disputes over health care.

Rules and Analogies

I will give special attention to the two most important methods for resolving disputes without obtaining agreement on first principles: rules and analogies. Both of these devices attempt to promote a major goal of a heterogeneous society: *to make it possible to obtain agreement where agreement is necessary, and to make it unnecessary to obtain agreement where agreement is impossible.* People can often agree on what rules mean even when they agree on very little else. And in the face of persistent disagreement or uncertainty about what morality generally requires, people can reason about particular cases by reference to analogies. They point to cases in which their judgments are firm. They proceed from those firm judgments to the more difficult ones. This is how judges often operate; it is also how ordinary people tend to think.

We might consider in this regard Justice Stephen Breyer's discussion of one of the key compromises reached by the seven members of the United States Sentencing Commission.[5] As Breyer describes it, a central issue was how to proceed in the face of highly disparate philosophical premises about the goals of criminal punishment. Some people asked the Commission to follow an approach to punishment based on "just desserts"—an approach that would rank criminal conduct in terms of severity. But different commissioners had very different views about how different crimes should be ranked. In these circumstances, there could be an odd form of deliberation in which criminal punishments became more, and more irrationally, severe, because some commissioners would insist that the crime under consideration was worse than the previously ranked crimes. In any case agreement on a rational system would be unlikely to follow from efforts by the seven commissioners to rank crimes in terms of severity.

Other people urged the Commission to use a model of deterrence. There were, however, major problems with this approach. We lack empirical evidence that could link detailed variations in punishment to prevention of crime, and the seven members of the Commission were unlikely to agree that deterrence provides a full account of the aims of criminal sentencing. An approach based on deterrence seemed no better than an approach based on just deserts.

In these circumstances, what route did the Commission follow? In fact the Commission abandoned large theories altogether. It adopted no general view about the appropriate aims of criminal sentencing. Instead, the Commision abandoned high theory and adopted a rule—one founded on precedent: "It decided to base the Guidelines primarily upon typical, or average, actual past practice." Consciously articulated explanations, not based on high theory, were used to support particular departures from the past.

Justice Breyer sees this effort as a necessary means of obtaining agreement and rationality within a multimember body charged with avoiding unjustifiably wide variations in sentencing. Thus his more colorful oral presentation: "Why didn't the Commission sit down and really go and rationalize this thing and not just take history? The short answer to that is: we couldn't. We couldn't because there are such good arguments all over the place pointing in opposite directions. . . . Try listing all the crimes that there are in rank order of punishable merit. . . . Then collect results from your friends and see if they all match. I will tell you they don't."[6]

This example suggests a more general point. Through both analogies and rules, it is often possible for people to converge on particular outcomes without resolving large-scale issues of the right or the good. People can decide what to do when they disagree on exactly how to think. For judges at least, this is an important virtue.

Agreements and Justice

The fact that people can obtain an agreement of this sort—about the value and meaning of a rule or about the existence of a sound analogy—is no guarantee of a good outcome, whatever may be our criteria for deciding whether an outcome is good. A rule may provide that no one over fifty is permitted to work, and we all may agree what it means; but such a rule would be pretty bad, since it would be neither just nor efficient. Perhaps the Sentencing Commission incorporated judgments that were based on ignorance, confusion, or prejudice. Certainly its judgment deserves support only if the average of past practice was not demonstrably wrong from the standpoint of appropriate theories of criminal justice. Perhaps the commission would have done better to think harder about those theories.

Some of the same things can be said about analogies. People in positions of authority may agree that a ban on same-sex marriages is acceptable, because it is analogous to a ban on marriages between uncles and nieces; but the analogy may be misconceived, because there are relevant differences between the two cases, and because the similarities are far from decisive. The fact that people agree that case A is analogous to case B does not mean that case A *or* case B is rightly decided. Perhaps case A should not be taken for granted. Perhaps case A should not be selected as the relevant foundation for analogical thinking; perhaps case z is more pertinent. Perhaps case B is not really like case A. Perhaps the outcomes in the cases should turn on a careful empirical assessment of social consequences of the possible legal rules, and analogy will not tell us much about those consequences. Problems with analogies and low-level thinking might lead us to be more ambitious. We may well be pushed in the direction of general theory—and toward broader and more controversial claims—precisely because analogical reasoners offer an inadequate and incompletely theorized account of relevant similarities or relevant differences.

All this should be sufficient to show that the virtues of decisions by rule and by analogy are partial. But no system of law is likely to be either just or efficient if it dispenses with rules and analogies. In fact it is not likely even to be feasible.

Rules and Cases? Rules Opposed to Cases?

Thus far I have discussed the contrast between ambitious theories and incompletely theorized judgments. Let us now turn to a quite different contrast, between rules and case-by-case judgments. The opposition will point the way toward some complexities in the old ideal of the rule of law. It will also lead toward a recognition of the virtues of casuistry. For lawyers, as for ordinary people dealing with ethical and political problems, casuistry—understood as analysis of cases unaccompanied by rules—continues to play an important, indeed indispensable role.

The opposition between rule-bound justice and casuistry is connected with two familiar conceptions of legal judgment. The first, associated with Jeremy Bentham[7] and more recently with Justices Hugo Black and Antonin Scalia, places a high premium on the creation and application of general rules. On this view, public authorities should avoid open-ended standards or close attention to individual circumstances. They should attempt instead to give guidance to lower courts, future legislators, and ordinary citizens through *clear, abstract rules laid down in advance of actual applications.*

The second conception, associated with William Blackstone and more recently with Justices Felix Frankfurter and John Marshall Harlan, places a high premium on *law-making at the point of application* through case-by-case decisions, narrowly tailored to the particulars of individual circumstances. On this view, judges should stay close to the details of the controversy before them and avoid broader rulings altogether. The problem with broad rulings is that they tend to overreach; they may be unreasonable as applied to cases not before the court. In the United States, this point marks an ongoing debate within the Supreme Court.[8]

It would not be easy to overstate the importance of the controversy between the two views. The choice between rules and rulelessness arises in every area of law; it often involves our most fundamental liberties. Should students be admitted into universities on the basis of rules or particularized judgments? May free speech be abridged when the government can show that it has good reasons for the abridgement in the particular case, or are categorical rules the best way to implement the free speech guarantee? Is sex discrimination always forbidden or might it be allowed if the particular circumstances make it seem justifiable and noninvidious? Should government employment, or grants of taxpayer money for the arts, be offered on the basis of a close assessment of particular cases, or instead on the basis of general rules?

In every area of legal regulation—the environment, occupational safety and health, energy policy, communications, control of monopoly power—it is necessary to choose between general rules and case-by-case decisions. In describing these choices, I explore a common dilemma for law, show how legal systems make space for both rules and rulelessness, and explain when legal systems are likely to move toward or away from rules.

Aside from description, I venture some claims about the appropriate place of rules and rulelessness and try to identify solutions to the problems posed by both. In its purest form, enthusiasm for genuinely case-specific decisions makes no sense. Any judgment about a particular case depends on the use of principles or reasons. Any principles or reasons are, by their very nature, broader than the case for which they are designed. We may acknowledge that nominees for the United States Supreme Court often answer hard questions—Where do you stand on abortion? On affirmative action? On electronic eavesdropping?—by saying: "That would depend on the circumstances of the particular case." But often, at least, this answer is rightly viewed as a dodge. Case-by-case particularism is not a promising foundation for law.

In some circumstances, however, enthusiasm for rules is senseless too.

Often general rules will be poorly suited to the new circumstances that turn up as a result of unanticipated developments. Can we really design good rules to govern developing communications technologies or to say what sorts of accommodations should be made for disabled people? Sometimes public authorities cannot design general rules because they lack relevant information. Sometimes general rules will fail because we seek subtle judgments about a range of particulars. In short, truly general rules are a mixed blessing for a system of law.

These considerations help point the way toward a more refined understanding of the rule of law. A system committed to that ideal is not committed to full specification of outcomes before actual cases arise. Untrammeled discretion is indeed inconsistent with the rule of law. But there are many advantages to close examination of particular cases, and the rule of law does not forbid the casuistical devices characteristic of many legal systems: analogical reasoning, guidelines, principles, judgment by reference to "standards" that do not qualify as rules, judgment by reference to "factors" rather than rules.

With an understanding of these devices, we will be able to appreciate the complexity of the idea of the rule of law, and hence to see the possibility of avoiding untrammeled discretion while also making space for particularistic forms of argument—where law is made, in part, at the point of application. We will also be able to identify solutions to the dilemmas posed by the pervasive need to choose between rules and rulelessness. Thus we will see the special virtues of *privately adaptable rules*, which allow flexibility for ordinary people; the existence, in well-functioning legal systems, of *legitimate rule revisions* by both public officials and private citizens; and the advantages of investigating particular contexts to see whether rules or rulelessness pose the more serious risks.

1

Reasoning and Legal Reasoning

Does law have special forms of logic? Does it offer a distinctive form of reasoning? To both questions, the simplest answer is no. The forms of logic and reasoning in law are entirely familiar—the same forms as elsewhere.

But the simplest answer is too simple. Participants in law do reason with their own conventions, and they do create and face special constraints. Participants in law have their own vocabularies and their own tools. They are concerned above all with issues of legitimate authority; they attempt to allocate power to the right people. And because of the particular social roles that lawyers and judges occupy, they think, in a sense, in their own ways. It is for this reason that legal thinking is not economics, or politics, or philosophy.

Much of what lawyers know is a set of practices, conventions, and outcomes that is hard to reduce to rules, that sometimes operates without being so reduced, and that is often just taken for granted. This background knowledge makes legal interpretation possible, and it sharply constrains legal judgment. If a law protects "the free exercise of religion," or if it forbids "unreasonable trade practices," it could, in the abstract, mean an infinitely wide range of things. Lawyers know how these terms are understood; they can point to a range of prototypical examples. If they are specialists, they have a clear sense of how these terms will be applied

13

to many particular cases, and they take for granted a set of understandings that, to nonlawyers or to people from other cultures, might seem weird or exotic.

This chapter deals with the classic sources of legal judgment—rules, standards, guidelines, principles, and analogies. It also discusses interpretive practices. An exploration of the sources of legal judgment will help to establish the relative independence of legal reasoning. It will also show that with the (incomplete) exception of rules, all of these sources make space for case-by-case judgments, in which the concrete details of the dispute at hand may matter a great deal.

It makes sense to begin, however, with ways of reasoning that have some place within law, and certainly within the academic criticism of law, but that cannot be described as special to law or as the traditional lawyer's tools. I offer a brief outline, one that is far from exhaustive, but that is designed to help us see what is special about legal thinking and also to set the stage for what is to come.

Theories and Deduction

Ethical, political, and even legal problems are often discussed in terms of some general theory. Indeed, this method seems to be increasingly popular in American law schools, though not in courts. By a general theory, I mean an approach to law that specifies a simple and (usually) unitary value, that operates at a high level of abstraction, and that decides cases by bringing the general theory to bear. Utilitarianism and economic analysis of law are especially familiar examples of this form of reasoning. Both utilitarianism and economics operate through specifying a single, general goal by which to evaluate outcomes. Thus we might ask whether a certain rule of contract law maximizes utility, and if we find this question too hard to answer, we might ask if the rule maximizes wealth. Some conceptions of autonomy or liberty have a similar function; consider the idea that the law of contract, or the law governing free speech, should be organized around a particular idea of autonomy. Perhaps judges should specify a certain conception of autonomy and decide free speech cases according to that conception.

An approach of this kind operates deductively. Results in particular cases are viewed as a logical consequence of the general theory. For example: The equal protection clause of the Constitution forbids legislation stigmatizing members of racial minorities; affirmative action imposes no stigma; therefore affirmative action is constitutionally acceptable. Or: The law should maximize efficiency; a system of negligence, in which people pay for harms they cause only if they behave unreasonably, is less efficient than one of strict liability, in which people pay for all harms they cause; the law should therefore be based on strict liability.

The general approach thus works by constructing a broad theory and then by approaching particular cases through the lens of that theory. The theory itself may be constructed on the basis of engagement with a range of particular cases or with appeal to "common sense." Thus many utilitarians claim that they are simply giving order and system to people's ordinary, concrete judgments; on this view, ordinary judgments about particular cases do play a role in generating the theory. But once the theory is in place—once it is established—individual cases are tested not by comparing one against another, but by exploring them in light of the theory. And some people who endorse general theories do not like to rely on people's ordinary judgments about particular cases, which are dismissed as "intuitions." Those who use general theory are often insistently anticasuistical and quite willing to disregard the fact that people are disturbed by particular outcomes that seem counterintuitive but that have been compelled by the general theory.

For example, some approaches, associated with the work of Kant, insist on truth telling in all cases and are willing to accept the possibility that truth telling is compelled even if (for example) many people will be killed as a result. The utilitarian analogue is the apparent obligation to kill an innocent person if social welfare will thereby be promoted. Cost-benefit analysis, or economic approaches to law, find a similar case in the acknowledgment that, on economic grounds, rape should be legalized if rapists would be willing to pay more to rape than victims would pay to avoid rape.[1]

Judgments of this kind make believers in general theories seem fanatical. Indeed, we can understand fanaticism in law as an insistence on applying general principles to particular cases in which they lead to palpable absurdity. The point is not that exponents of any of these views cannot avoid the seemingly bizarre counterexample; exponents of general theories are often very ingenious in doing just this. The point is instead that those who endorse general theories need not make existing convictions about particular cases a constituent part of the method through which principles are constructed.

Is this an objection to general theories? Not necessarily. Sometimes the judgment that a particular outcome is palpably absurd or palpably unjust should not be given decisive weight, because that judgment may be revised after it is subject to critical scrutiny. Often society's relatively particular judgments—calling for slavery, for racial segregation, for sex inequality—have been overcome by showing that those judgments cannot survive encounter with more general judgments about what is right or what is good. For a modern example, consider the fact that the perceived correctness of a legal prohibition on homosexual relations has often served as a "fixed point" for legal and political inquiry. As we will see, considered judgments about particular cases should count as such only if they have survived encounter with a good deal else that is both general and particular.

It is notable that advocates of theories often work very hard to show that deductions from the theory are indeed consistent with our judgments about particular cases. Consider Robert Bork's effort to explain why his controversial approach to constitutional interpretation—calling for reliance on the "original understanding" of the Constitution, taken up in Chapter 8—is consistent with the outcome in the great school desegregation case *Brown v. Board of Education*.[2] It seems that a belief in the correctness of *Brown* is now a fixed point for inquiry, so that to remain plausible, any theory of constitutional interpretation must offer an explanation of why *Brown* was right. So too a large part of the argument for the economic analysis of law is that economic analysis appears to "account for" or "explain" a large number of well-established and apparently satisfactory common law cases and principles.

General theories are a natural ally of codification, which tries to organize and systematize the law, and a natural enemy of the common law, which tends to be quite unruly and to resist explanation according to theory. (The economic analysis of law is an exception, since, as we have just seen, it does attempt to explain the common law as more systematic than it appears.) It is therefore no surprise that Jeremy Bentham was both the founder of utilitarianism and the most vigorous advocate of "codification," a word that in fact he coined. Thus Bentham wrote with palpable disgust about the disadvantages and irrationality of casuistry and the common law approach, in which "general inferences" are "deduced from particular decisions."[3] Of course it is possible to support codification without endorsing general theory, and it is possible too to support general theory without endorsing codification, on the ground that the relevant theory is best elaborated through encounters with particular cases.

It is apparent too that any theory may seem hubristic and sectarian to many people. Some people will think that another theory would be better. Others will insist on the need to give great weight to people's judgments about particular cases, and they will say that such judgments ought not to be rejected merely because some theory says that they should. Still others will believe that morality is based not on a single value, but on a variety of irreducibly independent values, which are plural and diverse. Hence some of the problems with single-valued theories might be alleviated with non-reductive theories that recognize a plurality of human goods.

The Search for Reflective Equilibrium

Ethical, political, and legal problems might be evaluated not by applying a general theory, but instead on the basis of a careful process of comparing apparently plausible general theories with apparently plausible outcomes in particular cases. Drawing on John Rawls's notion of reflective equilibrium,[4] we might understand much reasoning, in law and elsewhere, to entail an effort to engage with general principles and with considered judgments about particular cases and with all possible principles and judgments in between. There are many things—abstract, concrete, intermediate—that each of us thinks to be true. These beliefs qualify as provisional "fixed points" for inquiry, since we have a high degree of confidence in them and cannot readily imagine that they could be wrong. In searching for reflective equilibrium, what we think tentatively to be the general theory is adjusted to conform to what we think to be our considered views about particular cases. The particular views are adjusted to conform to the general theory and vice-versa. Eventually, views at all levels of generality are brought into line with one another. Through this process we hope finally to reach a form of equilibrium. On Rawls's view, neither the particular nor the general should have priority in this process. Neither is foundational.

Many different conceptions of reflective equilibrium are possible. We might accord great weight to particular judgments or little weight to them; make different decisions about what counts as a distortion of our judgment; stress or downplay the role of abstract philosophical arguments; and reject or approve apparently emotional reactions. In moral and political theory, the value of the search for reflective equilibrium is much disputed. Any particular person might well want to bring his considered judgments into a coherent structure. But perhaps an outsider could believe, with good reason, that someone who has reached reflective equilibrium is nonetheless wrong, since some of the provisional fixed points that generated his equilibrium are rooted in prejudice or confusion. Someone from America or England, for example, might reject the ethical views of someone from Iraq, even if those views are part of an overall position that embodies reflective equilibrium.

Some aspects of the search for reflective equilibrium do play an important role in thinking about law. In deciding hard cases, judges and lawyers make an effort to bring their convictions, both general and particular, into some coherent order, and this is one way that they think through legal problems. Much of the first year of law school operates in this way. Thus, for example, the notion that only political speech receives special constitutional protection under the First Amendment might be abandoned if and when it appears that that notion would allow censorship of great art and literature. The goal of the resulting method would be to produce, at once, a full set of confident judgments about specific cases, accompanied by an abstract theory, or a set of principles, that is able to account for all of them. (As we will see, however, there are sharp limits on the extent to which the search for reflective equilibrium can provide a model for legal thinking.)

In contrast to people who use general theories, those who search for reflective equilibrium may well place a high premium on judgments about particular cases. But this contrast should not be overstated. We have seen that many who use general theories try to justify such theories by reference to what people already believe about particular cases, and those who seek reflective equilibrium acknowledge that judgments about particular cases are revisable. But it is certainly useful to ask whether convictions about particular cases should play a role in legal (or moral) thinking. Sometimes people rebel against the idea that theories should be adjusted because they lead to unacceptable particular outcomes.[5] For them, the adjustment is a form of brinkmanship or strategic thinking and a violation of the necessary commitment to general principle and neutrality itself.

This is an objection to both analogical reasoning (discussed in Chapter 3) and the search for reflective equilibrium insofar as both of these allow judgments about particular cases to play a large role in developing governing principles. But there is nothing improper about giving weight to particular convictions in deciding on the appropriate content of ethical or political theories. If judgments by human beings are inevitably a product of what human beings think, it is hardly wrong to question your general theory when that theory brings about results that seem to be an unacceptable part of your approach to the subject.

To understand what morality requires, or what the law should be in hard cases, we need to canvass what we—each of us—actually believe; there is no other place to look. For example, many people could not accept a system of free expression that would allow suppression of a harmless political protest; that is indeed a fixed point for inquiry. And for some people, any general theory about the Constitution must fail if it entails the incorrectness of *Brown v. Board of Education*[6] the validation or overruling of the abortion decision, *Roe v. Wade*,[7] or a particular consequence for affirmative action. Here too we have some possible fixed points. It may well be wrong for any of these particular outcomes to have such foundational status; disagreement in law is often based on disagreement about what are the appropriate fixed points. But some particular outcomes occupy so central a role that they constrain the category of permissible general theories. This is a conventional feature of practical reason as it operates in law and elsewhere, and it is not at all a reason for embarrassment.

Investigating Consequences: Means–Ends Rationality

The content of law should turn a good deal on the consequences of law. Sometimes reasoning in law, or elsewhere, is simply a way of discovering the actual effects of legal rules and of figuring out the best means of achieving given ends. Suppose, for example, that a court is asked to decide whether to impose a warranty of decent conditions, or "habitability," on landlords. An important issue is: What would be the effects of such a warranty on the housing market? Will the result of a warranty be higher rents, with particularly severe consequences for the poor? Will such warranties decrease the stock of available housing? Or suppose that a court is asked to rule that the First Amendment forbids the use of the libel law in any case brought by a government official. A key question is the real extent of the "chilling effect" of libel law on public discussion. Do libel laws actually deter criticism of public officials? Do such laws prevent truths or only falsehoods? To answer such questions, courts must look at the facts.

Means–ends rationality, including an investigation of consequences, should play a large role in law, in courts and elsewhere. Indeed, it should play a much larger role than it now does. Frequently the empirical dimensions of legal issues are not even identified as such. Frequently courts approach questions about likely consequences as if they could be answered by reference to other judicial holdings. But judges can usually be interested in the question of consequences, and it is fair to say that such interest has increased in the last few decades. Social science plays a role in law, and the role should grow in the future.

Sources of Law

I now turn to the classic tools of Anglo-American lawyers. These tools are not, however, limited to lawyers. They are the stuff of daily life. People often work with rules, which they perceive to be mandatory. So too the inclusion and exclusion of certain factors, as reasons for action, are key aspects of practical thinking. Whether Jones goes to work on Saturday depends on no rule, but on a range of factors. These involve family matters, the weather, Jones's spirits in general, whether basketball is on television. It does not depend on whether it is cold in Australia, whether GNP is growing, or whether the Russian Constitutional Court is in session.

Law works with included and excluded reasons as well. In fact, law has a toolbox containing many devices. Academic lawyers have customarily opposed rules ("do not go over 60 miles per hour") to standards ("do not drive unreasonably fast"), with rules seeming hard and fast and standards seeming open-ended. There is indeed a difference between rules and standards—between a ban on bringing dogs into restaurants and a ban on offensive behavior in restaurants. But the rules–standards debate captures only a part of the picture, and it is important to have a fuller sense of the repertoire of available devices. In this section I outline a number of them.

First, however, a cautionary note. Whether a legal provision is a rule, a presumption, a principle, a standard, a set of factors—or something else—cannot be decided in the abstract or even on the basis of a reading of the provision. Everything depends on the understandings and practices of people who interpret the provision. The American Constitution, for example, says that "Congress shall make no law abridging the freedom of speech." This provision could mean many things. It could operate as a rule if people take it as a flat ban on certain sorts of regulations. It could operate as a presumption if people see it as saying that Congress can regulate speech only if it makes a demonstration of harm of certain kinds and degrees. Or it could turn out to be a set of factors; once we parse notions like "abridging" and "the freedom of speech," perhaps we will decide cases on the basis of an inquiry into two, three, or more relevant considerations.

In short, the content and nature of a legal provision cannot be read off the provision. It is necessary to see what people take it to be. For this reason we should distinguish among three kinds of actors. The first is the person or institution that *issues* the relevant legal provision. The second is the person or institution that is *subject to* the provision. The third is the person or institution charged with the power to *interpret* the provision. The lawmaker has some power over those practices, but that power is limited. Even if lawmakers issue rules for interpretation, those rules will themselves need interpretation, and such rules cannot be exhaustive.

The effect of interpretive practice on the nature of law is of immense importance; it leads to complex interactions among lawmakers, people subject to law, and interpreters. In fact, an understanding of prevailing interpretive practice is a large part of legal reasoning, as I will discuss in Chapter 8.

Untrammeled Discretion

By "untrammeled discretion," I mean the capacity to exercise official power as one chooses, by reference to such considerations as one wants to consider, weighted as one wants to weigh them. A legal system cannot avoid some degree of discretion, in the form of some power to choose according to one's moral or political convictions. But a legal system can certainly make choices about how much discretion it wants various people to have.

A system of untrammeled discretion exists when there are no limits on what officials may consider in reaching a decision, and on how much weight various considerations deserve; hence there are no limits on the officials' power to decide what to do and why to do it. Both inputs and outputs are unconstrained. Consider the old idea, with a narrow but continuing influence on Anglo-American law, that "the King can do no wrong." In the real world, untrammeled discretion is rare (fortunately). But perhaps some police officers, in some nations, come very close to this sort of authority, in light of common understandings about law enforcement and the practical unavailability of review of their decisions.

Rules

Often a system of rules is thought to be the polar opposite of a system of untrammeled discretion. But there is no such polar opposition. Rules do not eliminate discretion. There is a continuum from rules to untrammeled discretion, with factors, standards, and guidelines falling in between.

Definition

The key characteristic of rules is that they attempt to specify outcomes before particular cases arise. By a system of rules I mean to refer to something very simple: *approaches to law that aspire to make legal judgments in advance of actual cases.* We have rules, or (better) ruleness, to the extent that the content of the law has been set down in advance of applications of the law. In the extreme case, all of the content of the law is given before cases arise. A key function of law is to assign entitlements—to say who owns what, to establish who may do what to whom. If this is so, a rule can thus be defined as *the full or nearly full before-the-fact assignment of legal entitlements, or the complete or nearly complete before-the-fact specification of legal outcomes.*

This is an ambitious goal—impossibly ambitious. As we will see, no approach to law can avoid a degree of casuistry, in the form of judgments made in the context of deciding actual cases. Nonetheless, it is possible to ensure that a wide range of judgments about particular cases will occur in advance. In fact, much of law consists of rulelike assignments of authority to certain people in the government and in the private sphere—governors, parents, legislators, employers, drivers, voters, accused criminals, teachers, and spouses all have certain legally conferred rights and duties by virtue of their roles.

Consider some possible examples of rules: Laws that impose a speed limit of 55 miles per hour, prohibit continued employment of airline pilots over the age of seventy, ban dogs from restaurants, and tell people not to smoke on airplanes. Of course hard cases may arise under all of these laws. Suppose that someone goes over 55 miles per hour to get his friend, who has just had a heart attack, to the hospital quickly; or that a police officer seeks to bring a police dog into a restaurant in response to a bomb threat. But these are unusual cases.

We might compare rule-bound judgments with a system in which, for example, a judge decides whether someone is liable for wrongdoing by seeing whether his conduct was "unreasonable" (assuming this term has not been given precise content in advance) or in which a judge decides whether a particular restriction on abortion imposes an "undue burden" on women (making the same assumption). In the purest case of rule-bound judgment, the responsibility of the decisionmaker is to find only the facts; the law need not be found. When rules are operating, an assessment of facts, combined with an ordinary understanding of grammar, semantics, and diction—and with more substantive understandings on which there is no dispute—is enough to decide the case.

It is important to distinguish here between mandatory rules and rules of thumb.[8] Rules of thumb merely offer guidance. They show what it ordinarily makes sense to do, but they are not binding, and they are not taken by themselves to create reasons for action. For example, you might think that you should ordinarily drive under 70 miles per hour on a highway, or that you should not bring your word processor to dinner at a friend's house, but these thoughts may be mere guidance, subject to reconsideration under the particular circumstances. Perhaps it is safe to go over 70 miles per hour on this particular highway? Perhaps your friend would like to try out your word processor or to have the pleasure of seeing you working on it? A rule of thumb can be understood as a summary of individually wise decisions, a summary that can be reassessed in each case. By contrast, a mandatory rule, whether or not a summary of individually wise decisions, provides a reason for action by virtue of its status as a rule.

Despite this point, I have already suggested something that I will defend in detail below: Even under mandatory rules, decision of all cases in advance is unlikely, or close to impossible, because the limits of human foresight will make some degree of lawmaking nearly inevitable in the context of deciding actual cases. From this claim it follows that the distinction between rules of thumb and mandatory rules is one of degree rather than one of kind. From this it also follows that legal provisions are not either rules or something else, but instead fall on a continuum of casuistical liberty, where the "ruleness" of the provision depends on the extent to which decisions about cases have been made before cases actually arise.

Kinds of Rules

Rules may be *simple* or *complex*. A law could say, for example, that no one under eighteen may drive. It could be somewhat more complex, saying that people under eighteen may not drive unless they pass certain special tests. Or it could be quite complex, creating a *formula* for deciding who may drive. It might look, for example, to age, performance on a written examination, and performance on a driving test. Each of these three variables might be given a specified numerical weight, producing a complex rule. Complex rules are complex, but they are still rules. In applying a complex rule, a decisionmaker has some tallying to do, but he need not decide what factors count or to what weight they are entitled.

An important example of an attempt to move away from a highly discretionary system and in the direction of complex rules is the U.S. Sentencing Guidelines. These guidelines, produced after the process outlined above, offer formulas by which judges must decide on sentences, taking account of a range of variables. Some people think that the guidelines are too categorical and rigid; what is of interest here is the effort to discipline trial judges, by promoting greater uniformity in sentencing. A similar effort to create complex rules is the social security "disability grid." For most of its history, administrative law judges decided who was disabled, and hence entitled to disability benefits, on the basis of a fairly unstructured, ad hoc inquiry into the individual case. Vocational experts would testify, often invoking their own controversial judgments about who was entitled to benefits and who should be required to work. In 1983, the Department of Health and Human Services substituted a new, more rulelike system embodied in a grid looking at age, education, previous work experience, and physical abilities.[9] Each of these categories is in turn disciplined by rules setting out well-defined subcategories. What emerges is a complex formula in which the individual judge has limited discretion. The disability grid may not quite qualify as a rule, since it does not settle everything before the fact, but it is at least more rulelike insofar as it operates to limit the power to decide what factors count, and what weight relevant factors receive.

Rules can also be *specific* or *abstract*. Specific rules apply to a narrow class of cases; abstract rules apply to a broad class of cases. An abstract rule might say, for example, that no one may drive over 60 miles per hour, or that all cars must be equipped with catalytic converters. A more specific rule might say that President Nixon's papers are public property; that the First Amendment allows government to ban advertisements for smoking; or that sixth-grade students may be suspended without a hearing for a period of less than two weeks, if there has been a serious allegation of criminal activity. All rules are defined in terms of classes, but sometimes the rule is narrowly tailored so as to pick up only a few cases, or perhaps only one. Of course there is a continuum here rather than sharp categorical distinctions.

Rules, Politics, and the Vice of Formalism

Is legal reasoning independent of politics and morality? Some people think so. The vice of formalism is found whenever people in law *falsely* deny that they are making political and moral judgments. This is a common phenomenon. There is a pervasive impulse to formalism within the legal culture, though the impulse moves to the fore in particular periods, when judges find it especially necessary to say that their judgments about "what the law is" do not rest on political and moral claims.

The debate over formalism has a great deal to do with the debate over rules. In fact an honorable species of formalism—not a vice at all—can be found in the effort to constrain legal judgments in advance by reference to rules. The decision to constrain judgments in this way must itself be justified on political or moral grounds, but if the constraints are real, decisions in particular cases may depend much less, or perhaps not at all, on political or moral judgments. When a judge says that someone under the age of eighteen may not vote, because a law bans people under that age from voting, we have a form of legal reasoning that is deductive, and that, from the judge's point of view, does not rest on controversial moral or political grounds.

But this is not always true. Sometimes the relevant provision is not rulelike at all ("reasonable care," "the freedom of speech," "when feasible"), but on the contrary contemplates or requires a degree of substantive judgment about the content of the law. The American Constitution says that no state shall "deny any person the equal protection of the laws." The Supreme Court has said that in light of these words, affirmative action programs must be treated the same as ordinary racial discrimination, since the clause is phrased in terms of individuals—"any person"—rather than groups. But this is a dishonorable species of formalism. The fact that the text refers to "any person" does not say whether affirmative action programs are acceptable. The Court's claim to the contrary purports to be based on language, but in fact it is a product of undisclosed substantive judgments.

The vice of formalism may be found with apparent rules as well. Suppose—to return to our earlier example—that a Toyota Camry is found going 90 miles per hour, in a way that is said to violate an ordinance barring any motor vehicle from going over 55 miles per hour. On the facts stated, the case can be resolved by saying that the Toyota Camry is a motor vehicle and that it has exceeded the speed limit. If, on the other hand, the driver of the Camry asserts that she was escaping a vehicle with a murderer shooting at her, a purely semantic examination of the rule may well be inadequate. Perhaps the court is empowered, or ought to see itself as empowered, to decide whether there is an excuse in bizarre or extreme cases of this kind. If so, it is spurious for the court to say that it is deciding the case by reference to the rule alone. To decide the case, the court must actually be resorting to something other than the speed limit law. It will probably have to make some substantive judgments of its own.

Sometimes reasoning by reference to rules is indeed a sham, in the sense that some judgment of value, not found within the rules, is being made but not disclosed. This is a familiar and exceedingly unfortunate kind of formalism in law—the effort to decide cases in law solely by reference to decisions made by someone else, when one's own judgments are inevitably at work. Consider, for example, the (unsupportable) view that the liberty of contract is necessarily, and purely as a matter of semantics, part of the "liberty" protected by the due process clause.[10] The problem here is that the issue cannot be decided by reference to the word "liberty"; a supplemental value judgment is necessary. To conclude that liberty of contract is part of constitutional "liberty," the dictionary is insufficient. One has to make claims about morality, history, or probably both. The case is quite different from one in which someone decides that the category "dog" necessarily includes German shepherds.[11] Here ordinary understandings of language, unaccompanied by contestable substantive judgments, do the necessary work.

Rules with Excuses: Necessity or Emergency Defenses

Many rules have explicit or implicit exceptions for cases of necessity or emergency. For example, a person may be banned from taking the life of another; this can be phrased as a rule, but self-defense is a valid excuse. Many constitutions allow abridgments of individual rights in case of emergency. The American Constitution allows the government to suspend the writ of habeas corpus in time of war. Other constitutions say that certain rights can be abridged under unusual circumstances. We might go so far as to say that almost all rules have at least some implicit exceptions. Rules are not applied when the heavens will fall. As Justice Jackson wrote, the Bill of Rights is "not a suicide pact."[12] When rules allow excuses, the legal system may embark on a casuistical project of distinguishing contexts from one another by close reference to the details of particular cases.

The consequences of making exceptions depend on the details. An exception could be *narrow but vague*, as in the idea that reasonable limits on free speech can be made under conditions of war. The conditions are rarely met and the exception is therefore narrow, but the exception is vague (what are "reasonable limits?"). Or the exception could be *narrow and specific*, as in the idea that under conditions of war, members of the Communist Party may not work for the government in any capacity. An exception might be broad and vague or broad and specific. A specific exception might even convert the rule with exceptions into a complex rule or a formula.

It is often said that rules with exceptions are still rules, and in one sense this is true. But if the exception is vague, we may come very far from ruleness, and the content of law will come from the investigation of particular facts. Whether the existence of exceptions means that rules are not rules depends on the nature of the exceptions. "People under sixteen may not drive, unless their last name begins with s"—this is a rule. "People under sixteen may not drive, unless they can show that they are competent to do so"—this is not a rule at all.

Even when there are exceptions, people may understand that exceptions cannot be made unless something truly extraordinary is shown. They may also understand, at least roughly, what sorts of things do and do not count as extraordinary. These understandings are sufficient to allow a rule to remain close to a rule as understood here.

Presumptions

A legal system may contain presumptions or presumptive rules. The law may presume, for example, that when the government regulates speech on the basis of its content—consider a ban on speech by a Communist or a Nazi—the regulation is unconstitutional. But the presumption might be rebutted by a demonstration of a certain kind and strength, as when government can show a clear and present danger. The law might presume that an employer may not discriminate on the basis of race, but the presumption might be rebutted by showing that, for example, a black actor is necessary to play the part of Othello.

The line between presumptions and rules with emergency exceptions can be thin. A rule with necessity or emergency exceptions might be described as a strong presumption. With presumptions, we need to know what counts as a rebuttal, and whether it is specific or vague, broad or narrow.

Standards

Rules are often compared with standards.[13] A ban on "excessive" speeds on the highway is a standard; so is a requirement that pilots of airplanes be "competent," or that student behavior in the classroom be "reasonable." These might be compared with a 55-mile-per-hour speed limit, a ban on pilots who are over the age of seventy, or a requirement that students sit in assigned seats.

The contrast between rules and standards identifies the fact that with some legal provisions, interpreters have to do a great deal of work in order to give law real content. The meaning of a standard depends on what happens when it is applied, and those who decide what happens are likely to proceed casuistically. Of course casuistical judgments may well generate categories that provide great guidance for the future.

Here too the nature of the provision cannot be read from its text, and everything will depend on interpretive practices. Once we define the term "excessive," we may well end up with a rule. Perhaps officials will decide that a speed is excessive whenever it is over 60 miles per hour. Or we may instead end up with a set of factors or a presumption. Perhaps anyone who goes over 60 miles per hour will be presumed to have gone excessively fast, unless special circumstances can be shown.

An important illustration here comes from standards of proof and in particular from the notions of "clear and convincing evidence" and "beyond a reasonable doubt." Judges have refused to assign numbers to these ideas. Thus the legal system has standards rather than rules. Why should the "reasonable doubt" standard not be said to call for, say, 97 percent certainty of guilt? Part of the answer lies in the fact that this standard must be applied in many different contexts—different crimes, different police behavior, different defendants, and so forth—and across those contexts, a uniform formula may well be senseless. The "reasonable doubt" standard allows a degree of adaptation to individual circumstances, and this is part of its advantage over any single number.

Factors

In many legal contexts, particular judgments emerge *through the decisionmaker's assessment and weighing of a number of relevant factors, whose precise content has not been specified in advance.* Several factors are pertinent to the decision, but there is no rule, simple or complex, to apply. There is no rule because the factors are not described exhaustively and precisely in advance, and because their weight has not been fully specified. Hence the decisionmaker cannot rely simply on "finding the facts" and "applying the law."

Factors share with standards a refusal to specify outcomes in advance. But factors depart from standards in enumerating, at least to some extent, the sorts of considerations that are relevant in particular applications. It would not be right, however, to say that factors offer less discretion than standards. Some of the factors may even be standards. The amount of discretion depends on the context and on the content of the relevant provisions. Moreover, the difference between rules and factors is one of degree rather than kind. Since those who interpret most apparent rules sometimes must determine at least some of their content—since it is better to speak of "ruleness" than rules—factors are not at an opposite pole from rules.

Decisions by factors may ultimately occur through interpretation of legal standards, such as bans on "involuntary" confessions, on "excessive" speed in automobiles, on continued employment by "inadequate" employees, and on "undue burdens" on the right to choose abortion. The interpreter may well create and evaluate a range of variables in the process of deciding individual cases. She might evaluate those variables both by specifying what they are and by deciding what weight to accord to each of them. Of course a provision that looks like a set of factors might turn out to be a rule, if the interpreters understand it that way. Perhaps a set of factors will be understood as a complex rule or a formula. We cannot know before we see how the interpreters do their job.

A typical test by reference to factors refers to "the totality of the circumstances," in which courts look at three, four, five, or more relevant factors. A test of this kind operates in astonishingly many areas of the law. Thus a 1994 computer search of United States Supreme Court cases found no fewer than 149 cases referring to the "totality of the circumstances" test, and no fewer than 11,155 such cases in the federal courts since 1944.

Judgments can be based on factors even if the relevant considerations are fully *identified* in advance; if there is no advance *weighting*, we still lack a rule. If a statute says that whether speed is excessive will be determined through an examination of weather conditions, time of day, and popularity of the relevant route, we have a system of factors. Factors are converted into rules only if the relevant considerations are described exhaustively and specifically, and given assigned weights.

Consider the Emergency Petroleum Allocation Act of 1973, which regulated pricing and allocation of petroleum products in the United States from 1973 to 1981. The statute required the agency to "provide for" nine factors, "to the maximum extent practicable." These factors were (1) "protection of public health, safety, and welfare; (2) maintenance of all public services; (3) maintenance of agricultural operations; (4) preservation of an economically sound and competitive petroleum industry; (5) operation of all refineries at full capacity; (6) equitable distribution of crude oil and petroleum products; (7) maintenance of exploration and production of fuels; (8) economic efficiency; and (9) minimization of interference with market mechanisms."[14] Congress added that each of the nine factors is equally important. There is much to be said about this quite bizarre list. What is pertinent here is that an enumeration of factors may be possible, but weighting may not be because of qualitative differences.

In most contexts, no predetermined list of factors can be exhaustive. Life may turn up other factors that are hard to point out in advance. In most areas of law governed by factors rather than rules, it is understood that the identified factors, if described at a level of detail and specificity, are not complete—and if they are intended to be complete, they are stated in a sufficiently general way so as to allow unanticipated considerations to apply. Thus we might say that admission to law school will turn on college records, extracurricular activities, and issues of diversity, with an understanding that each of these factors will be a standard, requiring a lot of specification to operate in individual cases.

Is there a distinction between judgments based on factors and untrammeled discretion? The answer is yes, but it needs to be qualified. Since factors are usually not exhaustively listed ahead of time, and since their weights are not stipulated, a judge might seem able in every case to find a suitably weighted set of relevant-sounding factors to justify any conclusion that he wants. A set of factors might exclude a set of considerations deemed irrelevant, but this exclusion does not rule out any particular outcome.

So far, so good. But limits on legitimate inputs into decisions are important even if they do not exclude outputs. Such limits force people to talk in a certain way. They increase the psychological pressure to ensure that irrelevant factors do not bear on the outcome. The degree of constraint will depend on personnel and circumstances.

Principles

High-level moral principles are of course an important part of everyday thinking. Consider some examples: tell the truth; keep your promises; do not hurt other people's feelings. These principles are not really rules, since they are not taken by themselves as decisive of moral issues. They bear on moral issues, but by themselves they do not resolve particular cases. Their content emerges from their applications.

In law, high-level principles matter too. Legal principles are often said to be both deeper and more general than legal rules. We might say, for example, that rules are justified by principles. Government imposes a speed limit of 60 miles per hour; the reason for the rule—the principle behind it—is to promote safety. There is a principle to the effect that it is wrong not to keep your promises; hence the law contains a range of rules for enforcement of contractual obligations.

The justification of the rule, understood as the principle that lies behind it, could be used in interpretation. For example, the 60-mile-per-hour speed limit might not be applied to a police officer attempting to apprehend a fleeing felon, and the law of wills might not allow inheritance by someone who has murdered the testator in order to inherit a large sum of money. In both cases, we might say that the principle that accounts for the rule allows an exception. Hence a common use of the term "principle" in law involves the justifications behind rules.

There is another understanding of the notion of principle in law.[15] Any legal system contains explicitly formulated principles as well as rules; these principles do not lie behind or justify rules, but instead bear on the resolution of cases, in the sense that they are introduced as relevant factors. Thus courts say that laws should be interpreted, if possible, so as not to be retroactive; that no person may profit from his own wrong; that he who seeks equity must do equity; that ambiguous statutes should be construed so as not to apply outside the territorial boundaries of the nation. The status of legal principles of this sort is somewhat mysterious. Certainly they vary in their "weight," ranging from strong presumptions to mere tie-breakers when cases are otherwise in equipoise. Usually they operate as factors. They are not rules. We might say that principles are more flexible than rules, in the sense that principles bear on cases without disposing of them. This distinction should not be overstated. Since any given rule x is unlikely to resolve all cases that fall under the literal language of rule x, the difference between rules and principles (our now-familiar point) is one of degree rather than of kind.

What is the relationship between a principle and a standard? If we see a principle as the justification for a rule, the difference seems obvious: We have understood a standard not as a justification for an (already specified) rule, but instead as a legal provision that needs a good deal of specification to be used to resolve individual cases. If, on the other hand, we understand a principle as a relevant consideration in the decision of cases, the distinction between principles and standards is more complex. As I understand it here, a legal principle is different from a legal standard in the sense that the latter fully or nearly fully "covers" individual cases without specifying the content of the analysis in particular cases, whereas a principle is a background idea that does not by itself "cover" an individual case, but is instead brought to bear on it as one of a number of relevant factors.

One final point. It is sometimes said that a decision in a case turns on a "principle," as in the idea that speech may not be restricted unless there is a clear and present danger, that discrimination on the basis of race is presumed invalid, or that no contract is valid without consideration. In this usage, a principle is not distinguishable from a standard.

Guidelines

Sometimes the law establishes ceilings and floors, or it identifies outcomes from which officials (or citizens) can deviate only if they can demonstrate good cause in the particular case. Guidelines of these kinds include a mixture of possibilities. They may be mandatory or they may be merely suggestive. Mandatory guidelines may be preferred to rules, even to presumptive rules (which they closely resemble), because they allow a degree of flexibility in individual cases. They may be preferred to standards insofar as they can discipline behavior in a way that allows better monitoring of discretion. Thus guidelines may establish firm boundaries beyond which no one may go, and they may require reasons to be given publicly for any departure from the norm. On the other hand, the flexibility of guidelines can be a vice rather than a virtue, and hence there is often pressure to convert guidelines into rules.

Analogies

Analogical reasoning is the key to legal casuistry; I will discuss it in detail in Chapter 3. For the moment a few brief remarks should suffice. Sometimes a legal system proceeds by comparing the case at hand with a case (or cases) that have come before. The prior case is examined to see whether it "controls," is "distinguishable," or should be "extended to" the case at hand. The prior case will be accompanied by an opinion, which may *contain* a rule, a standard, a set of factors, or something else. The court deciding the present case will inspect relevant similarities and differences. That court, not bound by the previous opinion, may *produce* a rule, a standard, a set of factors, or something else.

With analogy, we do not have a decision by rule, because no rule is specified in advance of the process of analogical thinking. The governing legal requirement emerges from comparison of cases, and it is applied only after it has been identified. The nature of the requirement emerges by grappling with the precedent. Most of the time, an analogy will produce a standard, one that makes sense of the outcomes in the case at hand and the case that came before, and one whose ultimate meaning will become clear only as future cases are decided.

I have already discussed some connections between analogical reasoning and the search for reflective equilibrium. Both of these ways of proceeding emphasize the need to attend to our considered judgments about how particular cases should come out. But there are important distinctions. The search for reflective equilibrium places a high premium on, first, the capacity to develop a complete understanding of the basis for particular judgments and, second, the development of both abstract and general principles to account for those judgments. If reflective equilibrium could ever be obtained, we would have both horizontal and vertical consistency in our judgments. All cases would be harmonized with each other and with the general theory. Every particular judgment would become fully theorized and at a highly general level.

Analogical reasoning is far less ambitious, for it does not require anything like horizontal and vertical consistency. Local coherence is the most to which analogizers aspire. Why is analogical reasoning so unambitious? Part of the reason has to do with the distinctive constraints faced by participants in the legal system. Many precedents cannot be scrutinized by judges because of the limited authority of those judges; consider a lower court facing a Supreme Court precedent. For people thinking about morality or politics outside the legal system, by contrast, all judgments are merely provisional, in the sense that they are at least potentially subject to revision. In light of the system of precedent, reflective equilibrium is an unlikely ideal for law. Note in this regard that in the United States, lower courts cannot legitimately reject Supreme Court precedents and that the Supreme Court faces severe barriers to overruling its own precedents.

Interpretation

Knowledge of the law consists in large part of an understanding of prevailing interpretive practices within the legal community. Much of this understanding takes the form of what we might call "background knowledge," some of it made explicit, much of it taken for granted. As we have seen, legal provisions, read in the abstract, could mean a wide range of things. Consider, for example, a statute saying that no animals may be brought into parks, that conspiracies in restraint of trade are forbidden, or that the Environmental Protection Agency shall set air quality standards "necessary or appropriate to protect human health." Does the first provision apply to a blind person with a seeing eye dog? To a police officer with a German shepherd helping to see whether a bomb has been placed on the premises? Does the second provision apply to an agreement among car companies to lower prices? To establish a minimum wage? Does the third provision allow the Environmental Protection Agency to consider costs in setting air quality standards?

Though lawyers sometimes pretend otherwise, there is nothing inevitable to the selection of any particular approach to interpretation. There are choices everywhere. In interpreting statutes, for example, some people favor an emphasis on the "ordinary" meaning of the relevant words. Other people say that interpreters should look not for any "ordinary" meaning, but instead try to identify the intended meaning of the particular speaker—in the case of legislation, the meaning intended by the legislature. These are two of many alternatives. The stakes become especially high in debates over constitutional interpretation, when basic rights are at stake. I will return to these questions in Chapter 8.

We have now seen much of the lawyer's repertoire—the devices and strategies that underlie legal reasoning. Though most of it should be familiar, it would be wrong to say that legal reasoning lacks special features, or that it is reducible to some other field, like political science, philosophy, or economics. The concerns and projects of the law lead in distinctive directions. Lawyers ask questions that are different from those that would be asked by the politician, the philosopher, and the economist. The lawyer's questions have everything to do with constraints of competence and role. It is now time to explore how participants in a well-functioning legal culture try to limit large-scale debates over controversial issues—by taking a particular approach to the problem of political conflict.

2

Incompletely Theorized Agreements

Incompletely theorized agreements play a pervasive role in law and society. It is quite rare for a person or group completely to theorize any subject, that is, to accept both a general theory and a series of steps connecting that theory to concrete conclusions. Thus we often have in law an *incompletely theorized agreement on a general principle*—incompletely theorized in the sense that people who accept the principle need not agree on what it entails in particular cases.

This is the sense emphasized by Justice Oliver Wendell Holmes in his great aphorism, "General principles do not decide concrete cases."[1] Thus, for example, we know that murder is wrong, but disagree about whether abortion is wrong. We favor racial equality, but are divided on affirmative action. We believe in liberty, but disagree about increases in the minimum wage. Hence the pervasive legal and political phenomenon of an agreement on a general principle alongside disagreement about particular cases. The agreement is incompletely theorized in the sense that it is *incompletely specified*. Much of the key work must be done by others, often through casuistical judgments at the point of application.

Often constitution-making becomes possible through this form of incompletely theorized agreement. Many constitutions contain incompletely specified standards and avoid rules, at least when it comes to the description of basic rights. Consider the cases of Eastern Europe and

35

South Africa, where constitutional provisons include many abstract provisions on whose concrete specification there has been sharp dispute. Abstract provisions protect "freedom of speech," "religious liberty," and "equality under the law," and citizens agree on those abstractions in the midst of sharp dispute about what these provisions really entail.

Much lawmaking becomes possible only because of this phenomenon. Consider the fact that the creation of large regulatory agencies has often been feasible only because of incompletely specified agreements. In dealing with air and water pollution, occupational safety and health, or regulation of broadcasting, legislators converge on general, incompletely specified requirements—that regulation be "reasonable," or that it provide "a margin of safety." If the legislature attempted to specify these requirements—to decide what counts as reasonable regulation—there would be a predictably high level of dispute and conflict, and perhaps the relevant laws could not be enacted at all.

Incompletely specified agreements thus have important social uses. Many of their advantages are practical. They allow people to develop frameworks for decision and judgment despite large-scale disagreements. At the same time, they help produce a degree of social solidarity and shared commitment. People who are able to agree on political abstractions—freedom of speech, freedom from unreasonable searches and seizures—can also agree that they are embarking on shared projects. These forms of agreement help constitute a democratic culture. It is for this reason that they are so important to constitution-making. Incompletely specified agreements also have the advantage of allowing people to show one another a high degree of mutual respect. By refusing to settle concrete cases that raise fundamental issues of conscience, they permit citizens to announce to one another that society shall not take sides on such issues until it is required to do so.

So much for incompletely specified provisions. Let us turn to a second phenomenon. Sometimes people agree on a mid-level principle but disagree about both general theory and particular cases. These sorts of agreements are also incompletely theorized, but in a different way. Judges may believe, for example, that government cannot discriminate on the basis of race, without having a large-scale theory of equality, and also without agreeing whether government may enact affirmative action programs or segregate prisons when racial tensions are severe. Judges may think that government may not regulate speech unless it can show a clear and present danger—but disagree about whether this principle is founded in utilitarian or Kantian considerations, and disagree too about whether the principle allows government to regulate a particular speech by members of the Ku Klux Klan.

My particular interest here is in a third kind of phenomenon, of special interest for law: incompletely theorized agreements on particular outcomes, accompanied by agreements on the narrow or low-level principles that account for them. These terms contain some ambiguities. There is no algorithm by which to distinguish between a high-level theory and one that operates at an intermediate or lower level. We might consider, as conspicuous examples of high-level theories, Kantianism and utilitarianism, and see legal illustrations in the many distinguished (academic) efforts to understand such areas as tort law, contract law, free speech, and the law of equality as undergirded by highly abstract theories of the right or the good.[2] By contrast, we might think of low-level principles as including most of the ordinary material of legal "doctrine"—the general class of principles and justifications that are not said to derive from any large theories of the right or the good, that have ambiguous relations to large theories, and that are compatible with more than one such theory.

By the term "particular outcome," I mean the judgment about who wins and who loses a case. By the term "low-level principles," I refer to something relative, not absolute; I mean to do the same thing by the terms "theories" and "abstractions" (which I use interchangeably). In this setting, the notions "low-level," "high," and "abstract" are best understood in comparative terms, like the terms "big," "old," and "unusual." The "clear and present danger" standard is a relative abstraction when compared with the claim that members of the Nazi Party may march in Skokie, Illinois. But the "clear and present danger" idea is relatively particular when compared with the claim that nations should adopt the constitutional abstraction "freedom of speech." The term "freedom of speech" is a relative abstraction when measured against the claim that campaign finance laws are acceptable, but the same term is less abstract than the grounds that justify free speech, as in, for example, the principle of personal autonomy.

What I am emphasizing here is that when people diverge on some (relatively) high-level proposition, they might be able to agree when they lower the level of abstraction. Incompletely theorized judgments on particular cases are the ordinary material of law. And in law, the point of agreement is often highly particularized—absolutely as well as relatively particularized—in the sense that it involves a specific outcome and a set of reasons that do not venture far from the case at hand. High-level theories are rarely reflected explicitly in law.

Perhaps the participants in law endorse no such theory, or perhaps they believe that they have none, or perhaps they cannot, on a multimember court, reach agreement on a theory. Perhaps they find theoretical disputes confusing or annoying. What is critical is that they agree on how a case must come out. The argument very much applies to rules, which are, much of the time, incompletely theorized; indeed, this is one of the major advantages of rules. People may agree that a 60-mile-per-hour speed limit makes sense, and that it applies to defendant Jones, without having much of a theory about criminal punishment. They may agree that to receive social security benefits, people must show that they earn less than a certain sum of money, without having anything like a theory about who deserves what. Thus a key social function of rules is to allow people to agree on the meaning, authority, and even the soundness of a governing provision in the face of disagreements about much else.

Much the same can be said about rule-free decisions made under standards, factors, and analogical reasoning. Indeed, all of the lawyer's conventional tools allow incompletely theorized agreements on particular outcomes. Consider analogical thinking. People might think that A is like B and covered by the same low-level principle, without agreeing on a general theory to explain why the low-level principle is sound. They agree on the matter of similarity, without agreeing on a large-scale account of what makes the two things similar. In the law of discrimination, for example, many people think that sex discrimination is "like" race discrimination and should be treated similarly, even if they lack or cannot agree on a general theory of when discrimination is unacceptable. In the law of free speech, many people agree that a ban on speech by a Communist is "like" a ban on speech by a member of the Ku Klux Klan and should be treated similarly—even if they lack or cannot agree on a general theory about the foundations of the free speech principle.

Incomplete Theorization and the Constructive Uses of Silence

What might be said on behalf of incompletely theorized agreements, or incompletely theorized judgments, about particular cases? Some people think of incomplete theorization as quite unfortunate—as embarrassing or reflective of some important problem or defect. Perhaps people have not yet thought deeply enough. When people theorize, by raising the level of abstraction, they do so to reveal bias, confusion, or inconsistency. Surely participants in a legal system should not abandon this effort.

There is a good deal of truth in these usual thoughts. Sometimes more in the way of abstraction does reveal prejudice or confusion. But this is not the whole story. On the contrary, incompletely theorized judgments are an important and valuable part of both private and public life. They help make law possible; they even help make life possible. Most of their virtues involve *the constructive uses of silence*, an exceedingly important social and legal phenomenon. Silence—on something that may prove false, obtuse, or excessively contentious—can help minimize conflict, allow the present to learn from the future, and save a great deal of time and expense. In law, as elsewhere, what is said is no more important than what is left unsaid. Certainly this is true for ordinary courts, which have limited expertise and democratic accountability, and whose limits lead them to be cautious.

My principal concern is the question of how judges on a multimember body should justify their opinions in public; the argument therefore has a great deal to do with the problem of collective choice. But some of the relevant points bear on other issues as well. They have implications for the question of how an individual judge not faced with the problem of producing a majority opinion—a judge on a trial court, for example— might write; they bear on the question of how a single judge, whether or not a member of a collective body, might think in private; and they relate to appropriate methods of both thought and justification wholly outside of adjudication and even outside of law.

Multimember Institutions

Begin with the special problem of public justification on a multimember body. The first and most obvious point is that incompletely theorized agreements are well-suited to a world—and especially a legal world— containing social dissensus on large-scale issues. By definition, such agreements have the large advantage of allowing a convergence on particular outcomes by people unable to reach an accord on general principles. This advantage is associated not only with the simple need to decide cases, but also with social stability, which could not exist if fundamental disagreements broke out in every case of public or private dispute.[3]

Second, incompletely theorized agreements can promote two goals of a liberal democracy and a liberal legal system: to enable people to live together and to permit them to show each other a measure of reciprocity and mutual respect.[4] The use of low-level principles or rules generally allows judges on multimember bodies and hence citizens to find commonality and thus a common way of life without producing unnecessary antagonism. Both rules and low-level principles make it unnecessary to reach areas in which disagreement is fundamental.

Perhaps even more important, incompletely theorized agreements allow people to show each other a high degree of mutual respect, civility, or reciprocity. Frequently ordinary people disagree in some deep way on an issue—the Middle East, pornography, homosexual marriages—and sometimes they agree not to discuss that issue much, as a way of deferring to each other's strong convictions and showing a measure of reciprocity and respect (even if they do not at all respect the particular conviction that is at stake). If reciprocity and mutual respect are desirable, it follows that judges, perhaps even more than ordinary people, should not challenge a litigant's or another person's deepest and most defining commitments, at least if those commitments are reasonable and if there is no need for them to do so. Thus, for example, it would be better if judges intending to reaffirm *Roe v. Wade* could do so without challenging the judgment that the fetus is a human being.[5]

To be sure, some fundamental commitments might appropriately be challenged in the legal system or within other multimember bodies. Some commitments are ruled off-limits by the authoritative legal materials. Many provisions involving basic rights have this purpose. Of course it is not always disrespectful to disagree with someone in a fundamental way; on the contrary, such disagreements may sometimes reflect profound respect. When defining commitments are based on demonstrable errors of fact or logic, it is appropriate to contest them. So too when those commitments are rooted in a rejection of the basic dignity of all human beings, or when it is necessary to undertake the challenge to resolve a genuine problem. But many cases can be resolved in an incompletely theorized way, and that is all I am suggesting here.

Institutional arguments in law—especially those involving judicial restraint—are typically designed to bracket fundamental questions and to say that however those questions might be resolved in principle, courts should stand to one side. The allocation of certain roles has an important function of allowing outcomes to be reached without forcing courts to make decisions on fundamental issues. Those issues are resolved by reference to institutional competence, not on their merits.

In particular, the principle of stare decisis, which instructs courts to respect precedent, helps produce incompletely theorized agreements, and it helps to avoid constant struggle over basic principle. It serves this function precisely because it prevents people from having to build the world again, and together, every time a dispute arises. People can agree to follow precedent when they disagree on almost everything else. As a prominent example, consider the United States Supreme Court's refusal to overrule *Roe v. Wade*, where the justices emphasized the difficulties that would be produced by revisiting so large-scale a social controversy.[6] Members of the Court can accept the rule of precedent from diverse foundations and despite their many disagreements. Thus the justifications of the rule of precedent are diverse—involving predictability, efficiency, fairness, constraints on official discretion—and people who disagree on those justifications can agree on the practice, at least as a general rule.

Multimember Institutions and Individual Judges

Turn now to reasons that call for incompletely theorized agreements whether or not we are dealing with a multimember body. The first consideration here is that incompletely theorized agreements have the crucial function of reducing the political cost of enduring disagreements. If judges disavow large-scale theories, then losers in particular cases lose much less. They lose a decision, but not the world. They may win on another occasion. Their own theory has not been rejected or ruled inadmissible. When the authoritative rationale for the result is disconnected from abstract theories of the good or the right, the losers can submit to legal obligations, even if reluctantly, without being forced to renounce their largest ideals. I have said that some theories should be rejected or ruled inadmissible. But it is an advantage, from the standpoint of freedom and stability, for a legal system to be able to tell most losers—many of whom are operating from foundations that have something to offer or that cannot be ruled out a priori—that their own deepest convictions may play a role elsewhere in the law.

The second point is that incompletely theorized agreements are valuable when we seek moral evolution over time. Consider the area of constitutional equality, where considerable change has occurred in the past and will inevitably occur in the future. A completely theorized judgment would be unable to accommodate changes in facts or values. If the legal culture really did attain a theoretical end-state, it would become too rigid and calcified; we would know what we thought about everything. This would disserve posterity.

Incompletely theorized agreements are a key to debates over constitutional equality, with issues being raised about whether gender, sexual orientation, age, disability, and others are analogous to race; such agreements have the important advantage of allowing a large degree of openness to new facts and perspectives. At one point, we might think that homosexual relations are akin to incest; at another point, we might find the analogy bizarre. Of course a completely theorized judgment would have many virtues if it is correct. But at any particular moment in time, this is an unlikely prospect for human beings, not excluding judges.

A particular concern here is the effect of changing understandings of both facts and values. Consider ordinary life. At a certain time, you may well refuse to make decisions that seem foundational in character— for example, whether to get married within the next year, whether to have two, three, or four children, or whether to live in San Francisco or New York. Part of the reason for this refusal is knowledge that your understandings of both facts and values may well change. Indeed, your identity may itself change in important and relevant ways and for this reason a set of commitments in advance—something like a fully theorized conception of your life course—would make no sense.

Legal systems and nations are not so very different. If the Supreme Court is asked to offer a fully theorized conception of equality—in areas involving, for example, the rights of disabled people, children, and homosexuals—it may well respond that its job is to decide cases rather than to offer fully theorized accounts, partly because society should learn over time and partly because society's understandings of facts and values, in a sense its very identity, may well shift in unpredictable ways. This point bears on many legal issues. It helps support the case for incompletely theorized agreements.

The third point is practical. Incompletely theorized agreements may be the best approach that is available for people of limited time and capacities. Full theorization may be far too much to ask. A single judge faces this problem as much as a member of a multimember panel. Here too the rule of precedent is crucial; attention to precedent is liberating, not merely confining, since it frees busy people to deal with a restricted range of problems. Incompletely theorized agreements have the related advantage, for ordinary lawyers and judges, of humility and modesty. To engage in analogical reasoning, for example, one ordinarily need not take a stand on large, contested issues of social life, some of which can be resolved only on what will seem to many a sectarian basis (see Chapter 3).

Fourth, incompletely theorized agreements are well-adapted to a system that should or must take precedents as fixed points. This is a large advantage over more ambitious methods, since ambitious thinkers, in order to reach horizontal and vertical coherence, will probably be forced to disregard many decided cases. In light of the sheer number of decided cases and adjudicative officials, law cannot speak with one voice; full coherence in principle is unlikely in the extreme.

It is notable in this connection that for some judges and lawyers (lower court judges, for example), precedents truly are fixed (short of civil disobedience), whereas for others, including Supreme Court Justices, they are revisable, but only in extraordinary circumstances. If a judge or a lawyer were to attempt to reach full theorization, precedents would have at most the status of considered judgments about particular cases, and these might be revised when they run into conflict with something else that he believes and that is general or particular. This would cause many problems. Participants in a legal system aspiring to stability should not be so immodest as to reject judgments reached by others whenever those judgments could not be made part of reflective equilibrium for those particular participants. Thus the area of contract law is unlikely fully to cohere with the field of tort law or property; contract law is itself likely to contain multiple and sometimes inconsistent strands.

We can find many analogies in ordinary life. A parent's practices with his children may not fully cohere. Precedents with respect to bedtime, eating, homework, and much else are unlikely to be susceptible to systematization under a single principle. Of course, parents do not seek to be inconsistent. A child may feel justly aggrieved if a sibling is permitted to watch more hours of television for no apparent reason; but full coherence would be a lot to ask. The problem of reaching full consistency is all the more severe in law, where so many people have decided so many things, and where disagreements on large principles lurk in the background.

There is a more abstract point here. Human morality recognizes irreducibly diverse goods, which cannot be subsumed under a single "master" value.[7] The same is true for the moral values reflected in the law. Any simple, general, and monistic or single-valued theory of a large area of the law—free speech, contracts, property—is likely to be too crude to fit with our best understandings of the multiple values that are at stake in that area. It would be absurd to try to organize legal judgments through a single conception of value.

What can be said about law as a whole can be said about many particular areas of law. Monistic theories of free speech or property rights, for example, will fail to accommodate the range of values that speech and property implicate. Free speech promotes not simply democracy, but personal autonomy, economic progress, self-development, and other goals as well. Property rights are important not only for economic prosperity, but for democracy and autonomy too. We are unlikely to be able to appreciate the diverse values at stake, and to describe them with the specificity they deserve, unless we investigate the details of particular disputes.

This is not a decisive objection to general theories; a "top down" approach might reject monism and point to plural values.[8] Perhaps participants in democracy or law can describe a range of diverse values, each of them at a high level of abstraction; acknowledge that these values do not fall under a single master value; and use these values for assessing law. But even if correct, any such approach would run into difficulty because of an important practical fact: social disagreements about how best to describe or specify the relevant values. Moreover, any such approach is likely to owe its genesis and its proof—its point or points—to a range of particular cases on which it can build. Of course full theorization of an area of law would be acceptable, or even an occasion for great celebration, if it accounted for the plural values at issue. But this would be a most complex task, one that requires identification of a wide range of actual and likely cases. At least we can say that incompletely theorized judgments are well-suited to a moral universe that is diverse and pluralistic, not only in the sense that people disagree, but also in the sense that each of us is attuned to pluralism when we are thinking well about any area of law.

None of these points suggests that incompletely theorized agreements always deserve celebration. The virtues of such agreements are partial. Some incompletely theorized agreements are unjust. If an agreement is more fully theorized, it will provide greater notice to affected parties. Moreover, fuller theorization—in the form of wider and deeper inquiry into the grounds for judgment—may be valuable or even necessary to prevent inconsistency, bias, or self-interest. If judges on a panel have actually agreed on a general theory, and if they are really committed to it, they should say so. Judges and the general community will learn much more if they are able to discuss the true motivating grounds for outcomes. All these are valid considerations, and nothing I am saying here denies their importance.

Judges, Theory, and the Rule of Law

There is a close association between the effort to attain incompletely theorized agreements and the rule of law ideal. Insofar as a legal system involves rule by law rather than rule by individual human beings, it tries to constrain judgments in advance. Some people think that the rule of law, properly understood, is a law of rules; this claim will be discussed in later chapters. For the moment we can understand the rule of law more modestly. It is opposed to rule by individual human beings, who should not be permitted to govern as they wish through making law entirely of their choice in the context of actual disputes. Insofar as the rule of law prevents this from happening, it tries to prevent people in particular cases from invoking their own theories of the right or the good so as to make decisions according to their own most fundamental judgments.

Indeed, a prime purpose of the rule of law is to rule off-limits certain deep ideas of the right or the good, on the view that those ideas ought not to be invoked, most of the time, by judges and officials occupying particular social roles. Among the forbidden or presumptively forbidden ideas are, often, high-level views that are taken as too hubristic or sectarian precisely because they are so high-level. The presumption against high-level theories is an aspect of the ideal of the rule of law to the extent that it is an effort to limit the exercise of discretion at the point of application.

In this way we might make distinctions between the role of high theory within the courtroom and the role of high theory in the political branches of government. To be sure, incompletely theorized agreements play a role in democratic arenas; consider laws protecting endangered species or granting unions a right to organize. But in democratic arenas, there is no taboo, presumptive or otherwise, on invoking high-level theories of the good or the right.[9] On the contrary, such theories have played a key role in many social movements with defining effects on American constitutionalism, including the Civil War, the New Deal, the women's movement, and the environmental movement. Abstract, high-level ideas are an important part of democratic discussion, and sometimes they are ratified publicly and placed in a constitution.

By contrast, development of large-scale theories by ordinary courts is problematic and usually understood as such within the judiciary. The skepticism about large-scale theories is partly a result of the fact that such theories may require large-scale social reforms, and courts have enormous difficulties in implementing such reforms.[10] When courts invoke a large-scale theory as a reason for social change, they may well fail simply because they lack the tools to bring about change on their own. An important reason for judicial incapacity is that courts must decide on the legitimacy of rules that are aspects of complex systems. In invalidating or changing a single rule, courts may not do what they seek to do. They may produce unfortunate systemic effects, with unanticipated bad consequences that are not visible to them at the time of decision, and that may be impossible for them to correct thereafter.[11] Legislatures are in a much better position on this score. Consider, for example, an effort to reform landlord-tenant law. Judges may require landlords to provide decent housing for poor tenants, but the result may be to require landlords to raise rents, with detrimental effects on the poor. To say this is not to say that judge-initiated changes are always bad. But it is to say that the piecemeal quality of such changes is a reason for caution.

The claim that courts are ineffective in producing large-scale reform is a generalization, and it has the limits of all generalizations. The point does not count decisively against more ambitious judicial rulings when those rulings have a powerful legal and moral foundation. An ambitious ruling might announce an uncontestable high-level principle, and the announcement of the principle might be right even if courts lack implementing tools. What seems clear is that the difficulties of judge-led social reform provide a basis for judicial modesty (see Chapter 8 for more details).

More fundamentally, it is in the absence of a democratic pedigree that the system of precedent, analogy, and incompletely theorized agreement has such an important place. The need to discipline judicial judgment arises from the courts' complex and modest place in any well-functioning constitutional system. To be sure, judges have, in some societies, a duty to interpret the Constitution, and sometimes that duty authorizes them to invoke relatively large-scale principles, seen as part and parcel of the Constitution as democratically ratified. Many people think that judicial activity is best characterized by reference to use of such principles.[12] Certainly there are occasions on which this practice is legitimate and even glorious.

To identify those occasions it would be necessary to develop a full theory of legal interpretation. For present purposes we can say something more modest. Most of judicial activity does not involve constitutional interpretation, and the ordinary work of common law decision and statutory interpretation calls for low-level principles on which agreements are possible. Indeed, constitutional argument itself is based largely on low-level principles, not on high theory, except on those rare occasions when more ambitious thinking becomes necessary to resolve a case or when the case for the ambitious theory is so insistent that a range of judges converge on it. And there are good reasons for the presumption in favor of low-level principles—having to do with the limited capacities of judges, the need to develop principles over time, the failure of monistic theories of the law, and the other considerations traced above.

Overlapping Consensus and Incomplete Theorization

There is a relationship between the notion of incompletely theorized agreements and the well-known idea of an "overlapping consensus," set out by John Rawls.[13] Rawls urges that a constitutional democracy might seek a reasonable overlapping consensus on certain basic political principles— allowing people, from their own diverse foundations, to agree on those principles. The idea of an overlapping consensus, like the notion of incompletely theorized agreement, attempts to bring about stability and social agreement in the face of diverse "comprehensive views." Kantians, utilitarians, and Christians, for example, might all agree on the same political principles, though from their own starting points.

A prime goal of political liberalism is to ensure that operating with diverse perspectives, all citizens can endorse, as legitimate, certain exercises of political power. In developing the idea of an overlapping consensus, Rawls is particularly concerned with the question of social pluralism and with ways of enabling people to live together and to show a degree of reciprocity and mutual respect amid basic disagreement. Ideas of this kind are very much a part of what underlies the impetus toward incompletely theorized agreements. Social pluralism and the problem of legitimate disagreement make such agreements highly desirable; the same concerns underlie Rawls's formulation.

But the two ideas are far from the same. The distinctly legal solution to the problem of pluralism is to produce agreement on particulars, with the thought that often people who are puzzled by general principles, or who disagree on them, can agree on individual cases. When we disagree on the relatively abstract, we can often find agreement by moving to lower levels of generality. Rawls is more interested in the opposite possibility—that people who disagree on much else can agree on political abstractions and use that agreement for political purposes. Rawls emphasizes that when we find disagreement or confusion, or when "our shared political understandings . . . break down," we move toward political philosophy and become more abstract.[14] Thus Rawls writes that abstraction "is a way of continuing public discussion when shared understandings of lesser generality have broken down. We should be prepared to find that the deeper the conflict, the higher the level of abstraction to which we must ascend to get a clear and uncluttered view of its roots."[15]

Of course what Rawls says may be true: People can be moved toward greater abstraction by their disagreement on particulars. It is right too to emphasize the possibility that people who have different foundational commitments—liberal, Aristotelian, Catholic—may achieve an overlapping consensus on a political conception of justice including (for example) freedom of speech and the right to vote. Constitutionalism itself—a form of incompletely theorized agreement—is often made possible through this route, which leaves room for many possible specifications of underlying rights. But of course people may have trouble with abstractions. A special goal of the incompletely theorized agreement on particulars is to obtain a consensus on a concrete outcome among people who do not want to decide questions in political philosophy. They may be uncertain about how to choose among different forms of liberalism or about whether to select liberalism or a certain alternative. The lawyer's special goal—to allow people to solve problems while remaining agnostic (to the extent possible) on theoretical issues—animates the search for incompletely theorized agreements.

One of the basic aspirations of Rawls's approach is to avoid certain abstract debates in philosophy generally. Rawls wants to enable people to agree on political principles when they are uncertain how to think about many questions of philosophy or metaphysics. Thus Rawls seeks to ensure a political approach that "leaves philosophy as it is."[16] But if what I have said is right, judgments in law and politics sometimes bear the same relation to political philosophy as (on Rawls's view) do judgments in political philosophy to questions in general philosophy and metaphysics. The political philosopher may attempt not to take a stand on large philosophical or metaphysical questions; so too the lawyer, the judge, or the political participant may urge outcomes that make it unnecessary to solve large questions in political philosophy. Because of their limited role, judges in particular may very much want to leave political philosophy "as it is."

Sometimes it is too much to ask ordinary citizens—or ordinary lawyers and judges—to decide what sorts of abstractions they endorse or to arrive at a full understanding of what their abstract beliefs entail. In a liberal society committed to allowing people of different fundamental views to live together with mutual respect, the Rawlsian strategy may run up against confusion, limitations of time and capacity, and fears that political liberalism is itself too sectarian to serve as a defining political creed. I do not suggest that the Rawlsian project is unable to surmount these concerns. But participants in a liberal legal culture often seek agreement on what to do rather than exactly how to think. When they reach these agreements from diverse starting points, they can promote liberal goals in a way that has some distinctive advantages.

Of course some background abstractions, connected with liberty and equality, should limit the permissible set of incompletely theorized agreements. Otherwise there is no assurance that an incompletely theorized agreement is just, and we should design our legal and political systems so as to counteract the risk of unjust agreement. If we want to limit the category of incompletely theorized agreements, so as to ensure that they are defensible, we will have to make some movement in Rawls's direction, or at least toward more ambitious ways of thinking.

Hercules and Theory

An Ambitious Alternative

Enthusiasm for incompletely theorized agreements meets with many adversaries. Let us take Ronald Dworkin as an especially prominent example. In his illuminating work on legal reasoning, Dworkin urges, at least as an ideal, a high degree of theoretical self-consciousness in adjudication. Dworkin argues that when lawyers disagree about what the law is with respect to some hard question—Can the government ban hate speech? Cross-burning?—they are disagreeing about "the best constructive interpretation of the community's legal practice."[17] Thus Dworkin claims that interpretation in law consists of different efforts to make a governing text "the best it can be." This is Dworkin's conception of law as integrity. Under that conception, judges try to fit their rulings to preexisting legal materials, but they also invoke principle, in the sense that they try to cast those materials in their best light. The goal of the judge is to analyze the case at hand under the two dimensions of "fit" and "justification."

Hercules, Dworkin's infinitely patient and resourceful judge, approaches the law in this way. It is important for our purposes that on Dworkin's view, judges are obliged to account for the existing legal materials, whether judge-made or statutory, by weaving them together into a coherent framework.[18] Hence judges are not supposed to impose large-scale theories of their own making. Here we might appear to have the makings of an appreciation for incompletely theorized agreements, for reliance on precedent is a large part of those agreements.

But Dworkin does not defend incompletely theorized agreements. On the contrary, his account appears to require judges to develop high-level theories and does not (to say the least) favor theoretical modesty. In Dworkin's hands, the relevant theories are large and abstract; they sound just like political philosophy or moral theory.[19] On his view, the law of tort reflects a theory of equality, and the law of free speech a theory of autonomy. These theories are derived from and brought to bear on particular problems. But this is not how real lawyers proceed. They try to avoid broad and abstract questions. Such questions are too hard, large, and open-ended for legal actors to handle. They prevent people who disagree on large principles from reaching consensus on particular outcomes. In this way, Hercules could not really participate in ordinary judicial deliberations; he would be seen as a usurper, even an oddball.

In thinking about equal protection issues, for example, lawyers (and ordinary people) do not generate large-scale theories about the meaning of equality in a democracy. Instead they ask what particular sorts of practices seem clearly to violate the Fourteenth Amendment or the principle of equality, and then whether a measure discriminating against (for example) the handicapped is relevantly similar or relevantly different. Of course the description of relevant similarities and differences will have evaluative dimensions, and of course these should be made explicit. As we will see, an analogy depends for its plausibility on a principle of some sort. But lawyers and judges try not to engage in abstract political theorizing. They avoid such theorizing because it takes too much time and may be unnecessary; because it may go wrong insofar as it operates without close reference to actual cases; because it often prevents people from getting along at all; and because general theorizing can seem or be disrespectful insofar as it forces people to contend, unnecessarily, over their deepest and most defining moral commitments. Consider in this connection the idea that courts should not resolve constitutional issues unless they must in order to decide a case—an idea that imposes a presumptive taboo on judicial judgments about society's most basic or defining commitments.[20]

Dworkin anticipates an objection of this kind. He notes that it might be paralyzing for judges to seek a general theory for each area of law, and he acknowledges that Hercules is more methodical than any real-world judge can be. But Hercules, in Dworkin's view, "shows us the hidden structure of" ordinary "judgments and so lays these open to study and criticism."[21] Of course Hercules aims at a "comprehensive theory" of each area of law, whereas ordinary judges, unable to consider all lines of inquiry, must aim at a theory that is "partial." But Hercules's "judgments of fit and political morality are made on the same material and have the same character as theirs."

It is these points that I am denying here. The decisions of ordinary judges are based on different material and have a different character. They are less deeply theorized, not only because of limits of time and capacity, but also because of the distinctive morality of judging in a pluralistic society. I will qualify this claim below. But for the moment, the point suggests that the ordinary judge is no Hercules with less time on his hands, but a different sort of figure altogether.

Conceptual Ascent?

Borrowing from Henry Sidgwick's writings on ethical method,[22] an enthusiast for ambitious thinking might respond in the following way. There is often good reason for judges to raise the level of abstraction and ultimately to resort to large-scale theory. As a practical matter, concrete judgments about particular cases will prove inadequate for morality or law. Sometimes people do not have clear intuitions about how cases should come out; their intuitions are uncertain or shifting. Sometimes seemingly similar cases provoke different reactions, and it is necessary to raise the level of theoretical ambition to explain whether those different reactions are justified or to show that the seemingly similar cases are different after all. Sometimes people simply disagree. By looking at broader principles, we may be able to mediate the disagreement. In any case there is a problem of explaining our considered judgments about particular cases, in order to see whether they are not just a product of accident,[23] and at some point the law will want to offer that explanation.

For these reasons, a judge who does not theorize might end up being Herculean too. At least he had better have that aspiration in mind. When our modest judge joins an opinion that is incompletely theorized, he has to rely on a reason or a principle, justifying one outcome rather than another. The opinion must itself refer to a reason or principle; it cannot just announce a victor. Perhaps the low-level principle is wrong because it fails to fit with other cases or because it is not defensible as a matter of (legally relevant) political morality.

In short, the incompletely theorized agreement may be nothing to celebrate. It may be wrong or unreliable. The fact that people converge may be a kind of coincidence or an accident, and when they start thinking more deeply, they may be able to tell whether the judgment is really right. Thus if a judge is reasoning well, he should have before him a range of other cases, c through z, in which the principle is tested against others and refined. At least if he is a distinguished judge, he will experience a kind of "conceptual ascent," in which the more or less isolated and small low-level principle is finally made part of a more general theory. Perhaps this would be a paralyzing task, and perhaps our judge need not often attempt it. But it is an appropriate model for understanding law and an appropriate aspiration for judges.

The conceptual ascent seems especially desirable in light of the fact that incompletely theorized agreements will allow large pockets of inconsistency. Some areas of the law may appear coherent and make internal sense, but they may run into each other if they are compared. We may have a coherent category of law involving sex equality (though this would be fortunate indeed), and a coherent category involving racial equality (same qualification), but these categories may have a very strange and unsatisfactory relation to the categories involving sexual orientation and the handicapped. Various subcategories of tort law may make sense, but they may not fit together at all. More ambitious forms of reasoning seem necessary in order to test the low-level principles. In this way we might conclude that judges should think of incompletely theorized agreements as an early step toward something both wider and deeper. Many academic understandings of law, including economic analysis, undertake the task of showing that wider and deeper conception.[24]

There is some truth in this response. Moral reasoners should try to achieve vertical and horizontal consistency, not just the local pockets of coherence offered by incompletely theorized agreements. In democratic processes it is appropriate and sometimes indispensable to challenge existing practice in abstract terms. But the response ignores some of the distinctive characteristics of the arena in which real-world judges must do their work. Some of these limits involve bounded rationality and thus what should happen in a world in which judges face various constraints; some of them involve limits of role and appropriate judicial morality in a world in which judges are mere actors in a complex system, and in which people legitimately disagree on first principles. In light of these limits, incompletely theorized agreements have the many virtues described above, including the facilitation of convergence, the reduction of costs of disagreement, and the demonstration of humility and mutual respect.

As I have noted, incompletely theorized agreements are especially well-adapted to a system that must take precedents as fixed points; lawyers could not try to reach full integrity without severely compromising the system of precedent. Usually local coherence is the most to which lawyers may aspire. Just as legislation cannot be understood as if it came from a single mind, so too precedents, compiled by many people responding to different problems in many different periods, will not reflect a single authorial voice.

There are many lurking questions. How we do know whether moral or political judgments are right? What is the relation between provisional or considered judgments about particulars and corresponding judgments about abstractions?[25] Sometimes people write as if abstract theoretical judgments, or abstract theories, have a kind of reality and hardness that particular judgments lack, or as if abstract theories provide the answers to examination questions that particular judgments, frail as they are, may pass or fail. On this view, theories are searchlights that illuminate particular judgments and show them for what they really are. But we might think instead that there is no special magic in theories or abstractions, and that theories are simply the (humanly constructed) means by which people make sense of the judgments that constitute their ethical and political worlds. The abstract deserves no priority over the particular; neither should be treated as foundational. A (poor or crude) abstract theory may be a confused way of trying to make sense of our considered judgments about particular cases, which may be much better than the theory. In fact it is possible that moral judgments are best described not as an emanation of a broad theory, but instead as part of a process of reflection about prototypical cases or "precedents" from which moral thinkers—ordinary citizens and experts—work.[26]

Legitimacy

There is a final issue. Dworkin's conception of law as integrity contains a theory of what it means for law to be legitimate. Hercules, Dworkin's idealized judge, can produce vertical and horizontal consistency among judgments of principle in law. The same cannot be said of those who urge incompletely theorized agreements. A legal system pervaded by such agreements need not yield anything like full coherence. Perhaps this is a decisive defect. Perhaps it suffers from the standpoint of those who seek legitimacy in law.

Of course principled consistency should not be disparaged, and of course a regime of principled judgments has many advantages over imaginable alternatives. Of course problems of legitimacy may arise precisely because of the absence of such consistency. If you are treated differently from someone else—if you are treated worse or better—there should be a reason for the difference in treatment. In fact, however, the idea of integrity—insofar as it is focused on the judiciary—does not provide a convincing theory of legitimacy. Integrity, if a product of good judicial judgment, is neither necessary nor sufficient for legitimacy. Legitimacy stems not simply from principled consistency on the part of adjudicators, but from a justifiable exercise of authority, which requires a theory of just institutions. That theory should in turn be founded in democratic considerations, suitably constrained by an account of what interests should be immunized from democratic intrusion. Legitimacy is an outcome of well-functioning democratic processes, not of a system of distinction-making undertaken by judges. Even if done exceptionally well, distinction-making by principled judges is too court-centered as a source of legitimacy.

Those who stress incompletely theorized agreements insist that adjudication is part of a complex set of institutional arrangements, most prominently including democratic arenas. They attempt to design their theory of judicial judgment as an aspect of a far broader set of understandings about appropriate institutional arrangements and about forums in which the (suitably constrained) public can deliberate about its judgments. For reasons of both policy and principle, the development of large-scale theories of the right and the good is a democratic task, not a judicial one. These remarks should suggest the ingredients of an account of legitimacy of which incompletely theorized agreements would be a part.

Incompletely Theorized Agreements over Time

Incompletely theorized agreements have virtues, but their virtues are partial. Stability, for example, is brought about by such agreements, and stability is usually desirable; but a system that is stable and unjust should probably be made less stable. In this section I offer some qualifications to what has been said thus far. In brief: Some cases cannot be decided *at all* without introducing a fair amount in the way of theory. Moreover, some cases cannot be decided *well* without introducing theory. If a good theory is available and if judges can be persuaded that the theory is good, there should be no taboo on its judicial acceptance. The claims on behalf of incompletely theorized agreements are presumptive rather than conclusive.

Change

Thus far we have offered a static description of the legal process—a description in which judges are deciding what to do at a certain time. Of course low-level principles are developed over long periods, and a dynamic picture shows something different and more complex. The understanding may shift and perhaps deepen. What was once part of the uncontested background may be drawn into sharp question. At one point, commercial speech seems analogous to a threat and is therefore unprotected; at another point, it seems more analogous to political speech and is therefore protected.

A characteristic role of observers of the legal process is to try to systematize cases in order to see how to make best sense of them, or in order to show that no sense can be made of them at all. In any process of systematization, higher-level considerations might well be introduced. Observers will try to invoke some higher-level idea of the good or the right in order to show the deep structure of the case law, to move it in particular directions, or to reveal important, even fatal inconsistencies. Thus it might be shown that tort law reflects a commitment to economic efficiency, but the commitment is uncertain and wavering, and some aspects of the law might be changed. Or it might be urged that the law of free speech is basically founded on a principle of personal autonomy, but that some aspects of the law ignore that principle and hence should be revised. A demonstration that the law makes deep sense might be a source of comfort. A demonstration that the law makes no sense, or reflects an ad hoc compromise among competing principles, might produce discomfort and small or large-scale change.

Sometimes the law reflects more ambitious thinking on the part of judges or reacts to these more ambitious efforts by outsiders. The American law of antitrust, for example, is now based in large part on a principle of economic efficiency. This development occurred through the gradual incorporation of more modern economic thinking into the cases, beginning with the judicial suggestion, following academic observation, that some important cases "actually" or "implicitly" were founded on neoclassical economics, until the point where economics appeared to offer a large ordering role.[27] Some especially ambitious or creative judges invoke theories too. For example, some of the greatest American judges were principally nontheoretical thinkers (Harlan, Friendly, perhaps Cardozo), but some of them—Holmes, Brandeis, Marshall—had at least ingredients of a large-scale vision of the legal order. They used analogies, to be sure, but often with reference to at least a relatively high-level theory about some aspect of law. Many areas of law now show the influence of Holmes, Brandeis, and Marshall, and in part because courts, whether or not deploying low-level principles, have adopted aspects of the relevant theory.[28]

It is rare for any area of law to be highly theorized. Most of the time judges and lawyers operating from divergent starting points can accept legal outcomes. But small-scale, low-level principles can eventually become part of something more ambitious, and more ambitious thinking is not necessarily bad. A descriptive point first: After a time, the use of low-level principles can produce a more completely theorized system of law. To engage in analogy, for example, a reason is always required, and after a period, the low-level reasons may start to run into each other, perhaps producing debates at a higher level of abstraction. During those debates the concrete rulings may be synthesized and a more general principle may emerge. Sometimes the process of low-level judging will yield greater abstraction or a highly refined and coherent set of principles—the conceptual ascent. In the areas of free speech and discrimination, some such process has occurred in the United States, with occasionally ambitious claims, even if it would be far too much to say that full theorization or coherence can be found.

An especially interesting phenomenon occurs when a once-contestable analogy becomes part of the uncontested background for ordinary legal work—or when the uncontested background is drawn into sharp question, sometimes via analogies. Thus, for example, the view that bans on racial intermarriage are "like" segregation laws is taken largely for granted in the United States; it is part of the way that American lawyers order their conceptual world. So too perhaps with the view that sex discrimination is "like" race discrimination—a view that would have been unthinkable in United States Supreme Court opinions as late as, say, 1965. Ordinarily the slippage from the uncontested background to the contested occurs in law through encounters with particular cases that reveal gaps or problems with the conventional view. In American law, views that were taken as natural—not even as views at all—sometimes become dislodged in this way. The original attack on the monarchical legacy took this form; consider Gordon Wood's suggestion that before that attack "so distinctive and so separated was the aristocracy from ordinary folk that many still thought the two groups represented two orders of being. . . . Ordinary people were thought to be different physically, and because of varying diets and living conditions, no doubt in many cases they were different. People often assumed that a handsome child, though apparently a commoner, had to be some gentleman's bastard offspring."[29]

Similar changes accompanied and helped produce the continuing attack on racial hierarchy. So too for the New Deal, which depended on an insistence that common law categories were far from natural and prepolitical, but instead were a conscious social choice.[30] Eventually the contested can become uncontroversial as new categories emerge and harden through repeated encounters with particular cases.

Now let us turn to the question of what judges should do. If judges can agree on a high-level theory, and if the theory can be shown to be a good one, judicial acceptance of a high-level theory is hardly troubling; on the contrary, it is an occasion for celebration. Who could object to judicial adoption of what is by hypothesis a good theory? Perhaps this has happened with the triumph of economic thinking in the law of antitrust; perhaps it could be said for the eventual victory of a particular conception of equality in the law relating to discrimination on the basis of race, sex, and sexual orientation. But any resulting theory will likely have been developed through generalizing and clarifying incompletely theorized outcomes and doing so by constant reference to concrete cases, against which the theory is measured. At least part of the test of the theory—if it is a theory of law meant for judicial adoption—is how well it accounts for previous cases and for considered judgments about those cases, though of course judicial mistakes are possible, and these may be corrected by the theory, subject to the constraints of stare decisis.

I am thus declining to endorse what might be called a strong version of the argument offered here: a claim that incompletely theorized agreements are always the appropriate approach to law and that general theory is always illegitimate in law. What makes sense is a more modest point, keyed to the institutional characteristics of judges in any legal system we are likely to have. Judges should adopt a presumption rather than a taboo against high-level theorization. In many contexts they will not be able to think of a good theory. In many cases they will not be able to agree on any theory. The effort to reach agreement on an abstract theory may make it hard for judges or other people to live and work together, and unnecessary contests over theory can show an absence of respect for the deepest and most defining commitments of other people.

Of course there are intrapersonal parallels. In our ethical lives as individuals, each of us may avoid choice among theories if we do not need to choose in order to decide what to do in particular cases. But the interpersonal case is perhaps more vivid.

In many contexts, moreover, judges will not be able to know whether an apparently good theory really is right. The acceptance of a theory will create an excessive risk of future error. These possibilities are sufficient for the claims defended here. Judges should adopt a more complete theory for an area of law only if they are very sure that it is correct.

It may even happen that an area of judge-made law will become *less* theorized over time. A once-acceptable general theory may come to seem inadequate, and confrontations with particular cases may show its inadequacy and make it unravel. The American Supreme Court's decisions in the *Lochner* era, in which the Court struck down minimum wage and maximum hour laws, were well-theorized, in the sense that they were founded on a recognizable general theory of the permissible role of the state.[31] The general theory was not replaced with a new one all of a sudden, or even at all; instead it came apart through particular cases that attacked the periphery and then the core. This is a familiar phenomenon, as the process of case-by-case decision tests any general theory and exposes its limits. Over time, an area of law may become more theorized or less so. Over long periods of time, it may go from one to the other and back again.

If all this is right, we ought not to think of incompletely theorized agreements on particulars as a kind of unfortunate second-best, adapted for a world in which people disagree, are confused or biased, and have limited time. The alleged first-best—Hercules or the (exhausted?) judge who has reached reflective equilibrium—calls for an extrahuman conception of law. It is extrahuman because it is so obviously unsuited to the real world. To say the least, it is hard to know whether a top-down or highly theorized approach is appropriate for morality. But often, at least, it is easy to know that such an approach is inappropriate for law. The institutional features of the legal system—a human entity with distinctive constraints—require an account of law that is highly sensitive to the characteristics of the system in which it is situated. Among those characteristics are confusion or uncertainty about general theory; deep disputes about the right and the good; and a pressing need to make a wide range of particular decisions.

Disagreement

What of disagreement? The discussion thus far has focused on the need for convergence. There is indeed such a need, but it is only part of the picture. In law, as in politics, disagreement can be a productive and creative force, revealing error, showing gaps, moving discussion and results in good directions. The American political order has placed a high premium on "government by discussion," and when the process is working well, this is true for the judiciary as well as for other institutions. Progress in law is often fueled by failures of convergence and by sharp disagreement on both the particular and the general. Agreements in law may be a product of coercion, subtle or not, or of a failure of imagination.

Legal disagreements have many legitimate sources. Two of these sources are especially important. First, people may share general commitments but disagree on particular outcomes. In law as in morality, this is no less pervasive a social phenomenon than its converse, which I have stressed here. People may think, for example, that it is wrong to take an innocent life, but disagree about whether the Constitution protects the right to have an abortion. Second, people's disagreements on general principles may produce disagreement over particular outcomes and low-level propositions as well. People who think that an autonomy principle accounts for freedom of speech may also think that the government cannot regulate truthful, nondeceptive commercial advertising—whereas people who think that freedom of speech is basically a democratic idea, and is focused on political speech, may have no interest in protecting commercial advertising at all. Academic theorizing about law can have a salutary function in part because it tests low-level principles by reference to more ambitious claims. Disagreements can be productive by virtue of this process of testing.

Disagreements can thus be desirable, and incompletely theorized agreements may be nothing to celebrate. Certainly if everyone having a reasonable general view converges on a particular (by hypothesis reasonable) judgment, nothing is amiss. But if an agreement is incompletely theorized, there is a risk that everyone who participates in the agreement is mistaken, and hence that the outcome is mistaken. There is also a risk that someone who is reasonable has not participated, and that if that person were included, the agreement would break down. Over time, incompletely theorized agreements should be subject to scrutiny and critique. That process may result in more ambitious thinking than law ordinarily entails.

Nor is social consensus a consideration that outweighs everything else. Usually it would be much better to have a just outcome, rejected by many people, than an unjust outcome with which all or most agree. Consensus or agreement is important largely because of its connection with stability, itself a valuable but far from overriding social goal. As Thomas Jefferson wrote, a degree of turbulence is productive in a democracy.[32] We have seen that incompletely theorized agreements, even if stable and broadly supported, may conceal or reflect injustice. Certainly agreements should be more fully theorized when the relevant theory is plainly right, and people can be shown that it is right, or when the invocation of the theory is necessary to decide cases. None of this is inconsistent with what I have claimed here.

It would be foolish to say that no general theory can produce agreement, even more foolish to deny that some general theories deserve general support, and most foolish of all to say that incompletely theorized agreements warrant respect whatever their content. What seems plausible is something more modest: Except in unusual situations and for multiple reasons, general theories are an unlikely foundation for judge-made law, and caution and humility about general theory are appropriate for courts, at least when multiple theories can lead in the same direction. This more modest set of claims helps us to characterize incompletely theorized agreements as important phenomena with their own special virtues. They are the crucial part of the lawyer's distinctive solution to social pluralism.

Principle, Politics, Law

In the last generation in America, many people argued that courts engage in principled reasoning, elaborating basic social commitments, while the political process involves a kind of ad hoc set of judgments, producing unprincipled compromises.[33] This view finds its most dramatic statement in the suggestion that constitutional courts are "the forum of principle"[34] in American government.

This view is historically myopic. It reflects the spell cast by the Warren Court over the academic study of law. Courts do offer reasons and usually invoke principles, but those principles tend to be modest and low-level.

By contrast, high principle has had its most important and most defining moments inside the political branches of government, not within courtrooms. The American system is a deliberative democracy in which the system of electoral politics is combined with an aspiration to political reason-giving. The real forum of principle in American government has been democratic rather than adjudicative; consider the founding, the Civil War, the New Deal, and others—progressivism, the civil rights movement, the women's movement. Certainly the same basic point is true for other nations, including, to take some diverse and varied examples, England, France, Germany, South Africa, and Hungary. The basic democratic norms—political equality, broad deliberation, expansive rights of participation—are hard to transplant into judicial arenas.

The question might therefore be asked if it would be possible to reverse the conventional formulation, with the view that high principle plays an appropriately large role in the democratic arena, and that low-level principles are the more appropriate stuff of adjudication. Any such view would be too simple, but there is a good deal of truth to it. Of course high principle does not characterize ordinary politics, in which self-interest and logrolling play an important part. But high principle has had a defining role in American political life, and in any case the principles that mark American constitutionalism owe their origins to political rather than legal developments. Courts usually work from lower-level principles, even when they interpret the Constitution. There are important exceptions, with courts also making or referring to arguments of high principle, but ordinarily those exceptions consist of vindications of (certain readings of) constitutional judgments made by previous generations. The courts' usual reluctance to offer high-level principles stems from the judges' lack of democratic pedigree, which pushes them in the direction of incompletely theorized agreements, and from their limited remedial power, which properly makes judges reluctant to attempt large-scale social reforms on their own. As I have suggested, the argument on behalf of incompletely theorized agreements is therefore part of a theory of just institutions in general and deliberative democracy in particular, with a claim that fundamental principles are best developed politically rather than judicially.

There is, however, an exception to the general claim that I have made throughout this chapter. In order for participants in law (or democracy) to accept that general claim, they must accept at least one general theory: The theory that I have attempted to defend. This is the theory that tells them to favor incompletely theorized agreements. That theory should not itself be accepted without reference to general theoretical considerations, and its acceptance or rejection should not be incompletely theorized. Many people claim that law should reflect a high-level theory of the right or the good, and they will not be satisfied with incompletely theorized agreements.[35] The choice between the two approaches will turn on issues that are both high level and controversial.

This is an important matter. But it is notable that the belief in incompletely theorized agreements, while tacit, is quite widespread. The best evidence is the legal culture itself: Such agreements are the usual stuff of law, and participants in the legal culture are ordinarily suspicious of much in the way of theoretical ambition. There are reasons for their suspicion. What I have tried to do here is to spell out those reasons and to connect them to some of the most notable characteristics of thinking in law.

3

Analogical Reasoning

Much of legal reasoning is analogical: Is case A like case B? Or instead like case C? Is a ban on obscenity like a ban on political speech, or instead like a ban on threats? Is a prohibition on abortion like a prohibition on murder, or like a compulsory kidney transplant? Ordinary people make sense of the world by discerning patterns rooted in analogical thinking. The patterns found in the law also have analogical sources.

My principal interest in this chapter is legal reasoning within the court system. It is here that analogical reasoning finds its natural home. I shall argue that courts are drawn to analogical reasoning in large part because analogies allow people to reach incompletely theorized agreements. To say that one case is like another, we need a reason or a principle, but often, at least, we can offer a reason or a principle that operates at a low level of ambition.

Legislators use analogies all the time, but they often do and should reason in an ambitious way, and they often do and should set down rules in advance, rather than leaving things to judgments in individual cases. Imagine an effort to leave a tax code to be developed by courts through analogies or to identify the proper ingredients of the Clean Air Act via analogical thinking! Rules, like analogies, can be incompletely theorized, but rules are often favored over analogies precisely in order to cabin official discretion and to promote the traditional rule of law virtues.

A particularly interesting feature of analogical reasoning is its persistence within legal systems committed to the rule of law. In England and America, the common law places a premium on analogical thinking. In the United States, most constitutional cases are decided not by reference to constitutional text or history, but through analogies and thus through casuistical thinking. As we will see, analogies are often crucial in deciding on the meaning of rules themselves. We can therefore use analogical reasoning not only as a way of getting a better understanding of incompletely theorized agreements, but also in order to build a conception of the rule of law that allows a place for particularity as well as generality.

Features of Analogy

Analogical thinking is pervasive in law and in everyday life. In ordinary discussions of political and legal questions, people proceed analogically. You think that racial hate speech is not protected by the First Amendment. Does this mean that government can silence political extremists? A familiar argumentative technique is to show inconsistency between someone's claim about case x in light of his views on case y. The goal is to reveal hypocrisy or confusion, or to force the claimant to show how the apparently deep commitment on the case about which the discussants agree can be squared with the claimant's view about a case on which they disagree.

In analogical thinking as I understand it here, deep theories about the good or the right are not deployed. (Of course, it would be possible to reason analogically to justify or to build a large-scale theory, in science or ethics.) Such theories seem too sectarian, too large, too divisive, too obscure, too high-flown, too ambitious, too confusing, too contentious, too abstract. On the other hand, analogizers cannot reason from one particular to another particular without saying something at least a little abstract. They must say that case A was decided rightly *for a reason*, and they must say that that reason applies, or does not apply, in case B. I will try to show that this method of proceeding is ideally suited to a legal system consisting of numerous judges who disagree on first principles, who lack scales, and who must take most decided cases as fixed points from which to proceed.

In General

Analogies Outside of Law

Everyday thought is informed by analogical thinking; we see things as we do largely because of analogies. Much creativity depends on seeing patterns, or likenesses, where these had not been seen before. Advances in science are often founded on discerning new patterns of commonality. Human creativity might even be defined as "the capacity to see or interpret a problematic phenomenon as an unexpected or unusual instance of a prototypical pattern already in one's conceptual repertoire."[1] The point is not limited to human beings. Even nonhuman animals think analogically.[2]

Analogical reasoning helps to inform our judgments about factual issues on which we are uncertain. I have a German shepherd dog, and I know that he is gentle with children. When I see another German shepherd dog, I assume that he too will be gentle with children. I have a Toyota Camry, and I know that it starts even on cold days in winter. I assume that my friend's Toyota Camry will start on cold winter days as well. There is a simple structure to this kind of thinking. (1) A has some characteristic x, or characteristics x, y, and z. (2) B shares that characteristic or some or all of those characteristics. (3) A also has some characteristic Q. (4) Because A and B share some characteristic or characteristics, we conclude what is not yet known, that B shares characteristic Q as well.[3]

This is a usual form of reasoning in daily life, but it raises many questions. The problem or "target" case B has something in common with many possible "source" cases; it is a great puzzle how we decide what we will choose as the relevant source or prototypical case for comparison. Perhaps I should compare the unknown German shepherd not with my own dog, but with some other German shepherd in the neighborhood, who is not so gentle with children. Or perhaps I should compare the unknown German shepherd not with other German shepherds at all, but with a dog owned by someone "like" the person who owns that German shepherd. Or perhaps I should look to another of the innumerable facets of the situation. In law and elsewhere, there is often a simple, intuitive understanding that the puzzle case B is analogous to source cases A and C, but not to D and E. But greater reflection may show mistakes, bias, or inadequate care in the selection of source cases.

It will readily appear that analogical thinking does not guarantee truth. The existence of one or many shared characteristics does not mean that all characteristics are shared. Some German shepherd dogs are not gentle with children. Some Toyota Camrys do not start on cold days in winter. For analogical reasoning to work well, we have to say that the relevant, known similarities give us good reason to believe that there are further similarities as well and thus help to answer the open question. Of course this is not always so. At most, analogical thinking can give rise to a judgment about probabilities, and these are of uncertain magnitude.

Analogical Thinking in Law: Its Characteristic Form

Analogical reasoning has a simple structure in law. Consider some examples. We know that an employer may not fire an employee for agreeing to perform jury duty; it is said to "follow" that an employer is banned from firing an employee for refusing to commit perjury. We know that a speech by a member of the Ku Klux Klan, advocating racial hatred, cannot be regulated unless it is likely to incite and directed to inciting imminent lawless action;[4] it is said to follow that the government cannot forbid members of the Nazi Party to march in Skokie, Illinois. We know that there is no constitutional right to welfare, medical care, or housing;[5] it is said to follow that there is no constitutional right to government protection against domestic violence.

From a brief glance at these cases, we can get a sense of the characteristic form of analogical thought in law. The process appears to work in five simple steps. (1) Some fact pattern A—the "source" case—has certain characteristics; call them x, y, and z. (2) Fact pattern B—the "target" case—has characteristics x, y, and a, or characteristics x, y, z, and a. (3) A is treated a certain way in law. (4) Some principle, created or discovered in the process of thinking through A, B, and their interrelations, explains why A is treated the way that it is. (5) Because of what it shares in common with A, B should be treated the same way. It is covered by the same principle.

For example, someone asking for protection against domestic violence is requesting affirmative government assistance, just like someone asking the government for medical care. This is what the two cases have in common. If we know that there is no constitutional right to medical care, it might be said to follow that there is no constitutional right to protection against domestic violence, because of the principle to the effect that government need not furnish affirmative assistance to people in need.

Some people think that analogical reasoning is really a form of deduction, but this is a mistake. To be sure, analogical reasoning cannot proceed without identification of a governing idea—a principle, a standard, or a rule—to account for the results in the source and target cases. This is the crucial step (4). But the governing idea is not given in advance and applied to the new case. Instead, analogical reasoning helps identify the governing idea and is indispensable to the identification; we do not know what the idea is until we have assessed the cases. Analogy and disanalogy are created or discovered through the process of comparing cases, as people discern a principle that makes sense of their considered judgments.

Consider some issues in the law of free speech. Suppose that the government seeks to ban a speech by a member of the Ku Klux Klan, spreading racial hatred. Suppose too that the Supreme Court, not reasoning analogically, concludes that the speech cannot be regulated, on the ground that speech cannot be punished unless it creates a risk of likely, imminent violence.[6] A few years later members of the American Nazi Party propose to march in Skokie, Illinois, the home of survivors of concentration camps in Nazi Germany. The second case contains a large number of differences from the first. It involves the Nazis, not the Klan; it involves a march, not a speech; the audience is hostile rather than sympathetic. These or other differences might produce a refinement of the principle that speech cannot be regulated unless it creates a risk of likely, imminent violence. Suppose, however, that the Court decides that the differences are not relevant, and that the principle, as originally announced, covers the second case as well, and protects the Nazi march. In a third case, the question is raised whether the government can punish a threat to assassinate the president; let us suppose there is no risk of imminent violence because the speaker is hopelessly ineffectual. The Court might conclude that threats should be treated differently from political speeches, because (for example) threats do not qualify as a legitimate part of democratic deliberation. If the Court says something like this, it embarks on a casuistical process of refining the original principle, saying that the principle, as announced in the Klan case, makes sense only in certain restricted settings. Through some such process a complex body of law might emerge. The governing legal ideas are not given in advance, but emerge from the process of comparing cases.

We can now see an important difference between analogical reasoning in science and analogical reasoning in law and ethics. When scientists engage in analogy, they often use some case A to produce a probabilistic judgment that they think bears on case B. If dropped objects fall in New York, dropped objects will probably fall in London too. Analogical reasoning is imperfectly reliable in science because we do not (by hypothesis) have a full sense of the relevant causal mechanisms. If we had that full sense, we would not need analogies, though analogies might serve a heuristic function.[7]

Law and ethics are different. Here the key work is done not by a probabilistic judgment (based on known similarities), but by development of a normative principle (also based on known similarities). Of course no one should deny the creative function of analogical thinking in science, where new patterns are created or discovered, and where aesthetic judgments can play a role in evaluation.[8]

It should readily appear that analogical reasoning does not guarantee good outcomes in law. For analogical reasoning to operate properly, we have to know that cases A and B are "relevantly" similar, and that there are not "relevant" differences between them. Even seemingly similar cases are always different from each other and along innumerable dimensions. The Klan is involved in one case, the Nazis in another; is this not a relevant difference? When lawyers say that there are no relevant differences, they mean that any differences between the two cases (1) do not make a difference in light of the precedents, which foreclose certain possible grounds for distinction or (2) cannot be fashioned into the basis for a distinction that makes sense or is genuinely principled. A claim that one case is genuinely analogous to another—that it is "apposite" or cannot be "distinguished"—is parasitic on conclusion (1) or (2), and either of these must of course be justified.

The key task for analogical reasoners is to decide when there are relevant similarities and differences. Of course the judgment that a distinction is not genuinely principled requires a substantive argument of some kind. What, then, are the characteristics of a competent lawyer's inquiry into analogies?

The Features of Analogy

In law, analogical reasoning has four different but overlapping features: *principled consistency; a focus on particulars; incompletely theorized judgments; and principles operating at a low or intermediate level of abstraction.* Taken in concert, these features produce both the virtues and the vices of analogical reasoning in law. Here are some brief remarks on each of these features.

First, and most obviously, judgments about specific cases must be made consistent with one another. A requirement of principled consistency is a hallmark of analogical reasoning (as it is of reasoning of almost all sorts). It follows that in producing the necessary consistency, some principle, harmonizing seemingly disparate outcomes, will be invoked to explain the cases. The principle must of course be more general than the outcome for which it is designed.

Second, analogical reasoning is focused on particulars, and it develops from concrete controversies. Holmes put the point in this suggestive if somewhat misleading way: A common law court "decides the case first and determines the principle afterwards."⁹ Holmes' suggestion is misleading since in order to decide the case at all, one has to have the principle in some sense in mind; there can be no sequential operation of quite the kind Holmes describes. But Holmes is right to say that ideas are developed with close reference to the details, rather than imposed on them from above. In this sense, analogical reasoning, as a species of casuistry, is a form of "bottom-up" thinking.¹⁰ Unlike many kinds of reasoning, it does not operate from the top down.

Despite the analogizer's focus on particulars, we have seen that any description of a particular holding inevitably has some more general components. We cannot know anything about case x if we do not know something about the reasons that count in its favor. We cannot say whether case x has anything to do with case y unless we are able to abstract, a bit, from the facts and holding of case x. The key point is that analogical reasoning involves a process in which principles are developed from and with constant reference to particular cases.

Third, analogical reasoning in law operates without anything like a deep or comprehensive theory that would account for the particular outcomes it yields. The judgments that underlie convictions about the relevant case are incompletely theorized. Of course, there is a continuum from the most particularistic and low-level principles to the deepest and most general. I suggest only that analogizers in law avoid those approaches that come close to the deeply theorized or the foundational, and that to this extent, lawyers are generally analogizers and hence casuists.

Lawyers might firmly believe, for example, that the Constitution does not create a right to welfare, that political speech cannot be regulated without a showing of immediate and certain harm, or that government may impose environmental regulations on private companies. But usually lawyers are not able to explain the basis for these beliefs in great depth or detail or with full specification of the theory that accounts for those beliefs. Lawyers (and almost all other people) typically lack any large-scale theory.¹¹ They reason anyway, and their reasoning is analogical.

Consider in this connection a famous story of the early days of law and economics at the University of Chicago Law School. Edward Levi—a great champion of analogical reasoning—decided to introduce economics into his antitrust course, and he chose to do so by allowing every fifth class to be taught by the economist Aaron Director, in many ways the father of modern law and economics. As the story goes, Levi would spend four classes in the lawyer's fashion, brilliantly rationalizing the seemingly inconsistent judicial holdings. In the fifth class, Director would explain, with the economist's tools, why everything that Levi said was wrong.

Eventually—the story goes—even Levi was converted. The supposed moral of the story is that lawyers' reasoning, even by its most able practitioners, is far inferior to economics, most of all because it lacks clear criteria or a set of specified governing values. In the area of antitrust, this may well be true. But it is not true everywhere. And if this is so, there are places in which those now occupying the place of Levi should not be converted by those now occupying the place of Director.

Fourth, and finally, analogical reasoning produces principles that operate at a low or intermediate level of abstraction. If we say that an employer may not fire an employee for accepting jury duty, we might mean (for example) that an employer cannot require an employee to commit a crime. This is a standard, perhaps even a rule, and it does involve a degree of abstraction from the particular case; but it does not entail any high-level theory about labor markets, or about the appropriate relationship between employers and employees. If we say that a Nazi march cannot be banned, we might mean that political speech cannot be stopped without a showing of clear and immediate harm; but in so saying, we do not invoke any large theory about the purposes of the free speech guarantee, or about the relation between the citizen and the state. People can converge on the low-level principle from various foundations or without well-understood foundations at all.

If we put interpretation of rules to one side, as a partial exception, reasoning by analogy, understood in light of these four characteristics, is the mode through which the ordinary lawyer operates. He has no abstract theory to account for his convictions or for what he knows to be the law. But he knows that these are his convictions or that this is the law, and he is able to bring that knowledge to bear on undecided cases. For guidance, he looks to areas in which his judgment is firm.

Arguments, Constitutive Analogies, and Metaphors

Some claims of analogy depend on contested arguments. If you think that a ban on misleading commercial speech is "like" a ban on misleading political speech, and therefore to be protected by the Constitution, you need to offer an explanation. Other claims of analogy depend on arguments that might at some point be contested but that are, in the relevant communities, taken for granted and do not really need to be defended publicly. The idea that a restriction on the speech of socialists is like a restriction on speech by Republicans, and protected by the Constitution, has this form.

Still other analogies are simply constitutive of the thinking of people in the relevant community. Such analogies, or perceptions of likeness, do not depend on arguments, but rest instead on a widely shared way that human beings order their world. We do not really need an argument in order to say that one cat is, in its catness, relevantly like other cats. We take the point for granted; it is part of our language, our way of seeing the world. This form of categorization is different from the view, plausible but in need of an argument, that a ban on the work of the gay artist Robert Mapplethorpe is like a ban on *Ulysses*, or the claim, sharply disputed within the Supreme Court, that an affirmative action program is like discrimination against blacks.

Of course the distinction between analogies that depend on contestable arguments and analogies that constitute how people order their world is largely contingent and conventional—a function of existing social judgments. Sometimes the different kinds of analogies operate like points on a continuum, and there are important shifts over time from one category to another. A great deal of creativity in law consists of the effort to show that a judgment about likeness that seems constitutive of thought actually depends on contestable substantive judgments—and vice versa.

A good deal of recent attention has been devoted to the relationship between analogy and metaphor.[12] Here there is much room for further thought about both analogy and metaphor in law. I make one brief point here. Consider the statement "Abortion is murder," a statement that in the abstract could be intended and received either as a metaphor or as an analogy. If it is a metaphor, we know that the speaker believes that abortion is not literally murder, but is seeking to cast some light on the subject precisely by departing from literal description. ("Holmes was a lion of the law." "Michael Jordan is God.") But if the statement is an analogy, the speaker is claiming, and understood to be claiming, that abortion really is murder in the relevant respects; there is no acknowledgment that the statement is literally untrue. Here lies a large difference between metaphor and analogy.[13]

Fixed Points

Thus far I have suggested that analogical thinking operates by taking some precedents or judgments as "fixed points" for analysis. But the idea is more complex than it first appears. Begin by distinguishing three possibilities. (1) Some decided cases cannot legitimately be overruled by some judges. They must be taken as authoritative; they are truly "binding." This is the case with respect to lower court receptions of Supreme Court decisions. (2) Some cases can be overruled—they are not "binding"—but only in quite exceptional circumstances. This is the ordinary view about the responsibilities of the Supreme Court with respect to its own precedents. (3) Some judgments are not embodied in cases at all. They are not precedents, but they seem so obvious and irresistible that they have the status of a decided case. Consider the idea that government may not jail Christians because of their religion or force Hispanics alone to donate blood to people who need blood to survive.

These distinctions may clarify things, but a problem remains. Even if we know that some cases are authoritative in the sense that they are binding, and that others must be respected except in extreme circumstances, how do we know what past cases "stand for"? The distinction between a case's "holding" and the court's mere "dicta" is designed to handle this problem. The holding is usually described as the outcome in the case, accompanied by the narrowest rationale necessary to defend it. By contrast, the dicta consist of language in the opinion that is not necessary to the outcome. This distinction is not simple to apply, and it is therefore not so clear what it means to say that a holding is authoritative. Often we come to see that a court originally justified an outcome by an argument that turns out to be too broad, once other cases are brought forward. Often we conclude that the argument in favor of a certain outcome was too narrow, in the sense that once we consult other cases, we see that a broader principle will do much better. Those who come up with rationales for outcomes are rarely able to anticipate the full range of cases to which those rationales might apply.

The subsequent court's characterization of any "holding" in a past case is a constructive act, not a simple matter of finding something. Holdings are not given in advance. At the same time, one cannot characterize any holding absolutely any way at all, and the constraints on characterization are enough to undergird the enterprise of analogy.

Precedents as Rules and Analogies

A precedent can serve as *either a rule or an analogy*. It serves as a rule to the extent that it governs all identical cases, that is, all cases that are "on all fours" with it, in the sense that it is obvious that they are relevantly similar and there are no relevant differences between them.

A precedent serves not as a rule but as an analogy to the extent that it is at least plausibly distinguishable from the case at hand, but suggestive of a more general principle or policy that seems relevant to that case. Members of the Ku Klux Klan cannot be stopped from speaking. Does it not follow that members of the Nazi Party cannot be stopped from marching? Often it is hard to distinguish precedents as rules from precedents as analogies; we can see what we have only after we start to think and talk. We might ultimately conclude that a precedent that appears to be a mere analogy for case x is actually a rule for case x because there are clearly no differences between the precedent and case x—because the analogy is obviously "apposite." The subsequent court may therefore have to construct—to create for the first time—the precise factual predicate for the outcome in the course of deciding the subsequent case.

All this is a matter of shared understandings, and nothing more. When a precedent is said to be a rule, it is because it is believed so closely analogous to the case at hand, or because there are so clearly relevant similarities without relevant differences, that people agree that it "binds," and no one wants to suggest that it is "merely" an analogy. When a precedent is said to be an analogy, and not a rule, it is because there is at least plausibly a relevant difference between the two cases, and because there is no simple judgment that the precedent covers the case at hand. In the course of deciding the case, we might conclude that the analogy is "apposite," but here what emerges will be no simple (in the sense of obvious) statement of preexisting law, but instead a rule or a principle whose content was determined amid controversy and not given in advance.

All cases are potentially distinguishable; when we say that case B (involving, say, a march by Nazis) is identical to case A (involving a speech by members of the Klan), we have selected some characteristics that are shared and treated as irrelevant those characteristics that are unshared. When two cases appear identical to us, it is because we have suppressed, as irrelevant, their inevitable differences. It is the subsequent court that makes judgments about relevant similarities and relevant differences. And it will be readily apparent that because of the importance of shared understandings, whether the precedent is a rule or an analogy is an artifact of substantive ideas of some sort. We could imagine a community in which the Nazi speech was plausibly or even obviously different from the Klan speech. Or we could imagine a community in which a threat to assassinate the president is obviously similar to the Klan speech.

Analogical Confusion

Analogical reasoning can of course be done poorly. Sometimes the selection of a particular "source" case is inadequately justified; sometimes judges treat some case A as the obvious basis for analogical thinking, even though cases B and C would be a better place to begin. Sometimes the creative dimensions of analogical thought are downplayed, as people simply announce that case A is analogous to case B, when an unarticulated supplemental judgment is necessary and not defended. William James described a related phenomenon as "vicious abstractionism":

> We conceive a concrete situation by singling out some salient or important feature in it, and classing it under that; then, instead of adding to its previous characters all the positive consequences which the new way of conceiving it may bring, we proceed to use our concept privatively; reducing the originally rich phenomenon to the naked suggestions of that name abstractly taken, treating it as a case of "nothing but" that concept, and acting as if all the other characters from out of which the concept is abstracted were expunged. Abstraction, functioning in this way, becomes a means of arrest far more than a means of advance in thought. It mutilates things.[14]

Different factual situations are inarticulate; they do not impose order on themselves. The method of analogy is based on the question: Is case A relevantly similar to case B, or not? To answer such questions, one needs a theory of relevant similarities and differences. Everything is similar in innumerable ways to everything else, and different from everything else in the same number of ways. In the face of this fact, formalist analogical thinking—resting on an argument that is not offered—is no better than any other kind of bad formalism. Courts should always stand ready to explain and justify the claim that one thing is analogous to another.

Analogical reasoning can go wrong not simply because it is formalist, but also because it rests on an inadequately defended judgment about relevant similarities and differences. Consider, for example, Justice Holmes's notorious argument in *Buck v. Bell*,[15] the case upholding compulsory sterilization of the "feeble-minded":

> We have seen more than once that the public welfare may call upon the best citizens for their lives. It would be strange if it could not call upon those who already sap the strength of the State for these lesser sacrifices, often not felt to be such by those concerned. . . . The principle that sustains compulsory vaccination is broad enough to cover cutting the Fallopian tubes. Three generations of imbeciles are enough.

Holmes is arguing that if people can be conscripted during wartime or forced to obtain vaccinations, it follows that the state can require sterilization of the "feeble-minded." But this is a casual and unpersuasive claim. Many principles cover the first two cases without also covering the third. We might think that a vaccination is far less intrusive than sterilization, and conscription is plausibly a unique problem, unlike sterilization,

growing out of a nation's fundamental need to defend itself under conditions of war. Holmes does not explore the many possibly relevant similarities and differences among these various cases. He does not identify
the range of possible principles, much less argue for one rather than
another. Instead he invokes a principle of a high level of generality—"the
public welfare may call upon the best citizens for their lives"—that is
quite crude, and not evaluated by reference to low- or intermediate-level
principles that may also account for the apparently analogous cases.

The example shows that analogical reasoning can go wrong (1) when
one case is said to be analogous to another on the basis of a unifying
principle that is accepted without having been tested against other possibilities, or (2) when some similarities between two cases are deemed
decisive without enough investigation of relevant differences. This is of
course a pervasive problem, and it is the distinctive illogic of bad analogical reasoning.

A final problem is that analogical reasoning can distract attention from
the particular matter at hand, by persuading judges to grapple with other
cases and hypothetical examples that actually raise quite different issues.
If done poorly, analogical thinking can deflect the eye from the specific
problem and thus induce a kind of blindness to what is really at stake.
Note here Bishop Butler's phrase, "Everything is what it is, and not
another thing," which Wittgenstein considered as a motto for *Philosophical Investigations*.

Analogy and Democracy

In his classic discussion, Edward Levi also describes the process of legal
reasoning as analogical.[16] But the account here diverges from Levi's on
the important question of what happens when different analogies appear
to point in different directions. On the description just offered, the judge
must make some judgment about the appropriate "source" cases and
about the best controlling low-level principle. By contrast, Levi says that
in such cases, "words change to receive the content which the community
gives to them." Thus "peoples' wants change. . . . [T]he laws come to
express the ideas of the community. . . . Reasoning by example shows the
decisive role which the common ideas of the society and the distinctions
made by experts can have in shaping the law. . . . The process is one in
which the ideas of the community and of the social sciences, whether
correct or not, as they win acceptance in the community, control legal
decisions."[17] For Levi, reasoning by analogy therefore has a crucial dem-

ocratic component found through the use of public desires (and social science) to help decide the reach of analogies.

This is an arresting claim. It helps account for the enduring influence of Levi's account, for on Levi's view, analogical reasoning is not independent of the public will, even when it occurs within courtrooms. Levi did not, however, specify the mechanism by which community wishes help settle the conflict of analogies. There may be a historical explanation for Levi's seemingly odd suggestion. Levi's book was written at a distinctive time in American law. Its whole argument can be understood as a response to the legal realist attack on the autonomy of legal reasoning and to the realists' claim that legal reasoning is really "political"—and in the process to the associated claim, prominent in the aftermath of the New Deal, that legal reasoning is fatally undemocratic. When Levi was writing, it seemed crucial to establish the relative autonomy of law and especially of the common law method—to show that it had a logic and integrity of its own—but also and simultaneously to establish that it had a democratic feature. The continuing influence of Levi's account may stem from its ingenuity and apparent success in a seemingly doomed endeavor: connecting analogical thinking with democratic judgments.

It would, however, be most surprising if we could identify any mechanism translating democratic wishes into analogical reasoning. Perhaps the appointments process, disciplining the decision about who gets appointed to the bench, supplies some such mechanism. Surely there is some connection between community will and judicial outcomes. But any such connection is contingent and highly imperfect.

In hard cases, moreover, the community is badly divided. There may be no desire, on its part, to which courts can look in making decisions. What does the community think about difficult issues of contract or tort law? This is very hard to know. In fact the views of the community may be partly a function of what the courts say. The force of any argument by analogy really turns on underlying principles and not on community desires. Of course judges often care what people think, but usually the process works not by taking polls, but instead by a process in which judges ask themselves about the principles to which they are most deeply committed.

For these reasons Levi's account seems inadequate. But there are some valid and important points in the background. In analogical thinking, legal reasoning has a distinctive structure and faces distinctive constraints. Judges cannot think however they wish. This is not to deny that the judges' decisions about analogousness contain discretionary judgments with political dimensions, broadly speaking. Certainly those decisions turn on judgments about value. But this point does not dissolve the distinction between law and politics, and in challenging the realists on this claim, Levi was on firm ground. The realist slogan—"law is politics"—is far too crude. It offers no account of "law" or "politics."

Analogies and Precedent-Following

Why might we think analogically? Would it not be better to proceed directly to the merits, rather than to compare cases with one another? (Rules, another alternative to analogies, are explored in Chapter 4.) Part of the answer lies in the nature of human cognition; there is no such thing as proceeding "directly to the merits," since moral and legal thought is pervaded by prototypical cases. In any event the case for analogies is pragmatic; it involves an array of diverse social interests.

First, the analogizer is committed to consistency and equal treatment. A litigant in case A may not be treated differently from a litigant in case B unless there is a relevant difference between them. This idea operates as a barrier to certain forms of prejudice and irrationality. The conception of equal treatment underlying respect for precedent is closely related to the rule of law aspirations of analogical thinking.

Second, analogies can be a source of both principles and policies. A judge who looks at a stock of precedents should be able to learn a great deal by seeing what others have found persuasive. Investigation of analogies is hardly the best way to do policy science or to investigate issues of principle.[18] But it may contribute to that process.

Third, the resort to decided cases, as analogies, helps judges to avoid hubris. A judge who respects what others have done is less likely to overstep, by invoking theories that are confused, idiosyncratic, highly divisive, or sectarian.

Fourth, analogical reasoning, if based on precedent, promotes the important interests in fostering planning, maintaining predictability, and protecting expectations. Past cases encourage people to believe that the law is a certain way, and that they may act safely on that belief. A commitment to following precedent, and to reasoning analogically, enables those expectations to be vindicated and in that sense too it is associated with the rule of law. We might distinguish here between the interest in liberty, which entails predictability in law and hence the capacity to plan, and the interest in protecting against unfairness, which occurs when government ignores people's reliance on previous decisions. Both interests argue for respecting precedent.

Fifth, and relatedly, analogical thinking saves a great deal of time. If judges had to start from scratch in each case, the legal system would be overwhelmed. This might well be so even if the legal system consisted of a single judge. The project of putting one's own convictions into genuine order is (to say the least) time-consuming, and ordinary people often do well to think of their own past practices as precedents. This is all the more certainly true for a legal system consisting of thousands of people operating in a decentralized but mostly hierarchical judiciary. Following precedent enables judges to avoid recreating the law from the ground up, and thus ensures that people of limited time and capacities can take much for granted.

Finally—to return to our main theme—precedents and analogies facilitate the emergence of agreement among people who diverge on most or many matters. Judges A, B, and C may disagree on a great deal. But to say the least, it is helpful if judge A can invoke certain fixed points for everyone's analysis, so that judges B and C can join the discussion from shared premises. Perhaps judge B can invoke some fixed points that argue in a surprising direction. We cannot exclude the possibility that ultimately the judges really do disagree. But with analogies at least they can begin to talk.

Analogies in Law: Common, Constitutional, Statutory

The Common Law

Common law judges decide particular controversies by exploring how previous cases have been resolved. They rely on precedents. They look for relevant similarities and relevant differences. In the end, they will produce a rule or a standard, or more likely a series of rules and standards. But many rules are not given in advance of encounters with particulars; they are generated through close encounters with the details of cases. Moreover, what emerges from the cases is not rigid, for it is subject to revision at the moment of application, at least when the court encounters a case that seems to have new or unanticipated characteristics.

Consider, for example, recent developments with respect to the "contract at will." In the late nineteenth century, American courts decided that the general rule was that unless the contract specified otherwise, an employer could terminate an employee at his discretion. In this sense courts created something that looked and operated very much like a rule. In later cases judges slightly qualified this rule, saying that an employer could not fire an employee for failure to commit a crime on his behalf.[19] The new rule was that an employer could not use his authority over an employee so as to encourage criminal behavior. This notion was extended by analogy, so as to forbid an employer from firing an employee for filing a workers' compensation claim.[20] At this stage, the governing law—a standard rather than a rule—was that an employer could not discharge an employee in violation of clear legislative policy. But later cases extended the analogies still further, to cases in which an employee was fired for disclosing the employer's criminal behavior in the workplace and for failing to submit to sexual harassment by the employer.[21] As a result, the content of the "at will" rule is now unclear in many jurisdictions, with an uncertain boundary between cases marking the relevant divide. Here we have a characteristic example of the common law method at work.

The fact that the common law operates by analogy does not mean that the common law is without rules. Far from it. The common law is pervaded by rules, no less than in a civil law system. Many of these rules are followed even if a return to first principles, or to the justifications for the rules developed by common law courts, would call for some refashioning of the rules. Common law judges know that there is a large social interest in certainty and in protection of expectations. Thus if we look at the law of tort, contract, and property, we will find a wide range of so-called principles that really serve as rules.

Nonetheless, many common law courts do perceive themselves as authorized to change the rule, or to reconceive the rule, when the particulars of the case so require. Some common law judges believe that it is appropriate to treat the "rules" of the common law as rules of thumb, subject to fairly easy displacement when the circumstances of the new case so indicate. Hence, for example, some judges believe it very much in their domain to shift the "at will" rule when it fails to make sense; some courts have come very close to creating a new rule to the effect that an employer may not fire an employee without good cause. Other common law judges believe that the rule of law virtues, including the need for stability, predictability, and protection of expectations, mean that changes should come rarely and only on a compelling demonstration of need. Hence some judges resist change or recasting of the "at will" rule and on institutional grounds.

The point here is thus twofold. Much of the common law has rulelike features, even if the governing law has emerged through analogies and encounters with particulars. But the common law sometimes is not rulelike in practice because some judges believe it appropriate to define the law by elaborating and evaluating the justifications for the rule, and their applicability to the particular case, in the context of resolving controversies.

Some people think that the common law (especially of the nineteenth century) reflects a general commitment to economic efficiency or instead to some general conception of liberty or autonomy.[22] But these are doubtful claims. Undoubtedly the common law is not *very* inefficient from the economic point of view. To the extent that the common law generally respects freedom of contract, private property, and private ordering, it has many virtues from the standpoint of efficiency. Common law judgments also reflect intelligible understandings of liberty. Some familiar (though vague) understandings of liberty, allowing people to do as they choose so long as others are not at risk, overlap a great deal with some familiar understandings of economic efficiency.

But it is implausible to say that a general value like efficiency or liberty was the *goal* of common law courts, or to insist that specific common law decisions can be deduced from either general value. The norm of efficiency does not uniquely determine outcomes in all common law cases, certainly if we take account of the informational limits of the legal system, which make it hard for judges to know which outcome would be more efficient. Sometimes two or more outcomes are plausibly consistent with efficiency. And some common law doctrines seem disfavored from the standpoint of efficiency and to have been adopted for some reason independent of efficiency. Consider, for example, the generally held view that a rule of strict liability, accompanied by a contributory negligence defense, is more efficient than the old common law rule of negligence for torts.

The same doubts can be raised about the idea that liberty or autonomy explains common law cases. Is liberty promoted by a rule of strict liability or instead by a negligence regime? The common law reflects a complex set of judgments not uniquely derivable from a unitary value, but embodying instead a wide range of decisions based on mid-level principles, some of which do not cohere well with one another. This is the kind of outcome more reasonably to be expected from a heterogeneous group of judges, ill-equipped to think about first principles, and working in a more or less ad hoc way from particular situations.

The Constitution

Analogical reasoning is crucial in constitutional cases. Indeed, American constitutional law is often constructed from analogies—not from text or history, not from moral theory, and not from existing social consensus. Constitutional law is a form of casuistry. This is a controversial claim, and so it is worthwhile to spend time defending it here.

In American constitutional law, it is often suggested that the foundations of decision are text, structure, and history. The suggestion is not exactly wrong, but it is too simple, even a conceit.[23] Often text, structure, and history produce gaps, ambiguities, or otherwise insoluble interpretive difficulties. High-level ideas like "equal protection" must be specified in order to be useable. Does that idea doom affirmative action programs? Discrimination on the basis of sex or sexual orientation? Does "freedom of speech" include libel, commercial speech, or sexually explicit fiction on the Internet? Application of a general text to particular problems, many of which were quite unanticipated, will predictably yield uncertainty.

Investigation of structure leaves gaps as well. From the fact that the Constitution presupposes a federal structure, what follows, specifically, for the right to travel from one state to another? Any specific answer is likely to depend on something other than the structure itself.

So too history reveals many diverse judgments from the founding generation. These judgments can be described at different levels of generality, and the question, not easily answered historically, is what level of generality to select. Do we describe the equal protection clause as an effort to prevent discrimination against the newly freed slaves? Against the newly freed slaves and other groups defined in terms of race and ethnicity? Against whites too? Against women, noncitizens, or the handicapped? Surely courts should attend to history and try to get a sense of the problem at which the constitutional provision is aimed. But history will leave many open questions. (See Chapter 8 for more details.)

Hard constitutional cases, and many easy ones, turn on something other than text, structure, and history. People who accept this point sometimes suggest that constitutional law then becomes politics or philosophy, as large-scale moral or political claims solve constitutional questions. But this is doubtful, especially for a court consisting of people who are uncertain about or who disagree on first principles. As we have seen, judges try to avoid the largest and most disputable claims. This is a central aspect of the ethos of constitutional adjudication.

Consider, for example, how judges approach the question whether a ban on flag-burning violates the constitutional protection against laws abridging the freedom of speech. The constitutional text does not say whether flag-burning falls within "the freedom of speech," nor whether laws preventing flag-burning "abridge" any such freedom. The history behind the provision is not helpful. To come to terms with that history, we need to make complex judgments about the transplantation of the framers' commitments to a distinctive problem faced in a new era. There is no simple historical "fact" with which judges can work. This is so even if the framers did not specifically intend to ban laws criminalizing flag-burning. Many particular historical judgments are no longer binding; consider the founding view, no longer decisive today, that sex discrimination is unproblematic, or that laws restricting libel raise no First Amendment issue.

Moral and political argument can certainly help here. But if the argument is abstract, it may produce confusion or stalemate, and it may not be productive among heterogeneous judges who are not philosophers and who disagree on a great deal. Many judges will find high-level argument on the free speech principle—about liberty, democracy, utility—too abstract and confusing to be helpful. Others will disagree on the governing values. Judgments become far more tractable if constitutional interpreters try to proceed, as they do in fact, through analogies. There is general agreement—indeed there is a Supreme Court decision[24]—that draftcard burning is not protected by the constitution, *if* government is trying not to suppress messages but instead to make sure that people do not lose their draftcards. Is a ban on flagburning similar or different? This is a start of an inquiry into a large number of analogies, some involving decided cases, others involving hypothetical examples. This is also how actual judges proceed. The example suggests that our constitutional tradition is largely a common law tradition.[25] It has more in common with English constitutionalism and with Anglo-American common law than is generally appreciated.

This understanding of American constitutionalism raises a serious question of democratic legitimacy. Often the legitimacy of a constitution, and of constitutional law, is traced to the fact that the founding document reflects the considered judgments of the people as a whole. In this view, judicial review—the extraordinary process involving potential judicial invalidation of measures having a democratic pedigree—is justified by the fact that judicial decisions are a product of the people's will, indeed a deeper and more reliable product than ordinary legislative judgments. Those ordinary judgments come from mere representatives, who are not the people themselves. Constitutional law thus presupposes that the authority of the people is superior to that of their agents.

Of course this widely shared understanding is in some ways a charade, because judicial decisions are often not realistically traceable to the people's will, because the judgments reflected in constitutions can be very old, and because those judgments need not reflect real popular convictions; consider the fact that women and slaves were not involved in the ratification of the original Constitution. But theories of judicial review attempt to connect the Court's constitutional judgments to constitutional text and history. The absence of some plausible connection would be extremely disturbing to nearly everyone concerned with constitutional legitimacy. If we do not connect judicial review to past decisions of the public, on what authority do courts invalidate statutes?

There is no simple answer to this question. A partial response lies in the rule of law values associated with reasoning from precedent. The process of precedent-following disciplines judicial discretion and also makes it plausible to say that there has been public acceptance of, acquiescence in, or at least nonrejection of constitutional decisions from the Court. What disciplines judicial judgments, and part of what legitimates them, is the need, perceived by judges as well as by everyone else, to square current judicial decisions with previous judicial decisions that have survived the test of time. When a court concludes that a ban on flag-burning violates the constitutional protection of free speech, it may of course seek to connect its conclusion with constitutional text and history and also with a good conception of the free speech principle. But much of the apparatus behind the conclusion is not text or history, and not general principle, but previous judicial decisions—ruling some approaches off-limits, placing others on the table, and in any case establishing paths along which reasoning must go.

This is hardly a full solution to the problem of judicial legitimacy. The public's failure to overturn Supreme Court decisions does not show approval of those decisions. But it is important that in constitutional cases, judges rely on defining constitutional moments or defining constitutional precedents—the Civil War, the New Deal, the civil rights movement, and *Brown v. Board of Education*—that have a high degree of popular approval and that operate as fixed points for inquiry, whatever the judges think of them as a matter of political theory. Of course defining moments and defining precedents do not speak for themselves, and judgments about their meanings have large creative dimensions. Probably the best answer to the problem of legitimacy lies less in the *origins* of judicial review than in its *consequences*. To the extent that courts contribute to a well-functioning democratic regime, their powers are legitimate, at least if courts conform to the rule of law, receive general public support, and allow their judgments to grow in some diffuse sense out of aspirations laid down in other arenas.

Let us turn now to the role of moral judgments in constitutional law. Some people think that constitutional law is or should be deeply philosophical, in the sense that it should depend on deep thinking about basic principle. It is easy to understand the basis of this belief. How can we decide the meaning of the word "equal," "liberty," or "reasonable" without making philosophical claims? But there is a problem with this view, and the problem is connected to the fact that legal solutions must operate in a world with distinctive limitations. Some philosophers think, for example, that a free speech principle that places a special premium on political discussion is extremely attractive. But judges may not be able to agree on this idea, and some degree of agreement is indispensable in light of the fact that cases have to be decided. Perhaps too a political approach to the First Amendment would be too readily subject to abuse in the real world. Perhaps any judgments, within human institutions, about what counts as "the political" would be too biased and unreliable to be acceptable. For good institutional reasons, we might adopt a free speech principle of a low-level or philosophically inadequate sort simply because that approach is the only one we can safely administer. In this way there may be a significant split between a philosophically convincing account on the one hand and a legally correct approach on the other.

The example is not exotic. Suppose that we wanted to ensure that confessions are made under circumstances in which they are truly voluntary. Suppose that we can generate a philosophically adequate account of voluntariness, and that with respect to that account, some confessions that come after a police statement of the *Miranda* warnings are involuntary—while some confessions that are given without those warnings turn out to be voluntary after all. The *Miranda* rules, in short, turn out to be both overprotective and underprotective with reference to the best understanding of voluntariness.

Do we then have a sufficient reason to abandon *Miranda*? Surely not. The *Miranda* approach may be the best means of combining real-world administrability, by the officials we are likely to have, with substantive reasonableness. If so, it may be more than good enough despite its philosophical inadequacy. The phenomenon of philosophically inadequate but nonetheless justified legal strategies is a pervasive part of a well-functioning system of law.

All this suggests that deep philosophical justifications may not yield good law because of the institutional constraints faced by participants in any legal system. This point is connected with the role of analogies. Perhaps analogical thinking will not produce an adequate understanding of any area of law. Even if this is so, analogical reasoning is admirably well-adapted to some of the institutional disabilities of courts. We can see why this way of proceeding has such appeal among participants in law (and among ordinary people approaching moral questions as well).

Analogy Within Statutes and Rules

I have dealt thus far with the role of analogies in common law and constitutional cases. But in cases to be decided *under statutory rules*, courts also engage, much of the time, in a form of analogical reasoning.[26] This is a counterintuitive claim. Interpretation of rules is often said to be at an opposite pole from analogical reasoning. Of course common law courts engage in analogical thinking when dealing with precedents, but—it is often said—judges do nothing of the kind when they deal with statutes. The opposition is far too simple. Often interpretation of rules involves analogy too.[27] In this way we can vindicate Justice Holmes's striking suggestion that rules should be interpreted through examination of "the picture" that the words "evoke in the common mind."[28]

Some intriguing work in cognitive science and psychology supports Holmes's view. Because of how human beings think, rules and categories are defined by reference to characteristic instances. Suppose, for example, that we are investigating a single class of things—birds, vehicles, nations, works of art, or mammals. How do we know whether members of any such class are alike or different? It turns out that people have a mental picture of a model or typical example of the category, and they reason analogically, asking whether a member of the class is "like" or "unlike" that typical example. Thus people tend to think that a canary is more "bird" than a penguin, even though both are birds; a truck is more "vehicle" than an elevator; an apple is more "fruit" than a coconut.[29] Experiments show "the robust psychological reality of the typicality of a single exemplar of a given class. . . . The typicality of an exemplar is then routinely measured by the distance between the exemplar and the class as a whole."[30]

What these experiments reveal is that categories receive their human meaning by reference to typical instances. When we are asked whether a particular thing falls within a general category, we examine whether that thing is like or unlike the typical or defining instances. Very much the same is true in the interpretation of rules.

Consider these cases:

1. A statute enacted in 1920 forbids people to "sell babies." In 1993, Mr. and Ms. Jones hire Ms. Andrea Smith to be a surrogate mother. Does the contract violate the statute?[31]
2. A statute makes it a crime, with a thirty-year mandatory minimum sentence, for someone to "use a firearm in connection with a sale of an unlawful substance." Smith sells a firearm in return for cocaine, an unlawful substance. Has Smith violated the statute?[32]
3. In 1964, Congress enacted a law forbidding any employer from "discriminating on the basis of race." Bennett Industries has an affirmative action program offering preferential treatment to African-American

applicants. Does Bennett Industries discriminate on the basis of race, in violation of the 1964 statute?[33]

Here we have three cases involving the meaning of statutory terms. All three cases were hard. All of them produced divided courts. By what method should such cases be resolved? How were they resolved in fact? It would be especially good to be able to decide such cases without invoking large-scale theories of the good or the right. If to decide such cases, judges must develop a deep account of what lies behind the ban on discrimination, the prohibition on baby selling, or the ban on the use of guns in connection with drug transactions, things will become very difficult very quickly. But there is a feasible alternative, and it is roughly the same for all three cases, which should therefore be seen as variations on a single theme.

For the dissenting judge, the first case was especially easy. The statute forbids "baby selling." Smith sold her baby to the Jones couple. No controversial claim is necessary in order for us to see that a baby has been sold. The statute speaks unambiguously on the topic. We do not need analogies at all. Much less do we need deep theories of any kind. Here is a simple case of rule-following.

But perhaps things cannot proceed so quickly. Has Smith really sold "her" baby? How do we know whether it was ever hers? Mr. and Ms. Jones say that they are simply purchasing what might be called gestational services and not a baby at all. In this way, they say, the case is quite different from one in which a parent sells a born child who is unquestionably hers. Mr. and Ms. Jones say that the case is not covered by the statutory language at all. To be sure, it may seem natural to think that Smith's biological connection to the baby gives her ownership rights— whether whole or partial—in the child she has brought to term. But property rights do not come from the sky or even from nature; property rights as we understand them have legal sources. The claim that "x has a property right" means that x has a *legal* right of some sort to the interest in question.

The problem for the court is that when the case arose, the legal system had made no antecedent decision at all on the subject of ownership of the baby. The legal system had not allocated the child to Smith, or for that matter to Mr. and Ms. Jones. It follows that we do not really know whether we have a sale of a baby. Staring at the literal language of the statute—understood via the dictionary, in context, or both—will not be enough. The use of the literal language to resolve the case is therefore a version of bad formalism: the pretense of deciding a case by reference to legally authoritative language, when some kind of supplemental judgment is required, as in the idea that "liberty" necessarily includes freedom of contract. In such cases, we need an argument rather than a language lesson.

Is it therefore necessary, as some people suppose, to ask *why* baby selling is prohibited, or to develop "the best constructive account" of the prohibition, and then to ask whether that account bans surrogacy arrangements as well?[34] In a way the answer is yes; it is necessary to develop at least some understanding of why baby selling is banned in order to figure out how far the ban reaches. But that answer is too simple. In view of the difficulty and contested character of that issue, judges should avoid it if and to the extent that they possibly can. How did the court approach the problem?

In deciding the case, the majority of the court acknowledged that the text was not simple as applied to the situation of surrogacy. In determining its meaning, the court asked: Is a surrogacy arrangement relevantly similar to or relevantly different from the sale of a baby? The court therefore reasoned analogically. It held that the surrogacy arrangement was lawful. Its argument took the following form. There is at least a plausible difference between a surrogacy arrangement and the sale of a born child. In the former case, the child would not exist but for the arrangement. A ban on the sale of an existing child causes special risks for the child and for poor parents in general, who might be put under particular pressure to sell their children. The surrogacy situation is factually different on both of these counts. The child would not exist without the arrangement and may face lower risks from any deal, and the surrogate mother is in a quite different situation from parents who sell a born child.

In any case, the legislature that outlawed baby selling made no specific, considered judgment to ban surrogacy. The court thought that it ought not to take the language of the statute to foreclose a voluntary arrangement for which the legislature had made no considered judgment, at least where there is a plausible difference between that situation and the obvious or defining cases. The court interpreted the statute casuistically.

Does this approach take a theoretical stand? Does it does offer an account of why baby selling is banned? In a sense the answer to both questions is yes. To reason analogically, the court had to decide whether the sale of a baby is relevantly similar to or relevantly different from a surrogacy arrangement, and to make that decision it had to come up with an account of why the sale of a baby is banned. But notice the special form of the argument. There was no deep theoretical claim about the limits of the marketplace or about the sale of human beings. The court described the justification behind the ban at a relatively low, commonsensical level of abstraction. Moreover, the court did not say that a surrogacy arrangement was, in terms of basic principle, really different from a ban on baby selling. It said only that there were differences that might be thought relevant. Much of its decision had to do with the appropriate allocation of authority between courts and legislatures. In the court's view, a broadly worded criminal statute should not be applied to a controversial situation not within the contemplation of the enacting legislature, and plausibly different from the "picture" that inspired the legislation, unless and until there has been democratic deliberation on that question.

Despite the bow in the direction of literalism, the dissenting judges used a similar method. They reasoned analogically and found the analogy apposite. They said that a surrogacy arrangement poses all of the dangers posed by ordinary baby selling. They thought that surrogacy was unlawful because it was analogous to what was unambiguously unlawful. They reasoned that the statutory rule applied to the case at hand because that case was not relevantly different from the cases to which it unambiguously applied. They too were analogizers; they simply disagreed on the question of analogousness.

Now let us turn to the second case. In one understanding of the word "use," Smith has certainly "used" a firearm in connection with the sale of drugs. The gun was part of the transaction. But there is another linguistically possible conception of the word "use," one suggesting that if we read the law in its context, Smith has not really violated the statute. Perhaps someone "uses" a gun, as Congress understood the word "use," only if he uses it as a weapon. Smith did no such thing. Maybe the ordinary understanding of the word "use," taken in this particular context, requires the gun to be a weapon rather than an item of barter. The case is parallel to the surrogacy case in the sense that the ordinary understanding of the statutory term might call for its application in the situation at hand; but it might not, and the situation at hand was almost certainly not within the contemplation of those who wrote the term.

The Supreme Court held that Smith violated the statute. Despite a bow in the direction of literalism, the Supreme Court did not really pretend that the words of the statute were clear. Instead it reasoned partly in this way: We know that a gun may not be used as a weapon in connection with the sale of drugs. Is the use of a gun as an object of barter relevantly similar? The Court said that it was. It said that Smith's own use of a gun, as an item of barter, poses serious risks to life and limb, since that very use puts a gun into the stream of commerce with people engaged in unlawful activity. Even though this particular gun was used as an item of barter, it posed exactly the same dangers as other guns and was therefore very different from the use of mere cash. It follows that Smith must be convicted. Notice here that the Court did generate an account of what lay behind the ban on use of guns, but the account was quite commonsensical and low-level, and it worked by analogy.

Writing in dissent, Justice Scalia was incredulous. In part he relied on what he took to be the ordinary meaning of the word "use." But in part he too relied on an argument from analogy. In his view, Smith's conduct was different from that contemplated by the statute. Smith did not threaten to shoot anyone. He should therefore be treated differently from people whom Congress sought specifically to punish. The statute should not apply. Justice Scalia's argument paralleled that in the surrogacy case: For both, a statutory term should not be applied to a situation that reasonable people could think different from the most obvious instances of the term, at least if there is no reason to believe that the legislature intended it to apply to that situation.

Now let us go to the third case. The antidiscrimination law prohibits "discrimination on the basis of race." But is an affirmative action program "discrimination on the basis of race"? Are the words themselves decisive, in the sense that the literal meaning, or the words taken in context, admit of no dispute? Certainly not. If we consult any good dictionary, we will find that the word "discrimination" is ambiguous on the point, and in any case there are real hazards in relying on dictionaries. The word "discrimination" could be interpreted so as to forbid any form of differentiation and hence any racial differentiation—but it could also be interpreted to refer to invidious discrimination, or distinctions based on prejudice and hostility, in which case affirmative action programs might be unobjectionable.

Seeing the case like the majority in the surrogacy dispute and like Justice Scalia in *Smith*, the majority of the Supreme Court treated the words of the civil rights statute as ambiguous in their context. Instead of relying on a "plain" text, it proceeded roughly in the following way. We know that discrimination against members of racial minorities is unlawful. Is discrimination against whites similar or different? The Court said that it could be seen as relevantly different. In so saying, the Court relied on the legislative history and context, not for an unambiguous response to the issue at hand, but to get a sense of why the legislature thought that discrimination was wrong, and to test whether the justification for the law applied to affirmative action programs. The purpose and effect of the antidiscrimination law were to eliminate second-class citizenship for blacks, not to perpetuate it. The Court appeared to be arguing that the controversial issue of affirmative action should not be resolved through the broad interpretation of an ambiguous term, if that issue had never been squarely faced by the enacting legislature. The Court reasoned in a casuistical way.

The three cases are hard, and they could be analyzed in many different ways. I believe that in each of them, the statutory barrier should have been found inapplicable. This is not for deeply theoretical reasons, but because of institutional concerns: If it is reasonable to see a relevant difference between the obvious instances covered by the statute and the case at hand, if application to the case at hand would outlaw a voluntary social practice, and if there is good reason to doubt that the case at hand was or would have been within the contemplation of the enacting legislature, courts should not apply the statutory term. For this reason the "use" case was relatively easy and Justice Scalia was right: A thirty-year mandatory minimum sentence should not have been applied to a case that was plausibly quite different from the applications Congress had in mind.

The surrogacy case was similar. The ban on baby selling was certainly not enacted with surrogacy in mind, and surrogacy is plausibly different from baby selling. The court was correct to refuse to apply a criminal prohibition in the absence of focused legislative attention on the plausibly different case. The affirmative action case was a bit harder because it did not involve the criminal law, but it too was rightly decided. Congress had not really thought about affirmative action programs, and the term "discrimination" need not include such programs, which again are quite plausibly different in principle. The Supreme Court was correct to require focused legislative attention before applying a barrier to a plausibly different case.

Whether or not we think these cases were rightly decided, they support a simple point. Sometimes a statute is ambiguous. Perhaps its words are unclear on their face, or unclear in context, or perhaps there is a question whether they should be interpreted literally when the literal terms extend to apparently unreasonable or unanticipated applications. A conventional and honorable approach to interpretation takes the following form. The court examines what it takes to be the standard or defining applications of the statute—the cases to which it obviously applies. Then it asks whether the application at hand is relevantly similar or relevantly different. In so doing, the court is engaging in a form of analogical reasoning. The unambiguous applications of the statute serve as fixed points. The court cannot question those applications. The applications operate very much like holdings in decided cases or like precedents. But on the question at hand, there is no rule at all. This is a pervasive phenomenon in the interpretation of rules. It is pervasive not only in law, but in everyday life when the meaning of rules becomes unclear.

It is often said that courts can distinguish precedents but that they cannot distinguish statutes, and that for this reason the interpretation of statutes is quite different from case-by-case judgments. But we have just seen that this contrast is far too simple. Often courts do distinguish statutes—by saying that their rationale does not apply, just as in the case of a precedent.

Thus far the discussion has involved hard cases, but we can go further. In easy cases, analogy is at work too. When a judge says that a rule does apply—that discrimination against women in Ohio is impermissible under a law banning sex discrimination—he might be taken to be saying that there is no difference between the application at hand and the simple or defining cases. In the easy cases of rule-application, an implicit analogical process occurs too. It happens very quickly. But the case is easy only because it is so obvious that there is no difference between the application and the core or defining case. What counts as an easy case can of course change over time; as substantive understandings shift, understandings of analogy shift as well, and hence a case that appeared at one point identical to the defining cases might later appear quite different from them.

All this is not to say that the interpretation of rules is the same as the interpretation of precedents. In interpreting statutes, courts might rely on the literal meaning of the statutory term or the ordinary meaning of the term in its context—if there is one—and stick with that meaning even if the particular application is or seems very odd. Or courts might refer more generally to statutory purpose or legislative intent, without engaging in the analogical process. All I mean to suggest is that there is an approach to statutory cases—a familiar and in many ways an attractive one—that involves analogical argument. Analogies play a prominent role in common law and constitutional cases, but they are important in statutory cases too. In this way, the line between the common law and statutory interpretation is shifting and ill-defined. With an understanding of analogy, we can thus help vindicate the old notion that legal reasoning is all of a piece, and that it has distinctive and identifiable features.

Analogy and Incompletely Theorized Agreements

In this section, I defend analogical reasoning against certain alternatives and complaints. At this stage I will not compare the use of analogies with the use of rules laid down in advance. It should be clear that rules have many advantages over case-by-case judgments unaccompanied by rules.

This will emerge from Chapter 4; for the moment I put the point to one side.

Analogy and Legal Realism

On a view associated with legal realism, reasoning by analogy suffers from a fatal defect: It is utterly indeterminate in the absence of social consensus. Without a good deal of agreement in advance, analogical reasoning cannot even get started. According to this account, we can reason analogically only if we already agree on certain fundamental questions. Otherwise people will simply differ, and there will be no way to reason through their differences. If so, reasoning by analogy merely uncovers agreement where it already existed. Very little can be said on behalf of something so unambitious as that.

To some degree the objection is valid. We have seen that any two cases are alike and different, and both in innumerable ways. A claim of relevant similarity requires a judgment of principle. If someone thinks that the government can punish political speech whenever that speech poses any risk of any degree to the government, it will be hard to reason with him, through analogies, to a sensible system of free expression.[35] (Note, however, that it may be possible to undermine this very position with analogies.) In this sense it is right to think that reasoning by analogy depends on a degree of commonality among participants in the discussion. If people have little or nothing in common, they may be unable to talk.

We might ask, however, whether this really amounts to an objection at all. The need for a degree of consensus is hardly a problem distinctive to analogy. It applies to all forms of reasoning.

In coming to terms with the objection, we need to distinguish between analogical reasoning in law and analogical reasoning elsewhere. In law, there are greater constraints on the process. Existing legal holdings sometimes provide the necessary commonality and the necessary consensus. People who disagree with those holdings usually agree that they must be respected; the principle of stare decisis so requires. Within the legal culture, analogical reasoning imposes a certain discipline, and a widespread moral or political consensus is therefore unnecessary. Hence people who could not use analogies to reach closure in politics or morality can often do so in law.

Analogies may well be less helpful in politics or morality simply because of the possible absence of precedents that can help generate an incompletely theorized agreement on particular outcomes. The differences lead to two important conclusions. First, the method of analogy may indeed be less determinate outside of law. Second, there can be a real difference between the legally correct outcome and the morally correct outcome. The difference lies in the fact that analogies will operate as entirely "fixed points" in legal reasoning, whereas many of these are revisable in morality. Consider, for example, the fact that lawyers must take *Roe v. Wade* as authoritative so long as it stands, even if they think the decision abhorrent from a moral point of view. If *Roe* is authoritative, it disciplines discussion of certain topics—the right to withdraw medical equipment, the right to use contraceptives, the right to euthanasia—and the discipline would be removed if the abortion issue itself were up for moral judgment.

Even outside of law, however, the objection from indeterminacy is not entirely persuasive. Very diverse people may have sufficient commonality, on fundamental matters, to permit considerable progress. When there appears not to be such commonality, a good deal of movement can occur through simultaneous engagement with what various participants in the discussion say and think—engagement that includes narratives about diverse experiences or history, personal and otherwise, as well as more conventional "reasons." (Note that the case method operates in part through narratives.) Much of moral discussion involves this form of casuistry, in which people test their provisional judgment by reference to a range of actual or hypothetical cases. We have no reason to disparage the process in advance.

In order to provide relevant information and to counteract parochialism and bias, it is important to ensure that people with different perspectives and experiences are permitted to participate. It is equally important to ensure that judges are alert to the range of possible low-level principles, and that they attempt to compare those principles against one another. But through some such route people who initially disagree so strongly as to make conversation seem difficult can sometimes be brought together, at least to the point where analogical reasoning can start. Nearly everyone has had this experience.

In any case we cannot know that the optimistic view is false until we try to talk. And here the very concreteness of analogical reasoning is a large advantage. When there are major differences in starting points, people can often think far better about particular problems than about large-scale approaches to the world. None of this means that people will always be able to reach closure. Sometimes they really do disagree. But analogical reasoning can at least help to discover exactly where they do and exactly why.

We should note also that it does not follow, from the mere fact of disagreement, that there are not correct answers to disputed questions in law or ethics, any more than in science. The fact that people disagree does not mean that no one is right. Nor does it follow, from the fact that legal categories are after all our categories and revisable by us, that everything is up for grabs or that we are in some sort of abyss. It is true that human beings, including lawyers, see things through interpretive frameworks created by human beings. But this need not entail any form of skepticism or relativism. It would do so only if the only possible knowledge were external or transcendental, and there is no reason to think that. Indeed, people who think that the absence of external or transcendental foundations leads to relativism or skepticism often have a great deal in common with their purported transcendentalist adversaries. They have the same odd conception about what correct answers must be to count as such. The prominence of analogical reasoning offers no reason for relativism or skepticism in law.

Realism and Judicial Psychology

At this point a legal realist might raise the stakes. If we are really interested in describing legal reasoning, we have to recognize that judges are often motivated by their own political judgments about how they want a case to come out. On this view, the picture of analogy and incompletely theorized agreement is hopelessly sanitized—inconsistent with the true psychology of judging. For many judges, so-called legal reasoning really reflects a process in which politically preferred solutions are sought and reached except to the extent that they are "blocked" by authoritative legal materials. Judges may write as if they are analogizers, but the analogies are often boilerplate disguising a political judgment, rather than a helpful guide to judicial reasoning. In any event not all judges are the same; there are many different methods at work in cases. Thus the picture is not only sanitized but far too uniform.

There is truth in these claims. Certainly judicial practice varies. What I have offered here is a general picture that does not fit all judges. Some judges do not favor theoretical modesty, and some judges are not analogizers. No one should deny that judges often have strong initial reactions to cases, and those reactions can be based on what are, broadly speaking, political grounds. If we are seeking an account of the psychology of judging, analogy and incompletely theorized agreement are only part of the picture. How much a part depends on the particular judge.

But the realist view is easy to overstate. The judge's "political" preference is not a brute fact. It has sources. In fact it is a product of judgments, and those judgments are in turn a product, at least in part, of the legal culture, including the system of precedent, incompletely theorized agreement, and analogy. If judges do not "want" to say that siblings have a right to marry one another, it is partly because of their judgments about appropriate analogies and about the proper role of courts in a democracy. And if the account offered here seems to underplay the role of political judgments in law, we should say once again that claims of analogousness are a product of those very judgments, disciplined as they are by authoritative legal materials.

In any case there is a difference between the psychology of judging—the internal process that leads to decisions—and the process of public justification in law. The effort to describe legal reasoning is not an attempt at uncovering judicial psychology—a task for biographers—but instead an attempt, with inevitable evaluative features, to capture how lawyers and judges offer public justifications.

Analogy and Burke

A separate challenge, traceable to Jeremy Bentham, is that the method of analogy is insufficiently scientific, unduly tied to existing intuitions, and partly for these reasons static or celebratory of existing social practice.[36] On this view, analogical reasoning works too modestly from existing holdings and convictions, to which it is unduly attached. It needs to be replaced by something like a general theory—in short, by something like science. For the critics, analogizers are Burkeans, and their approach suffers from all the flaws associated with Edmund Burke's celebration of the English common law. It is too insistently backward-looking, too skeptical of theory, too lacking in criteria by which to assess legal practices critically.

At first glance, the claim seems mysterious. Analogical reasoning cannot work without criteria. Whether analogical reasoning calls for the continuation of existing practice turns on the convictions or holdings from which analogical reasoning takes place. Without identifying those convictions or holdings, we cannot say whether existing practices will be celebrated. The process of testing initial judgments by reference to analogies can produce sharp criticism of many social practices and, eventually, can yield reform. Legal holdings that are critical of some social practices can turn out, through analogy, to be critical of other practices as well.

In fact analogical thinking has often produced large-scale change. *Brown v. Board of Education* invalidated racial segregation in education. By analogy to *Brown,* American courts invalidated racial segregation elsewhere too. Even more than that, they reformed prisons and mental institutions; struck down many racial classifications, including affirmative action programs; invalidated sex discrimination; and prevented states from discriminating on the basis of alienage and legitimacy. The analogical process has hardly run its course. Consider the (highly controversial) view that if miscegenation laws are unconstitutional under the equal protection clause, it follows by analogy that the ban on same-sex marriages is unconstitutional too.[37] Whether analogical reasoning is conservative or not depends not on the fact that it is analogical, but on the nature of the principles brought to bear on disputed cases.[38]

On the other hand, analogical reasoning does start from existing convictions or holdings, and judgments of sameness or difference receive their content from current thinking. In this way, analogical reasoning can have a backward-looking, conservative, incremental character. Whether this is a bad thing for courts depends on the virtues and vices of different institutions of government, on the society in question, and on the weight to be accorded to stability. But insofar as analogical reasoning takes current legal materials as the basis for reasoning, it might indeed be an obstacle to justified change through law. Thus Gulliver comments:

> It is a maxim among . . . lawyers that whatever hath been done before may legally be done again; and therefore they take special care to record all the decisions formerly made against common justice and the general reason of mankind. These, under the name of precedents, they produce as authorities to justify the most inequitous opinions; and the judges never fail to direct accordingly.[39]

The most important lesson to draw from this objection is that a full theory of legal reasoning should make it possible to say which holdings are wrong, and which holdings should be overruled because they are wrong. Analogical reasoning, at least as thus far described, is unhelpful here. It might therefore be said that efforts to reason from analogies are stuck in existing holdings or convictions, which are sometimes a morass, and that such efforts are for this reason severely deficient in comparison to forms of reasoning that provide better resources for critical evaluation.

There is truth in these complaints. As I have noted, analogical reasoning is especially unlikely to help us in figuring out the consequences of legal rules, and knowledge of consequences is crucial. But sometimes reasoning by analogy does help to reveal mistakes. Reference to other cases helps show us that our initial judgments are inconsistent with what we actually think. Much of legal education consists in the testing of initial judgments by reference to other cases, and sometimes it can be shown that those judgments must yield. If those judgments are reflected in judicial holdings, then it is necessary for courts to decide whether to overrule them. Of course every legal system must make many decisions on how to weigh the interest in stability against the interest in getting things right (with the acknowledgment that what is now thought to be right might not in fact be right).

Analogy and Hercules

I have discussed Ronald Dworkin's use of the Hercules metaphor, and I have tried to show why incompletely theorized agreements have distinctive advantages. For present purposes, it is important to say that analogies may have virtues as compared with the search for what Dworkin calls "integrity." Courts do need principles to think analogically, and sometimes a conceptual ascent will be required. But analogical thinking in law places a premium on low-level principles, and it is well-adapted to the institutional limits of the legal system. Analogical reasoning might therefore be defended on the ground that the best approaches to certain areas of law call for principled consistency with respect to individual cases and low-level principles. For judges, at least, the search for integrity is too difficult to complete, and it is also inconsistent with the morality of judging in a pluralistic society.

Top Down, Bottom Up

We might look, finally, at efforts to replace legal reasoning with highly general non- or extralegal approaches, especially those that apply a broad theory "top down" to particular legal disputes.

Efforts of this kind could take many forms. Consider the effort to ask what sorts of legal rules will promote economic efficiency.[40] The advantage of economic analysis of law is that it casts a critical light on ordinary intuitions altogether, showing that they are too crude to be a basis for law. Intuitions about the effects of legal rules may be completely wrong; a rise in the minimum wage, for example, could increase unemployment, and in that sense hurt many of the people one is trying to help. In a sharp restatement of Bentham's attack on the common law, economic analysts sometimes claim that traditional legal reasoning is not reasoning at all, but instead an encrusted system of disorganized and perhaps barely processed intuitions.

Policies, Principles, Analogies

Judge Richard Posner uses ideas of this kind against analogical reasoning. In his view, we cannot really reason from one particular to another. Instead we need to give an account of the policy that underlies the first particular. Once we are doing this, we are engaged in "policy science." "One can call this reasoning by analogy if one likes but what is really involved is querying (or quarrying) the earlier case for policies that may be applicable to the later one and then deciding the later one by reference to those policies."[41] Judge Posner's complaint is that if we are going to do policy science, we should really do it, rather than investigate prior cases, which "often constitute an impoverished repository of fact and policy for the decision of the present one." In his view, analogical reasoning is pervasively formalistic, that is, it treats law as a self-contained system, when legal decisions should be based on an investigation of what really matters, on which policy analysts would be far more helpful.

Judge Posner is right to insist that insofar as we are doing policy analysis, past legal decisions are at best a start. But as it occurs in courts, law is not only policy analysis, for which judges are imperfectly equipped; and we should not undervalue the process of ordering judgments about legal problems by seeing if one's judgment in the case at hand can be squared with judicial or hypothetical judgments in other cases. This process is especially well-adapted for the context of adjudication, in which current judges seek to produce consistency and equal treatment; to save their own time and resources; to protect expectations and reliance; and to avoid hubris and sectarianism. Recall here that any account of reasoning is likely to have a great deal to do with the particular role in which particular reasoners find themselves.

Analogies and Economics

At this point we might compare analogical thinking with economic analysis of law. There can be no question that economic analysis has led to major advances. For many purposes, it is much better than analogical thinking. Above all, economic analysis helps untangle the social consequences of legal rules, some of which are counterintuitive, and many of which are relevant to the evaluation. Compare, for example, economic analysis of antitrust law with analogical thinking in that area. Here economic analysis has a major advantage over analogical reasoning.

If it is intended to exhaust the concerns of law, however, economic analysis depends on far too thin a repertoire for inquiry: the notion, held by some of its practitioners, that legal rules should be designed so as to maximize wealth. This intuition can be shown to be too crude and general to be right, and by reference to particular cases that disprove it. There are many cases in which wealth-maximization, as a social goal, runs afoul of people's considered judgments about particular cases. Should religious groups be banned if nonbelievers would pay more to "buy" the ban than religious groups would pay to "buy" their liberty? Would criminal acts—rape, assault, incest—be justified if it turned out that the victim would pay less to avoid them than the criminal would pay to be permitted to engage in them? We could ask many similar questions.

If economic analysis is intended as a complete guide to the goals of a legal system, it is far too sectarian for lawyers and judges to accept. In a heterogeneous society, people disagree too deeply about the maximization of wealth. They find it too high-level or simply unappealing. Analogical reasoning, by contrast, does not force people to make broad or deep claims about the good or the right. By itself, it embodies no general theory of value. Instead it builds on a range of low-level judgments.

Of course this is a vice as well as a virtue. Analogizers may be quite confused. They may use ideas about value that are inconsistent with one another, unsound, or evil. Analogies are no better than the principles and policies that make them work. But it is important that analogical reasoners, unlike economic analysts, need not insist that plural and diverse social goods should be assessed according to the same metric. Analogical thinkers usually accept the plurality and diversity of human goods and acknowledge the frequent absence of any metrics that allow for commensurability. To make diverse goods commensurable is often to do violence to our considered judgments about how all these should be characterized.[42] Those considered judgments are far from embarrassing; they are part of what it means to think well. Consider, for example, the view that we should see all of the following as "costs": unemployment, the loss of a species, higher prices for pencils, the adaptation of workplaces to accommodate people in wheelchairs, environmental degradation, sexual assault, and chilling effects on speech.

If we understand all these things simply as "costs," to be assessed via the same metric, we will disable ourselves from making important qualitative distinctions. A serious problem with economic analysis of law is that it runs afoul of the plurality of values and the phenomenon of value-incommensurability. It might be objected that a more differentiated approach, one that insists on the plurality and diversity of goods and therefore rejects commensurability, is fatally unscientific. To this we should respond that this conception of science is ill-suited to good thinking about a certain range of legal problems. What is required is not science, but practical reason.[43]

The hard question remains: How does one make choices when incommensurable social goods are at stake, and when some of these must be sacrificed? No answer can be found from the mere fact of analogical thinking; but an exploration of how analogical reasoning actually works may well be helpful. Unequipped with and unburdened by a unitary theory of the good or the right, the analogical thinker is in a position to see diverse and plural goods for themselves and to make choices among them without ignoring qualitative differences. The very search for relevant similarities and differences places a premium on this process.

Analogies and Top-Down Theories

Economic analysis of law is an especially controversial top-down approach; but the vices of the economic approach may be vices of other approaches as well, at least if they are monistic in the sense that they posit a single value by which to understand any area of law. In particular, the vice of sectarianism characterizes many other single-valued, top-down theories of law. Consider the distinguished efforts to approach the free speech principle through the lens of a general theory of autonomy or democracy.[44] The autonomy principle has considerable appeal, but it seems to run afoul of many considered judgments about particular cases, and its most prominent defender has repudiated it as a complete account.[45] A democratic approach to free speech runs into similar difficulties. By itself, all this may prove little. But it suggests the possibility that if it is monistic, any top-down approach to certain areas of law will be inadequate because it will be ill-suited both to the extent of social heterogeneity and to the plurality of the relevant values at stake.

From this point we can offer a general conclusion. Analogical reasoning lies at the heart of legal thinking and for good reasons. It is admirably well-suited to the particular roles in which lawyers and judges find themselves—to a system in which heterogeneous people must reach closure despite their limitations of time and capacity and despite their disagreements on fundamental issues. There is nothing static to the analogical process; it leaves room for flexibility and indeed for an enormous amount of creativity. Much creativity in law comes from the ability to see novel analogies. And no matter how sophisticated a legal culture becomes, and no matter how committed it is to the rule of law, it is likely to make a large space for analogical thinking. The persistence of analogical thinking in day-to-day life is thus mirrored in law.

4

Understanding
(and Misunderstanding)
the Rule of Law

Thus far we have seen that legal systems try to resolve cases rather than choose between abstractions, and that for this reason participants in law try for low-level or mid-level justifications on which broad agreement is possible. In this light analogical reasoning is well-suited to the goals of the legal system in a pluralistic society. Analogical thinking also helps show how legal systems might make space for a process of thinking in which we do not have clear, general rules laid down in advance. This point complicates some familiar understandings of the rule of law.

We have not, however, yet dealt with the important conflict between case-by-case judgments and rule-bound justice. My ultimate aim is to provide a defense of the former, though as we will see, any such defense must be qualified. The case for rules is too insistent in too many contexts. In the criminal law, for example, decisions are generally made by reference to rules rather than analogies, and it is well-appreciated that people should be entitled to know, in advance and for certain, whether what they are doing might be considered a crime.[1] This form of advance notice is a large part of liberty under law.

In this chapter and the next, I will be paying special attention to two appealing and widely held conceptions of procedural justice. The first conception, often identified with the rule of law, calls for firm, clear rules laid down publicly and in advance. The second conception prizes the absence of fixed rules and the opportunity to argue that one's own case is different from all that have come before. We will see that even in legal systems committed to the rule of law, there is a continuing place for casuistry, understood as rule-free judgments based on careful comparison of individual cases.

Prefatory Note

Whether we should have rules or something else is partly a function of the identity of the particular institution charged with making that decision. It is familiarly thought that legislatures make rules, while courts decide cases, and administrators do some of both. This thought is too simple. Legislatures often avoid rules and rest content with standards or factors. Courts often issue rules. But the conventional idea captures some truth. Legislatures may well be in an especially good position to set out rules, because they are capable of getting a systematic overview of a whole area of law, and they can see how its various parts fit together. Judges are often incapable of obtaining that overview; they have only the litigants before them and can make rulings only about the issues that the litigants present. This institutional disability rightly leads courts sometimes to avoid rulemaking and to decide the case instead through some narrow rationale that leaves many questions open.

I will speak here of the advantages of proceeding through rules. My principal interest is in the question why a legislature should seek or even be required to issue rules, but I will discuss the obligations of administrators and judges as well.

Description

A system of rules is often thought to be the signal virtue of a regime of law. Indeed, the rule of law might seem to require a system of rules. In American law, the idea has a constitutional source. The due process clause of the American Constitution is sometimes interpreted to require rules, or rulelike provisions, and to forbid a system based on analogies, standards, or factors. This is particularly important in the area of criminal justice and freedom of speech, where the "void for vagueness" doctrine is said to require clear rules before the state may regulate private conduct.

It is not an overstatement to say that the void for vagueness doctrine is among the most important guarantees of liberty under law. Consider the great case of *Papachristou v. City of Jacksonville*,[2] which is exemplary on the point.

In the early 1970s, it was a crime to engage in "vagrancy" in Jacksonville, Florida. The category of "vagrancy" covered "Rogues and vagabonds, or dissolute persons who go about begging, common gamblers, persons who use juggling or unlawful games or plays, common drunkards, common night walkers . . . persons wandering or strolling around from place to place without any lawful purpose or object, habitual loafers, disorderly persons, . . . persons able to work but habitually living upon the earnings of their wives or minor children. . . ." A number of people were arrested under this law. Among them were two white women, Papachristou and Calloway, who had been traveling in a car with two black men, Melton and Johnson.

The Supreme Court reversed the convictions on the theory that the Jacksonville ordinance was inconsistent with the due process clause. It was "void for vagueness" because it failed to provide fair notice of what conduct is unlawful, and because "it encourage[d] arbitrary and erratic arrests and convictions." The Court emphasized several points: "The poor among us, the minorities, the average householder are not in business and not alerted to the regulatory schemes of vagrancy laws; and we assume that they would have no understanding of their meaning and impact if they read them." Moreover, the "ordinance makes criminal activities that by modern standards are normally innocent." Thus "[p]ersons 'wandering or strolling' from place to place have been extolled by Walt Whitman and Vachel Lindsay. . . . The difficulty is that these activities are historically part of the amenities of life as we have known them."

The ordinance was also unlawful because it put "unfettered discretion . . . in the hands of the Jacksonville police." To say this is not to deny that the ordinance could serve important law enforcement purposes. The Court said: "Of course, vagrancy statutes are useful to the police. Of course, they are nets making easy the round-up of so-called undesirables. But the rule of law implies equality and justice in its application."

Notably, the Court quoted a law review article to the effect that "'Algeria is rejecting the flexibility introduced in the Soviet criminal code by the 'analogy' principle, as have the East-Central European and black African states.'" Many systems of criminal justice have made it an offense to engage in conduct that is "analogous" to what is specifically prohibited. The analogical principle has played a large role in Chinese criminal law.[3] Apparently the Supreme Court believed that this analogical approach to the criminal law raises severe problems under the due process clause.

We can take *Papachristou* to exemplify a failure of the rule of law. But what specifically does this concept entail? It is possible to identify several characteristics.[4] Many of them are connected with the traditional view, signaled by many representations of the goddess herself, that justice is *blindfolded*. This is a vivid and puzzling metaphor. The solution to the puzzle lies in determining what the blindness of justice represents.

1. *Clear, general, publicly accessible rules laid down in advance.* It is plain from *Papachristou* that the rule of law requires rules that are *clear*, in the sense that people need not guess about their meaning, and that are *general*, in the sense that they apply to classes rather than particular people or groups. The "rule of lenity" provides that in the face of ambiguity, criminal statutes will be construed favorably to the criminal defendant. This principle is an outgrowth of the requirement that laws be clear so as to provide notice. The ban on bills of attainder—measures singling out particular people for punishment—is a traditional requirement of generality.

Laws should be publicly accessible as well as clear and general. It follows that there is a ban on "secret law." In America, the Freedom of Information Act is justified in part as a barrier to secret law. Of course vague laws—banning, for example, "excessive" or "unreasonable" behavior— are unacceptable, at least in the criminal context; they are akin to secret law in the sense that people are unlikely to know what they entail.

In the real world of law, many complexities arise on these counts. It is a fiction to say that would-be criminals actually consult the lawbooks in advance of the crime. We do not know the extent to which criminal statutes are understood by the general public. Undoubtedly the answer varies from area to area, and in many cases people could not describe the law with much accuracy. Despite *Papachristou*, many laws, including criminal statutes, have a high degree of ambiguity. No legal system can eliminate official discretion to give content to law at points of application, and this means that ruleness will be limited even in legal systems highly committed to the rule of law. To some extent this is a failure of the rule of law, but it is also a product of the limitations of human language and foresight.

2. *Prospectivity; no retroactivity.* In a system of rules, retroactive lawmaking is disfavored, and it is banned altogether in the context of criminal prohibitions. The ban on ex post facto laws is the clearest prohibition on retroactivity. More modestly, American law includes an interpretive principle to the effect that civil laws will ordinarily apply prospectively.[5] If the legislature wants to apply a law retroactively, it must do so unambiguously, and if it does so unambiguously, there is at least an issue under the due process clause.

3. *Conformity between law on the books and law in the world.* If the law does

not operate in the books as it does in the world, the rule of law is compromised. If there is little or no resemblance between enacted law and real law, the rule of law cannot exist. If the real law is different from the enacted law, generality, clarity, predictability, fair notice, and public accessibility are all sacrificed. People must be permitted to monitor official conduct by testing it against enacted law.

In many legal systems, of course, there is an occasional split between what the law says and what the law is, and the split can be severe. The frequency of the phenomenon should not deflect attention from the fact that this is a failure of the rule of law. In Chapter 7 we will see, however, that some legal systems allow a form of legitimate rule revision by officials and citizens, and this phenomenon does create some acceptable gaps between enacted law and real-world law.

4. *Hearing rights and availability of review by independent adjudicative officials.* The rule of law requires a right to a hearing in which people can contest the government's claim that their conduct meets legal requirements for either the imposition of harm or the denial of benefits. Someone who is alleged to have committed a crime, or to have forfeited rights to social security benefits or a driver's license, is entitled to some forum in which he can claim that the legal standards have not in fact been violated. Ordinarily the purpose of the hearing is to ensure that the facts have been accurately found. There should also be some form of review by independent officials, usually judges entitled to a degree of independence from political pressures.

5. *Separation between lawmaking and law-implementation.* The *Papachristou* case embodies a tacit but important understanding of the separation of powers, sometimes known as the "nondelegation" principle. The nondelegation principle requires that the legislature lay down rules in advance; it therefore prohibits laws from being created by the people who execute them. In this way, there is a guarantee of political accountability, at least in democratic systems.

In the United States, the nondelegation principle is rarely enforced by courts, in part because there are no clear criteria by which to distinguish lawmaking from law-implementation. But in some areas of law, people engaged in enforcement activity are constitutionally constrained from giving content to the law. The area of criminal justice is an important example. Law enforcement officers are not supposed to decide what the law is, though in practice they do have a degree of law-making authority.

6. *No rapid changes in the content of law; no contradictions or inconsistency in the law.* If the law changes too quickly, the rule of law cannot exist. People will not be able to adapt their conduct to what is required. And if the law

contains inconsistency or contradiction, it can be hard or impossible to know what the rules are. Needless to say, people should not be placed under mutually incompatible obligations. The problem of rapidly changing law was a prime impetus behind the adoption of the American Constitution. Hence James Madison wrote:

> The mutability of the laws of the States is found to be a serious evil. The injustice of them has been so frequent and so flagrant as to alarm the most steadfast friends of Republicanism. I am persuaded that I do not err in saying that the evils issuing from these sources contributed more to the uneasiness which produced the Convention, and prepared the public mind for a general reform, than those which accrued to our national character and interest from the inadequacy of the Confederation to its immediate objects.[6]

Most unfortunately, both of these phenomena—unstable law and inconsistent law—are part of the fabric of the modern regulatory state. Sometimes regulatory law changes very quickly, thus making it difficult for people to plan. Sometimes regulatory law imposes conflicting obligations, so that it is hard for people to know what they are supposed to do. These are important pathologies of modern law, and they exact a high toll on both liberty and prosperity.

The Case for Rules

A great virtue of rules is that they limit permissible grounds for both action and argument. I have said that in a heterogeneous society, containing people of limited time and capacities, this is an enormous advantage. It saves effort, time, and expense. By truncating the sorts of value-disputes that can arise in law, it also ensures that disagreements will occur along a narrowly restricted range. On this count, rules have tremendous advantages over the alternatives.

It is very hard, for example, to decide who is poor, and who, among the class of poor, is entitled to what. It would be particularly hard to decide who is poor through case-by-case judgments based on analogy, and even harder to make decisions about appropriate social entitlements in that fashion. But if the legislature says that people who earn more than $10,000 cannot qualify for food stamps, officials need not decide when people are poor or when they deserve food stamps. If people who steal money commit a felony of a certain identified sort, then particular officials need not decide how bad it is to steal money. They need not compare cases similar in some respects and different in others; and they need not ask whether criminal punishment is designed to deter harmful conduct, embody retribution, confine dangerous people, or something else. (Recall Justice Breyer's discussion of the Sentencing Commission.)

Rules are sometimes said to be a product of "balancing" of relevant factors. There is something to this. But it is more accurate to say that rules are a product of judgments of what sorts of considerations are relevant in different contexts. Rules are, and are products of, *exclusionary reasons*, to the effect that certain factors should not be relevant in certain circumstances.[7] Consider an example: We might think that it is never appropriate to breach a friend's confidence in order to have fun gossiping with other friends. If this is what we think, then the fun of gossiping is entirely excluded as a reason for breaching a confidence. On the other hand, we might think that the confidence should be breached if it is necessary in order to save a friend's life. The rule against breaching a confidence allows you to act in situations of emergency. This is just a simple example of how a rule operates in personal relations. It is not the product of balancing, nor is it the occasion for balancing.

There are many analogues in law. Legal rules are exclusionary reasons, and they result from judgments about what reasons ought to count in what contexts. For example, American law provides that offense at the content of ideas is never a justified reason for regulating speech. Courts do not think that offense at the content of ideas is an insufficiently weighty justification for regulating speech; they think that it is an illegitimate justification. That judgment, itself a rule, is reflected in the more specific rules governing permissible regulation of speech.

This does not mean that free speech is an absolute. Speech can be regulated for good and sufficiently weighty reasons, but those reasons do not include offense at the content of ideas. Flag-burning may thus be prohibited if this is a way of protecting people's ownership rights in flags, but flag-burning may not be prohibited if this is a way of stopping a particular form of political protest. Everything depends on why government is trying to prohibit flag-burning. So too a jury in a contracts case, deciding whether the defendant had sufficient reason to breach the agreement, may not consider the skin color of the parties, or their political views, even though the members of a jury may certainly consider political views and even skin colors when choosing friends. So too a law allowing emergency exceptions will not allow national leaders to identify, as cases of emergency, situations in which their own political popularity is at risk.

The key point is that rules generally say that considerations that are relevant in many settings are not relevant here. Rules will say what sorts of considerations bear on what issues, and what sorts of considerations do not. Rules decide questions of appropriate role, and they say what is relevant for people in different social roles.

Different Kinds of Rules

Rules fall in several different categories. Here is an account, far from exhaustive and tied to our special concerns here.

1. Often rules are a summary of wise decisions; they are defended on the grounds that they are a good summary, and that they are desirable as rules, rather than mere advice or rules of thumb, so as to save the costs of making individualized decisions. If people over the age of sixty are banned from being commercial pilots, it is because this is a pretty accurate summary of good individual decisions and less costly to administer than any alternative. If we say that people under the age of sixteen may not drive, it is for a similar reason.

Many legal rules are best defended as generalizations, admittedly somewhat crude, that operate as a good proxy for individualized inquiries, but that are much less costly and much more efficient than individualized inquiries. Perhaps such inquiries would be expensive to undertake and would not yield much in the way of additional accuracy. Or perhaps such inquiries would go wrong because of the ignorance, confusion, bias, or venality of some or many of the inquirers.

It is worth emphasizing in this regard that we do not have rules at all if rules are taken as a mere summary of wise decisions or as a factor to be taken into account, and if interpreters feel free to disregard rules when their rationale does not apply or when reasons of substance so suggest. Instead we have guidance, advice, or maxims. A defining characteristic of rules is that they are entrenched, and that they bind even if a decisionmaker, probing into the ground for the rules, would conclude that the rule should not apply.

2. Often rules establish *conventions* or otherwise enable people to coordinate their behavior. This is true, for example, with respect to rules of the road. The rule that people must drive on the left-hand side of the road is valuable because it tells people where to drive, not because it is any better than its opposite. We do not think that people must drive on the left because it is a wise decision, in the individual case unaccompanied by rules, to drive on the left.

So too rules may respond to situations in which individually rational decisions can lead to social disaster. The rules governing emission of pollutants are an example. If each polluter makes an individually rational decision, there would be too much pollution in view of the fact that the full costs of pollution are not borne by polluters. And if each polluter felt free to revisit the justification for the rule, the problem might not be solved. If everyone thought that it was legitimate to modify a rule, or to give it special content, in a context in which modification made sense, then no one could know what everyone else would do. The best solution may be to fix a rule and to require everyone to adhere to it. Of course rules of this kind may be over- or underinclusive. To require people to drive on the left-hand side of the road makes little sense when there are boulders and trees on the left-hand side, or when all traffic is going in the same direction.

3. Some rules have an *expressive function*; they make statements about governing social values. The rules governing who may marry whom, for example, say something about the institution of marriage and about social convictions governing who is entitled to public recognition of a relational commitment. Three people cannot be married, nor can people of the same sex. These rules do not summarize individually wise decisions, but instead express a social judgment about appropriate relations. Many people argue for rules because they think that the statement in those rules will make good "statements" or have good social consequences, by pressing social attitudes and norms in the right direction. Consider, for example, the view that government should ban racial hate speech, require recycling, protect endangered species, or impose capital punishment.

4. Sometimes rules are constitutive of social practices.[8] Constitutive rules do not regulate conduct that preexists the rules at issue, but instead create new practices and new forms of behavior. A law banning homicide is a regulative rule; homicide exists before the rule does (even if the term and the category are constructs of the rule). Compare the rule that says a touchdown in football is worth six points. The notion of a touchdown does not precede the rule; when a person runs across the goal line, his conduct is meaningless without the rules establishing what a touchdown is.

Sometimes legal rules have similar features. Consider the rules for making wills, getting married, creating money, making laws, and making contracts. Wills, marriage, money, and laws exist only because of social understandings brought about through law. They do not predate law.[9] When we say that in the United States a law exists if and only if two houses of Congress act according to certain procedures and if the president agrees, we do not mean to summarize individually wise decisions about how to make laws. Instead we say, in defense of the rules, something like this: The law-making enterprise of democracy works best if such rules are observed. That claim must be justified by reference to a claim about the characteristics of democracy as best understood. The same is true of rules of contract and wills.

Of course some particular rules in these areas may stand or fall in accordance with their plausibility as a summary of wise decisions, and for this reason there may be sharp internal disputes about whether to shift from rules to case-by-case judgments. We might adopt a rule to the effect that a will is unenforceable without two witnesses, but when confronted with some particular cases, we may conclude that some wills with only one witness are enforceable because (for example) there is no doubt about their reliability.

5. Some rules overcome the problem of *time inconsistency*. Suppose that in order to succeed in your plans, you need to engage in consistent behavior over time. Perhaps an exercise program requires you to work out for one hour, and just one hour, every day. Or perhaps a good diet requires you to eat the same things, more or less, at the same time for a period. People may unduly discount the future when they make individual decisions. In these circumstances, a rule that is enforceable through some mechanism—perhaps social sanctions from your friends—may be the best way to proceed.

Societies can face similar problems. Perhaps good monetary policy for a certain period requires the Federal Reserve Board to do the same thing each month; suppose too that without a rule, and with particularized judgments about what to do each month, the Board would do inconsistent things. Adoption of a rule may ensure the requisite consistency, perhaps by overcoming excessive discounting of the future, or perhaps by ensuring against strategic behavior on the part of politicians. In this way, a rule may be a *precommitment strategy* that overcomes predictable problems with ruleless decisions.

Defending Rules as Rules

Rules might produce incompletely theorized agreements, and in three different ways. First, people can agree that a rule is binding, or authoritative, without agreeing on a theory of why it is binding, and without agreeing that the rule is good. Theories of legitimate authority are varied and pluralistic, and acceptance of rules can proceed from diverse foundations. Second, people can often judge that a certain rule is reasonable, without taking a stand on large issues of the right or the good. People can urge a 60-mile-per-hour speed limit, a prohibition on bringing elephants into restaurants, a ten-year minimum sentence for attempted rape, and much more without taking a stand on debates between Kantians and utilitarians. Third, rules sharply diminish the level of disagreement among people who are subject to them and among people who must interpret and apply them. When rules are in place, high-level theories need not be invoked in order for us to know what rules mean, and whether they are binding.

1. *Rules minimize the informational and political costs of reaching decisions in particular cases.* Without rules, decisions are extremely expensive; rules can produce enormous efficiency gains. Every day we operate as we do because of rules, legal and nonlegal, and often the rules are so internalized that they become second-nature, greatly easing the costs of decisions and making it possible to devote our attention to other matters. With a speed limit law, for example, we do not have to decide how fast to drive. With rules, the complex and sometimes morally charged question of *what issues are relevant* itself has been decided in advance.

Rules are disabling for just this reason; they constrain us, but they are enabling, even liberating too.[10] Like the rules of grammar, they help make social life possible. If we know that there will be one and only one president, we do not have to decide how many presidents there will be. If we know that a will must have two witnesses, we do not have to decide, in each case, how many witnesses there must be to a will. Rules both free up time for other matters and facilitate private and public decisions by establishing the frameworks within which they can be made.

By adopting rules, people can also overcome their own myopia, weakness of will, confusion, venality, or bias in individual cases. This holds true for individuals and societies alike. Societies and their representatives too may be subject to myopia, weakness of will, confusion, venality, or bias, and rules safeguard against all of these problems.

These ideas justify the general idea that rules should be entrenched in the sense that they apply even if their rationale does not. If we substitute for rules an investigation of whether their justification applies in each instance, we are engaging in a form of case-by-case decisionmaking, and it is easy to underestimate the often enormous costs of that way of proceeding. Officials may be pressed by the exigencies of a particular case to seek individualized justice, without seeing the expense, and risk of unfairness, of that goal. It is notable that in the 1960s and 1970s American administrative agencies shifted dramatically from adjudication to rulemaking, largely because of their understanding that through issuing rules, they could decide hundreds or even thousands of cases at once and thus eliminate the various expenses of case-by-case decisions.[11]

Some of the costs of rulelessness are simply a matter of compiling information. To know whether a particular pilot is able to fly competently, we need to know a lot of details. But some of the costs are of a different character. Suppose that we are deciding on emissions levels for substances that contribute to destruction of the ozone layer, or that we are thinking about when to go forward with projects that threaten endangered species. Information is important here, but it is also necessary for multiple people to reach closure on hard and even tragic matters. For this reason, there may be, for lawmakers, high political costs or great difficulty in producing a rule. But once a rule is in place, individual enforcement officials can bracket those matters and take the decision as a given.

The high costs—informational and political—of ruleless decisions are often not visible to those who are deciding whether to lay down rules in the first instance. The Supreme Court, for example, can see that rules will bind its members, perhaps unfortunately, in subsequent cases, and the Court therefore might avoid rulemaking in the interest of maintaining flexibility for the future. The Court might so decide without easily seeing that the absence of rules will force litigants and lower courts to guess, possibly for a generation or more, about the real content of the law. In this way the Court can internalize the benefits of flexibility while "exporting" to others the costs of rulelessness. So too legislatures can see that rules would contain major mistakes, or that they cannot be compiled without large informational and political costs—without, perhaps, fully understanding that the absence of rules will force administrative agencies and private citizens to devote enormous effort to giving the law some concrete content.

2. *Rules are impersonal and blind; they promote equal treatment and reduce the likelihood of bias and arbitrariness.* Rules are associated with impartiality. Their impartiality is captured in the notion that the Goddess justice is blindfolded. Rules are blind to many features of a case that might otherwise be relevant and that are relevant in some social contexts—religion, social class, good looks, height, and so forth—and also to many things on whose relevance people have great difficulty in agreeing.

In *Papachristou*, for example, the Court was especially concerned to diminish bias and arbitrariness, by requiring the legislature to lay down clear rules that limit the discretion of police officers. A comparative disadvantage of rule-free decisions is that they increase the risk that illegitimate considerations will influence decisions. The administrative law judge awarding disability benefits on the basis of factors or standards may well be affected by his feelings for the particular claimant, issues of race, his opinion of the social security program in general, or even his mood on the day of decision. With rules, people who are similarly situated are more likely to be similarly treated.

Many debates about constitutional "doctrine" are related to this claim. For a period, the law governing the First Amendment consisted not of rules but of a set of factors: the government interest; the value of the speech; and the likelihood of harm.[12] But in the last generation, the Court has shifted in the direction of "categorical balancing," consisting of rules that determine how different forms of speech will be treated and also of distinctions among different categories of restrictions on speech. The categories are somewhat crude and may in particular cases produce inferior results to a more fine-grained approach. But the very existence of the categories usefully disciplines judges in politically sensitive free speech cases.

The claim that rules promote generality and in that sense equal treatment requires an important qualification. In a way rules prevent equal treatment. Of course rules suppress many differences among cases; they single out a particular feature of a range of cases and subsume all such cases under a single umbrella. In this sense, rules make irrelevant features of cases that might turn out, on reflection by people making particular judgments, to be relevant indeed. Should everyone who has exceeded 60 miles per hour be treated the same way? Should everyone falling in a particular unfortunate spot on a social security grid be denied benefits? If equality requires the similarly situated to be treated similarly, the question is whether people are similarly situated, and rules do not permit a particularized and perhaps more accurate inquiry on that score. In this way rules may actually fail to promote equal treatment as compared with rulelessness.[13]

3. *Rules serve appropriately both to embolden and to constrain decisionmakers in particular cases.*[14] A special advantage of rules is that judges (and others) can be emboldened to enforce them even when the particular stakes and the particular political costs are high. Rules may provide the basis for courageous decisions that might otherwise be difficult to reach and to legitimate.

Suppose, for example, that the Supreme Court has set out the *Miranda* rules, and that everyone knows that they will be applied mechanically to every criminal defendant. If so, judges can refer to those rules, and in a sense hide behind them, even if the defendant is especially despised, and even if it is tempting to say that the rules should yield in the particular case. Or if the rule banning discrimination against viewpoints is well-entrenched in the law of free speech, judges can refer to that rule in invalidating laws banning flag-burning, even in the face of severe and otherwise irresistible public pressure.

The key advantage here (one that can be a disadvantage too) is that rules make it unnecessary and even illegitimate to return to first principles. If judges decided on the content of law at the point of (politically charged) application, and if they had to go back to first principles, they might not adhere to those principles at all when the stakes are high.

In one sense rules reduce responsibility for particular cases, by allowing the authority to claim that it is not his choice, but the choice of others who have laid down the rule. Officials can claim that the previous choice is not being made but simply followed. When the rule is ambiguous, this claim is fraudulent. But it is true when the rule is clear. In a system in which rules are binding and are seen to be binding, the law can usefully stiffen the judicial spine in cases in which this is a valuable guarantor of individual liberty against public attack.

4. *Rules promote predictability and planning for private actors, legislators, and others.* From the standpoint of people who are subject to public regulation, it is especially important to know what the law is before the point of application. Indeed, it may be more important to know what the law is than to have a law of any particular kind. When cases are settled in advance, people are able to plan their affairs and to do so with knowledge of what government may and may not do.

In modern regulation, a pervasive problem is that members of regulated classes face ambiguous and conflicting guidelines, so that they do not know how to plan. Under a standard or a set of factors, neither the government nor affected citizens may know about their obligations. Consider, by contrast, the *Miranda* rules, instructing police officers how to deal with those charged with a crime. A special virtue of those rules is that they tell the police what must be done and therefore eliminate guessing-games that can be so destructive to planning. So too in the environmental area, where rules are often far better than the open-ended "reasonableness" inquiry characteristic of the common law.

5. *Rules increase visibility and accountability.* When rules are at work, it is clear who is responsible, and who is to be blamed if things go wrong. This is especially valuable when the rulemaker has a high degree of accountability and legitimacy. A large problem with a system based on standards or factors is that no one knows who is really responsible if, for example, the air stays dirty or the crime rate goes up. If the *Miranda* rules create a problem, the Supreme Court is obviously the problem. But if the Court sets out no rules, but a test based on factors, and if that

test produces mistakes of various sorts, the Court may escape the scrutiny it deserves.

There is a related point. Without rules, the exercise of discretion can be invisible or at least less visible. By contrast, rules allow the public more easily to monitor compliance.

6. *Rules avoid the humiliation of subjecting people to exercises of official discretion in their particular case.* A special advantage of rules is that because of their fixity and generality, they make it unnecessary for citizens to ask an official for permission to engage in certain conduct. Rules turn citizens into right-holders. Discretion, standards, or factors make citizens into supplicants. Importantly, factors and standards allow mercy in the form of relief from rigid rules. But rules have the comparative advantage of forbidding officials from being punitive, or unmoved, for irrelevant or invidious reasons, by a particular applicant's request.

Compare, for example, a mandatory retirement for people over the age of seventy with a law permitting employers to discharge employees who, because of their age, are no longer able to perform their job adequately. If you are an employee, it is especially humiliating and stigmatizing to have employers decide whether you have been rendered incompetent by age. A rule avoids this inquiry altogether, and it might be favored for this reason even if it is both over- and underinclusive. Or consider a situation in which officials can give out jobs at their discretion, as compared with one in which officials must hire and fire in accordance with rules laid down in advance. In the first system, employees are in the humiliating position of asking for grace.

From all these considerations we see that the case for rules can be very insistent, especially in a world in which officials and citizens cannot always be trusted, and in light of the enormous simplifying effects of rules for busy people with many things to do. We will soon raise many questions about the project of making and following rules. But first, some clarifications are in order.

Misunderstandings of the Rule of Law

The ideas outlined here cast doubt on many imaginable legislative initiatives. They support bans on retroactive law, on vague law, on secret law. They help explain the prohibition on bills of attainder. They offer reasons to question open-ended delegations of power to administrative officials (even though American law is pervaded by such delegations, which are, interestingly, forbidden under the German constitution). They also call for principles of interpretation that favor the availability of judicial review, "prospective only" legislation, and the rule of lenity for criminal provisions, giving the defendant the benefit of the doubt.

But some people go further. They think that the requirements of the rule of law provide an important check on what they see as partisanship or selectivity insofar as these are reflected in law. On this view, the rule of law is a requirement of generality, and the requirement of generality forbids law from imposing selective benefits or selective burdens. In this notion lies much of the debate over the ideas of impartiality and neutrality in law.

An influential discussion appears in Justice Robert Jackson's concurring opinion in the *Railway Express* case.[15] New York City prohibited anyone from operating an "advertising vehicle" on the streets, that is, a vehicle that sells its exterior for advertising purposes. But the New York law exempted from the general prohibition the use of advertising on vehicles that are engaged in the ordinary business of the owner, and not used mainly or only for advertising.

Railway Express, a company operating nearly 2000 trucks for advertising purposes, challenged the New York law under the due process and equal protection clauses of the American Constitution. The Supreme Court upheld the law. The Court emphasized that judges should defer to legislatures and noted that the local authorities might have believed that people who advertise their own wares on trucks do not present the same traffic problems as people in the business of advertising. The Court added that "the fact that New York City sees fit to eliminate from traffic this kind of distraction but does not touch what may be even greater ones in a different category, such as the vivid displays on Times Square, is immaterial. It is no requirement of equal protection that all evils of the same genus be eradicated or none at all." In this way the Court rejected the idea that the principle of generality imposed serious limits on legislative classifications.

Justice Jackson saw things differently. He took this seemingly mundane case as an occasion for celebrating the use of the equal protection clause as a guarantor of the rule of law—understood as a ban on selectivity. The equal protection clause, as part of the rule of law, "means that the prohibition or regulation must have a broader impact." The requirement of breadth in turn serves a democratic function.

[T]here is no more effective practical guaranty against arbitrary or unreasonable government than to require that the principles of law which officials would impose upon a minority must be imposed generally. Conversely, nothing opens the door to arbitrary action so effectively as to allow those officials to pick and choose only a few to whom they will apply legislation and thus to escape the political retribution that might be visited upon them if larger numbers were affected. Courts can take no better step to assure that laws will be just than to require that laws be equal in operation.

There is much good sense here. A system of law ought to require public-regarding justifications for the denial of benefits or the imposition of burdens. In a fair legal system, interest-group pressure or legislative self-interest is an inadequate basis for law. The requirement of generality can bring into effect political checks that would otherwise be too weak to prevent oppressive legislation from going forward. Consider a law requiring people of a certain race to go through onerous procedures before obtaining drivers' licenses. If the procedural requirements were imposed generally, they might not be imposed at all. And if such laws were imposed on everyone, we have a guarantee that they are not so oppressive after all.

But how are we to know whether a seemingly narrow enactment must be applied generally? Many laws are narrow, and because their narrowness is justified, they need not be extended more generally. Children cannot vote; electric cars are not subject to pollution controls; labor unions are exempted from antitrust laws. Are these forms of selectivity unacceptable? Is it illegitimate to say that blind people cannot receive drivers' licenses?

To know whether generality is required, we have to know whether there are relevant similarities and relevant differences between those burdened and those not burdened by legislation. The notion of the rule of law by itself cannot supply this knowledge. No one thinks that "generality" should be required when there are relevant differences. No one supposes that the speed limit laws are unacceptable if they do not apply to police officers and ambulance drivers operating within the course of their official duties.

Any requirement of equal treatment depends on a set of ideas establishing whether there are relevant differences between the cases to which a law is applied and the cases to which it is not. If a law says that in order to receive federal employment, everyone who is not white must take certain tests, we can easily see that the grounds for the distinction are illegitimate. If a law says that women must take strength tests to be police officers, but that men need not, we can conclude that there is insufficient generality in the law. But sometimes selectivity is legitimate. When we ask whether it is, we come far from rules and the rule of law. We are not merely requiring generality, but second-guessing judgments about who is similar to whom. The rule of law does not have the resources to resolve the resulting debates.[16]

Is the Rule of Law Associated with Free Markets?

These points provide reason to question some prominent ideas about the rule of law. Consider, for example, Friedrich Hayek's influential discussion.[17] Hayek identifies the rule of law with an idea of "impartiality." Its antonym is a system of "planning," in which the state picks winners and losers. Because the rule of law does not pick out particular winners and losers, it does not play favorites, and in this sense it is impartial. But what does the requirement of generality forbid? Hayek does not disapprove of all that is done in the name of the regulatory state. Government provision of public services is on his view unobjectionable. Nor does he disapprove of maximum hour laws, laws banning dangerous products, and laws protecting conditions in the workplace.

What, then, is prohibited? Hayek is concerned about those measures that "involve arbitrary discrimination between persons." This category includes most importantly "decisions as to who is to be allowed to provide different services or commodities, at what prices or in what quantities— in other words, measures designed to control the access to different trades and occupations, the terms of sale, and the amounts to be produced or sold." But how do we know whether these decisions, or any others, are arbitrary? Certainly it is not impermissible for the state to require taxi drivers to show that they have good eyesight, or to ban people from practicing medicine without meeting certain requirements of medical competence. It therefore emerges that the state is banned from imposing qualifications only when they are arbitrary on their merits. But to decide this question, we need a theory of appropriate qualifications. The rule of law, standing by itself, does not supply that theory.

What about price controls? So long as the prices are stable, controls seem consistent with the rule of law (which is not at all to say that they are good policy). Hayek thinks that since they abandon the touchstone of supply and demand, any governmentally fixed prices "will not be the same for all sellers" and that they will "discriminate between persons on essentially arbitrary grounds." Of course there is much to be said against government controls of prices and quantities, and much of what can be said against them relates to their rejection of the forces of supply and demand. But the judgment that price controls are "arbitrary" comes not from the rule of law, but from the idea that the appropriate prices and quantities of goods and services are set by the market. That is a reasonable judgment, but it is not part of the rule of law.

It might be tempting at this point to suggest that much of Hayek's discussion is simply confused, and that the rule of law has nothing to do with markets at all. This conclusion is mostly right, but a bit too simple. There are at least three features shared by the rule of law and free markets. First, the rule of law does not make after-the-fact adjustments. Rules operate prospectively. The same is true for markets. Second, there is a sense in which both rules and markets are "no respecter of persons." For advocates of the rule of law, government, like justice, should be "blind." Markets are similarly blind. Third, both rules and markets work against measures that impose inappropriate informational demands on government. Price-fixing is especially objectionable because it requires government to do something that it lacks information to do well. The same argument can be invoked on behalf of (at least many) rules. By setting out rules of the road or requirements for the transfer of land, government can appropriately allocate informational burdens between itself and others.

On the other hand, the metaphor of "blindness" should not be overstated. All laws do, in a sense, pick winners and losers. Certainly this is true for maximum hour laws; it is also true for the provision of governmental services. And though free markets may not pick winners and losers, it is often quite predictable who will be favored and who will be disfavored under the ordinary rules of property, tort, and contract, which make markets possible. We know, for example, that severely disabled people are unlikely to do well in a market system.

It is also a theoretical possibility that a system of planning could comply with the rule of law, at least if the "plans" were announced in advance and if expectations were firmly protected. Probably most real-world systems of planning must shift too rapidly to conform to these requirements. This point is part of the enduring argument against socialist systems. But the argument has nothing to do with the rule of law.

These points cast doubt not only on Hayek's view but also and for the same reasons as Marxist-inspired attacks on the rule of law. Consider Morton Horwitz's suggestion that

> I do not see how a Man of the Left can describe the rule of law as "an unqualified human good"! It undoubtedly restrains power, but it also prevents power's benevolent exercise. It creates formal equality—a not inconsiderable virtue—but it promotes substantive inequality by creating a consciousness that radically separates law from politics, means from ends,

processes from outcomes. By promoting procedural justice it enables the shrewd, the calculating, and the wealthy to manipulate its forms to their own advantage. And it ratifies and legitimates an adversarial, competitive, and atomistic conception of human relations.[18]

This passage takes the rule of law to require much more than in fact it does. Does the rule of law forbid the pursuit of substantive equality through, for example, progressive income taxes, welfare and employment programs, antidiscrimination laws, and much more? Like Hayek, Horwitz appears to identify the rule of law with (a particular conception of) free markets. The identification is unwarranted.

The rule of law does not have the features that Hayek and his Marxist opponents understand it to have. A familiar challenge to rules—that they are connected with merely "formal" equality—is therefore unpersuasive. Rules could provide that no person may have more than one dollar more than anyone else, that the average income of men and women must be the same, or that all racial groups must have the same per capita wealth. There is no association between rules on the one hand and conservatism, free markets, or inequality on the other.

The rule of law has many virtues, but we should not overstate what it entails. As we will now see, the virtues of rules are inseparable from the vices of rules. A great task of a well-functioning legal system is to come to terms with the resulting puzzles, which arise every day, and which can involve our most fundamental liberties.

5

In Defense
of Casuistry

In this chapter I offer two arguments against rules. Both of these arguments are intended to challenge the virtue claimed for rules—that they operate as mid- or low-level generalizations that settle all cases in advance.

First: Rules cannot do what they are supposed to do, since substantive disagreements may break out at the moment of application. Rules are not quite what they appear to be. They do not settle all cases in advance. The inevitability of interpretation undermines the aspiration to rule-bound justice.

Second: The generality of rules, and their blindness to particulars, is not always a virtue but is often a political vice, because a just system allows equity or adaptation to the particulars of individual cases. Rules are obtuse; ideal justice is flexible and based on the situation at hand.

Taken together, these arguments do not show that rules are generally a bad idea. But they do point the way toward casuistry, and emphasis on particulars, as important aspects of law.

Against Rules, I: Are Rules Feasible?

Challenges

If rules are understood as complete, before-the-fact judgments about legal rights, rules are pretty much impossible.[1] Encounters with unforeseen cases will confound the view that things have been fully settled in advance. The need for interpretation, and the likelihood of competing interpretations founded on disagreements about substance, will likely defeat the project of following rules.

On Language and Invitations

Because of the nature of language, legal rules will leave a variety of gaps and ambiguities. Even when the meaning of a legal term is clear in the abstract or in the dictionary, uncertainty may break out at the point of application. This is because the meaning of legal (and other) language is a function of both *context* and *culture*. Words do not have acontextual meanings. The word "bat," for example, could mean a great many things. If a law says that bats must be made of wood, the meaning is probably transparent and clear, but only because of context; so too with a law saying that "bats" may not be imported from South America. The same can be said for the words "feasible," "equal," and "free." To interpret words, we must know a great deal more than dictionary meanings. We must also know the particular setting in which words are uttered. We must similarly identify cultural understandings. The English word "cricket" may have one meaning in Ireland and another in the United States.

Thus far I have spoken of single words. To understand a whole sentence, people must make extremely complex but amazingly rapid judgments, in which countless possibilities, some of them based on literal or dictionary meaning, are disregarded as implausible in the context. Consider the sentence, "take out the garbage." This sentence is likely to have a clear meaning when placed in a familiar context—a request for a chore within the household—but the dictionary will reveal numerous indeterminacies, and in other contexts (a book reviewer reading a manuscript, for example, or a tennis instructor commenting on a serve), the meaning could be altogether different.

In short, background understandings of various sorts make words intelligible. The operations of the human brain in this regard are crucial, omnipresent, even a bit miraculous, and sometimes the background understandings are disputed or shift over time. The word "bat" is intelligible to sports fans because of what they know about baseball; the word "equal" is intelligible or transparent to certain communities because of what they know, or think they know, about issues of justice. For heuristic purposes, we might put background understandings into two categories, the *semantic* and the *substantive*. Sometimes a dispute about the meaning of a legal term really involves semantic practice; sometimes the dispute is largely independent of moral or political claims. We might quarrel over the meaning of the word "bat" because we are puzzled about the kind of sports equipment to which it refers—are we discussing baseball, table tennis, or badminton? We might be confused because we do not know enough about the particular context. Or we might puzzle over a question of statutory meaning because we disagree about the relevance of the placement of a comma, about the implications of the omission of a certain word, or about how a term is commonly understood in a certain community.

Some people think that the contextual character of meaning undermines the project of rule-following. But this is a mistake. "Bat" may mean one thing in connection with baseball and another thing in connection with a zoo, but the term, taken in its context, may well be determinate, and its meaning need not depend on a moral or political argument of any sort. The contextual character of meaning warns us not to make "a fortress out of the dictionary,"[2] and thus to avoid mechanical reliance on dictionary definitions when the context suggests that the dictionary meaning is not apt. But the need to refer to context should not be troubling to enthusiasts for rules. On the contrary, it is usually the context that makes meaning plain.

So, too, the dependence of meaning on a range of background understandings does not undermine the project of rule-following. Background understandings are what make the project of rule-following feasible in the first instance.

But sometimes substantive disagreements, rooted in political or moral considerations, lie behind interpretive debates. Nonlawyers may not know the meaning of the term "freedom of speech" because they are not part of the community that defines this term, with (and this is the key point) its accepted prototypical cases and its shared but contingent background assumptions about substantive issues. Any particular understanding of the words "freedom of speech" or "equal" will require much more than a dictionary or a language lesson. Thus we cannot say whether affirmative action is compelled or prohibited by a requirement of "equality" without knowing much more than dictionaries tell us. Perhaps the legal materials authoritatively resolve that question; if they do not, a view on that point will require not a language lesson but a substantive moral or political argument, often rooted in analogy. The same is true of the term "reasonable" in the law of tort or environmental protection. Some people think that conduct is reasonable if it passes a cost-benefit test; other people think that the term calls for compliance with community norms; still others believe that it requires respect for certain understandings of individual autonomy. Dictionaries cannot resolve this question.

Words like "equality" and "reasonable" are vague because they need a great deal of specification to have meaning for particular cases. Abstract terms have to be applied to endlessly varied cases that cannot be captured exhaustively by rules. We might say that substantive debates are invited by such terms. But substantive debates can also lie behind the interpretation of apparently clearer and more specific terms such as "discrimination," "use," or "carcinogen." Such terms are given meaning by reference to prototypical cases as well; recall the discussion of analogy in Chapter 3. Thus the last term could be understood literally (has the substance caused cancer in anyone, ever?), but perhaps the prototypical case is a substance that creates a serious risk, and perhaps it should not be understood literally if the result would be to increase overall risks (as in a case in which a ban on low-level "carcinogens," causing trivially low risks, prevents people from obtaining products that are actually safer than those now on the market).

In some cases, we might think that the interpretation of an apparently clear term cannot depend on dictionaries or on "ordinary" meaning. The act of interpreting the law, properly understood, requires people to use analogies and to make substantive claims—about what speakers should be taken to intend or about what makes best sense. If we are fanatical about limiting interpretive discretion, we will be disturbed to find that laws that apparently amount to rules often call for moral or political judgments by interpreters at the point of application.

The Problem of the Single Exception

We can understand the argument thus far to suggest that in order for many rules to be interpreted, there need be nothing like an invitation for moral or political judgments from the (shared understanding of the) text of the rule itself, or from the (shared understanding of the goal of the) people who wrote the rule. Laws that appear confining and quite rulelike will require interpreters to give them content at the point of application. The interpretation of rules *generally* requires substantive moral or political judgments of some kind—not only the substantive moral judgment to be bound by law itself, but also substantive understandings that inevitably go into the reading of legal terms. These understandings are invisible only because (and if) they are widely shared.

Let us try to extend this argument. In brief: The very fact that a rule has at least one exception, and the very fact that the finding of an exception is part of ordinary interpretation, means that in every case a judge is presented with the question whether the rule is best interpreted to cover the application at hand. Any judgment on this matter depends on a moral or political claim about relevant differences and relevant similarities— between the case where an exception has been or would be found and the case now under consideration. We can return in this way to the role of analogical thinking in the interpretation of rules.

Some of this seems to follow from an adaptation of a famous argument about the open texture of language offered by Friedrich Waismann.[3] Waismann claims that even the most apparently precise and specific language can become uncertain because of our limited knowledge of the future and because of the possibility that new events will unsettle present understandings. Sooner or later, clear language will confront an unanticipated problem. When the confrontation occurs, we are unlikely to know what to do, since the language will no longer be clear. For example, a law requiring "all cars" to be equipped with catalytic converters seems unambiguous. But its meaning becomes unclear when electric cars come onto the market. A law forbidding dogs to come into restaurants seems like a genuine rule. But it may be unclear when applied to a police officer using a German shepherd to find a bomb. (We shall see shortly that in the legal context, Waismann's argument is erroneous or at least based on a contentious assumption, but let us accept the claim for now.)

It may be right to say, as some do, that when an exception is made to literal language, a judge is "legislating" or "making law." But the finding of an exception seems to be a part of ordinary legal interpretation. Indeed, many legal systems include a principle to the effect that literal language will not be applied to a case if the application would produce absurdity or gross injustice.[4] If a judge is legislating whenever he finds an exception, then judges legislate often, and indeed a judge is in a sense legislating everywhere, because in every case a judge must decide whether to make an exception, and that decision usually turns on a moral or political argument. The failure to find an exception in ordinary cases is not an exception to this general claim. The failure to find an exception amounts to a judgment that the case at hand is different from the truly exceptional cases, and not truly different from the ordinary cases.

I have said that literal language will never, or almost never, be interpreted so as to reach applications in a way that would produce absurdity or gross injustice. There is an old maxim from Chief Justice Coke: *Cessante rationae, cessat ipsa lex*. This idea is embodied in some statutes. California law says that "when the reason of a rule ceases, so should the rule itself." Return to our law forbidding people from driving over 65 miles per hour on a certain street. Jones goes 75 miles per hour because he is driving an ambulance, with a comatose accident victim, to the hospital; Smith goes 90 because she is a police officer following a fleeing felon; Wilson goes 80 because he is being chased by a madman with a gun. In all these cases, the driver may well have a legally acceptable excuse, especially if there is a general "necessity" exception to criminal punishment, but even if there is no law "on the books" allowing an exception in these circumstances. And if rules have exceptions in cases of palpable absurdity or injustice, the denial of an exception depends on a moral or political judgment to the effect that the particular result is not palpably absurd or unjust.

We might call this *the problem of the single exception*. Once an exception is made, or would be made, a degree of casuistry becomes inevitable, as judges interpret rules by seeing whether the case at hand is different from or similar to the case in which an exception is made or would be made.

Consider a real case, *Church of the Holy Trinity v. United States*.[5] In that case the Court interpreted an apparently unambiguous statutory provision making it unlawful for "any person, company, partnership, or corporation, in any manner whatsoever, to prepay the transportation, or in any way assist or encourage the importation or migration of any alien or aliens, any foreigner or foreigners, into the United States . . . under contract or agreement . . . made previous to the importation or migration . . . to perform labor or service of any kind in the United States." The Court said that despite this language, it was acceptable for the Holy Trinity church to pay for the transportation of a rector to the United States. The Court held that the statute should not apply to the church, because that application would be unreasonable in light of the statute's purposes and was not likely intended. But what if a further case arose involving a hospital paying the travel expenses of a doctor, or a university paying the travel expenses of a scientist, or a charity paying the expenses of an expert on the relief of poverty? If an exception would not be made in those cases as well, it would not be because of the binding nature of the literal language of the statutory "rule"—that issue was settled by *Holy Trinity*—but because the argument for an exception would be found weaker or less plausible in those cases than in the *Holy Trinity* case.

Of course the strength of any claim for an exception cannot depend on anything other than social judgments and understandings. We can imagine a culture in which the absurdity of the application would be more obvious for a hospital than for a church or more obvious for a charity than for anything else. And on this score, we can imagine changes across space and time, as different social judgments enter into assessments of absurdity.

The argument I am making raises problems for Frederick Schauer's preferred solution to some of the problems posed by rules and ruleless-ness.[6] Schauer points to the many advantages of rule-following and to the many dangers of treating a rule as coextensive with its justifications. As we have seen, the justification for a rule is a standard, and if rules are confused with their justifications, they are not rules at all. But Schauer is aware that rules can produce weird or palpably unjust outcomes in partic-ular cases. He therefore urges what he calls "presumptive positivism," that is, an approach to rules that refuses to investigate the justifications for rules in ordinary cases, but that allows exceptions to be made when-ever there is genuine absurdity, or when the cases for making exceptions is exceptionally strong. In this way Schauer hopes to have a system of rules, but also to allow an exit from rules in extreme cases.

This solution may be the best that we can do—whether it is depends on a set of contextual issues discussed in Chapter 7—but its interesting feature is that it produces a regime of casuistry rather than one of rule-bound justice. If exceptions will be made in cases of absurdity, then it is possible to ask, in every case, whether the particular application is absurd. To do this, we will have to embark on a form of analogical reasoning in which the apparent rulelessness of the rule does not really settle things before the fact. The content of the law, even under Schauer's system of presumptive positivism, depends on political or moral judgments made at the point of application. In this way presumptive positivism is not an antonym to casuistical judgment but instead a species of it. It may be a species of casuistry that allows few deviations from rules, but it depends critically on particular judgments about absurdity and analogy.

Now it is possible to say that for an observer of legal behavior, it is usually possible to "say what the law is" without making substantive judgments. Perhaps acute outsiders know which arguments are most like-ly to move Supreme Court justices, and they may be able to offer a good prediction that, for example, an excuse will be found for Jones but not for Wilson. The prediction is not itself moral in character. A description of an evaluative judgment is still a description.[7] But even if that claim—intended as a defense of legal positivism— is right, it is not responsive to the point here, which is that for participants in the legal system, moral or political judgments underlie claims about what the law is. Participants in law cannot ask what the law is by asking what moral arguments will move participants in law. They have to ask what moral arguments are most persuasive *to them*, and they cannot answer that question as if it were a matter of fact.

There is a further issue. When judges are faced with more than one rule, cases become problematic, and unless priority rules have been laid down in advance, they must be settled at the point of application. Suppose the Supreme Court says that in the face of interpretive doubt, statutes will be construed so as not to apply outside the territorial boundaries of the United States, and also that in the face of interpretive doubt, statutes will be interpreted in accordance with the views of the administrative agency charged with enforcing them. Suppose that a case arises in which the agency charged with enforcing a civil rights law concludes that the law applies outside the United States. The two interpretive rules conflict. What should a court do? A legal system may contain no rulelike answer to this question. If it does not, disputes may break out at the point of application, when judges try to accommodate the two rules. Of course if judges or others are concerned to ensure that the system really is one of rules, they may come up with rules of priority, so that conflicts between rules can be resolved by reference to rules. But it is most unlikely that rules of priority can be specified exhaustively in advance.

The meaning of rules is thus a product of substantive judgments, often at least partly moral or political in character. This point is decisive against approaches that insist from the internal point of view, it is possible to say what the law is without making judgments about what the law should be.

The Rule of Law Chastened

How damaging is this to the project of following rules or to the rule of law? The simplest point here is that almost all real-world cases involving the meaning of rules are very easy. This is because the substantive judgments that underlie readings of rules are often widely shared. Usually the literal application of statutory language does not produce absurdity.

In any case it may be feasible to rely on the literal or ordinary understanding of legal terms, and courts could do this even in cases in which such reliance leads to apparently unreasonable applications. We might urge literalism or ordinary meaning for pragmatic purposes, indeed for some of the same pragmatic reasons that support ruleness in general—as a means of promoting predictability and limiting judicial discretion at the point of application. Waismann's argument about the open texture of language does not undermine this point. To be sure, some legal terms are open-ended in the sense that they invite discretionary judgments at the point of application: "reasonable," "equal," "feasible," "safe." But other terms might be interpreted literally and applied even to cases not foreseen at the time of enactment. Many legal terms are applied to situations not specifically contemplated when they were enacted.

For example, the statutory term "motor vehicle" would apply to a Saturn or a Ford Taurus, even if those cars did not exist until recently. The existence of an unforeseen case causes interpretive doubt only when two conditions are met: (1) the interpreters believe that the case is relevantly different from the foreseen cases and (2) the interpreters believe that statutory terms should not be applied to unanticipated cases that are relevantly different. Since (1) and (2) are often true in Anglo-American law, unforeseen cases can produce interpretive doubt. But it would be feasible to adopt an approach to interpretation that would deny (2). Thus Waismann's insistence on the possibility of unforeseen and relevantly different cases does not show that literalism is not feasible.

If judges cannot look into the reasonableness of the particular application, some unfortunate results will follow, but we might believe that the results will be better, in the aggregate, than those that would follow from allowing judges to apply rules literally only in cases in which the application makes sense (to them). We might fear a situation in which judges felt free to explore the justification for the rule and the reasonableness of the application when deciding whether to apply the rule. Part of the point of any rule is not only to serve substantive purposes but also to obtain the distinctive benefit of ruleness.[8]

Read literally, rules are almost always over- and underinclusive if assessed by reference to their purposes. Indeed, there is a plurality of plausible justifications for every rule, with some very specific ("to ensure that people do not drive dangerously") to some very general ("to make the world better"); this plurality of justifications makes the use of justifications quite problematic for those who want to interpret rules. But it is hardly an argument that literal readings are not feasible.

Whether literal readings, when feasible, are reasonable or right is a complex issue having to do with our faith in interpreters, our faith in those who make rules in the first place, the aggregate risk of error, and the possibility of legislative corrections of absurd results in particular cases. That judgment—the judgment whether to allow for exceptions from literalism—will itself be based on moral and political considerations. But this is not a point about feasibility.

We have concluded, then, that rules cannot be interpreted without resort to shared background understandings, and usually they cannot be interpreted without resort to substantive arguments of certain kinds. A degree of casuistical judgment is most likely to be exercised at the point of application, at least in a system in which literal language will not be understood to produce absurdity or gross injustice. In this way—the way suggested by the problem of the single exception—the case for rules must be chastened. Whether rule-bound decisions are preferable to the alternatives is another question; it is to this question that I now turn.

Against Rules, II: Are Rules Obtuse?

In many spheres of law, people do not rely on rules at all. They rely on a complex set of judgments and understandings not reducible to any simple verbal formulation. A rule-book for telling jokes may be helpful, but if you really tried to tell jokes by following clear rules laid down in advance, you probably would not be very funny. There are no clear rules for dealing with friends in distress. Doctors are said to follow rules, and surely they do, but some illuminating accounts treat clinical medicine as a matter of casuistry, in which experienced people build up judgments analogically and from experience with past cases. They rely on rules of thumb rather than mandatory rules.[9] People who write by reference to rules are likely to be poor writers. Indeed, a rule-oriented approach to writing reflects insecurity, and this is visible to readers.

These examples help explain the inadequacy or obtuseness of many rules in law. They help show the virtues of asking whether rules make sense, or nonsense, in particular instances. They indicate that at least in principle, individualized, rule-free judgments are more just than rule-bound decisions. Here, then, are the basic problems with rules.

1. *Rules are both over- and underinclusive if assessed by reference to the reasons that justify them.* If you have ever been frustrated by modern government, you know that rules can produce arbitrary outcomes. Experience is likely to turn up considerations that make it odd or worse to apply the rule. Particularized decisions may be just, and rule-bound decisions may be unjust, because the latter could not sufficiently take account of individual circumstances. This was a large part of the argument in the important case of *Woodson v. North Carolina*,[10] in which the Supreme Court invalidated mandatory death sentences (see Chapter 6).

For similar reasons it is sometimes inefficient to make decisions by rule, because any rule that we can generate will produce too much inaccuracy in particular cases. Individualized decisions would be better. If people can adapt their behavior to the rules, and thus avoid the inefficient outcome, this problem can be minimized. But sometimes private adaptation is not a realistic or adequate response.

Consider, for example, the case of college admissions. It is reasonable to think that any simple rule would produce too many errors from the standpoint of the goal of obtaining a good student body. Even a complex rule or formula, allowing several factors to count but also weighting them and hence minimizing discretion, might well produce many mistakes. Or consider the matter of criminal sentencing. While open-ended discretion has been persuasively criticized, the range of relevant variables is very wide, and rigidly rule-bound decisions would produce much injustice. Or consider the rigidly rule-bound enforcement of the laws against drunk driving in Norway, when people were sent to jail for three weeks for having a relatively low blood alcohol content over 0.05 percent—even when driving to back their cars into the garage or to save lives.[11]

In modern regulatory law, this problem is associated with the pervasive and damaging phenomenon of "site level unreasonableness."[12] This phenomenon occurs when a general rule is applied to situations in which it makes no sense. Consider a requirement that all eating places have two fire exits, that all places of employment be equipped with ramps as well as staircases, or that all pollution sources use certain expensive antipollution devices. (Many more examples could be added.) The general rule can produce enormous costs for few benefits in the particular site, yet administrators insist on mechanical compliance with the general rule. Perhaps it would be best to dispense with rules and instead to allow firms to comply by showing adequate performance under a set of factors, a process to be overseen by flexible inspectors.

The legal philosopher Roscoe Pound thought that the over- and under-inclusiveness of rules called for a special attitude from the American judge. In Pound's view, the good judge "conceives of the legal rule as a general guide to the judge, leading him to the just result, but insists that within wide limits he should be free to deal with the individual case, so as to meet the demands of justice between the parties and accord with the general reason of the ordinary man."[13]

2. Rules can be outrun by changing circumstances. People who issue rules cannot know the full range of particular situations to which the rules will be applied, and in the new circumstances, the rules may be hopelessly anachronistic. Even well-designed rules in the 1970s may be utterly inadequate for the twenty-first century. Consider the regulation of banking and telecommunications. With the development of automated teller machines, prohibitions on "branch banking" make absolutely no sense; with the rise of cable television, a regulatory framework designed for three television networks is built on wildly false assumptions. For this reason it may be best to avoid rules altogether, or at least to create a few simple rules that allow room for private adaptation.

John Dewey thought the point counted against use of abstract rules and principles in law generally: "Failure to recognize that general legal rules and principles are working hypotheses, needing to be constantly tested by the way in which they work out in application to concrete situations, explains the otherwise paradoxical fact that the slogans of the liberalism of one period often become the bulworks of reaction in a subsequent era."[14]

3. *Abstraction and generality sometimes mask bias.* When people are differently situated, it may be unfair or otherwise wrong to treat them the same, that is, to apply the identical rule to them. Anatole France's remark on this count has become a platitude: the poor "have to labor in the face of the majestic neutrality of the law, which forbids the rich as well as the poor to sleep under bridges, to beg in the streets, and to steal bread."[15] The platitude brings out a common problem with apparently neutral rules. If everyone must use stairs, people in wheelchairs will face special disadvantages. If everyone must pay to enter museums, people without money will be unable to go to museums. If every employee must lack the capacity to become pregnant, most women will be frozen out of the workforce.

By ignoring individual circumstances, general rules can harm members of identifiable groups with distinctive characteristics, and in that sense reflect bias despite or even because of their generality. A familiar understanding of equality requires the similarly situated to be treated the same; a less familiar but also important understanding requires the differently situated to be treated differently, also in the interest of equality. The civil rights movement for handicapped people has this feature. So too with certain claims in the area of sex equality, where women seek treatment that fairly reflects sex differences, and that does not turn their differences into disadvantages. General rules might abridge equality to the extent that they do not allow people to speak of relevant differences.

4. *Rules drive discretion underground.* When rules produce inaccuracy in particular cases, people in a position of authority may simply ignore them. Discretion is exercised through a mild form of civil disobedience, which is hard to police or even to see. Thus in *Woodson v. North Carolina*,[16] discussed in Chapter 6, the Court invalidated the mandatory death penalty in part on the ground that the mandatory rule could not possibly be mandatory in practice. In fact juries would refuse to sentence people to death, but for reasons that would not be visible and accessible to the public.

"Jury nullification" of broad and rigid rules is a familiar and often celebrated phenomenon. Similarly, enforcement agencies can simply refuse to enforce statutes when they are too rulelike in nature. Prosecutors may fail to enforce laws that contain mandatory rules. This has happened in the United States, for example, with officials refusing to enforce the "three strikes, and you're out" policy threatening life imprisonment for people convicted of three felonies. Thus the American Clean Air Act's severe provisions for listed pollutants, operating in rulelike fashion, led the Environmental Protection Agency to stop listing pollutants at all. "[T]he act's absolute duties to respond to danger prompted officials not to recognize the dangers in the first place."[17] It is hard to police selective prosecution, and the resulting exercise of discretion may be far worse than what would be produced in a system of factors or standards.

5. *Rules allow evasion by wrongdoers.* Because rules have clear edges, they allow people to "evade" them, by engaging in conduct that is technically exempted and hence not covered by the rules themselves. But this evasive conduct can create the same or analogous harms as are prohibited by the rules. In the notorious area of tax law, clear rules can allow taxpayers to escape taxation by imaginatively designed tax-evasion schemes; a system of standards has advantages on this count. As Charles Black writes, "Some lawyers talk as though they thought maximum clarity always desirable even though they wouldn't have to probe very deeply to find that fraud, and fiduciary obligation, and undue influence, have been carefully isolated from exact definition, because such exact definition would simply point out safe ways of immunity, and, to the birds of prey, make the law 'their perch and not their terror.'"[18]

We have seen that rules are underinclusive as well as overinclusive if we refer to their background justifications. In this light things may be much better if the justifications (in the form of a standard) are enacted rather than the rule. A serious problem with rules is that if judges cannot proceed by analogy and extend the rule where the justification so suggests, people will be able to engage in harmful conduct because of a mere technicality. Sometimes judges have interpreted statutes beyond the instances that gave rise to them, and even beyond their literal language, in a process of analogical reasoning designed to overcome the problem of evasion.[19]

6. *Rules can be dehumanizing and procedurally unfair; sometimes it is necessary or appropriate to seek individualized tailoring.* A prominent conception of procedural justice—embodied in the due process clause—says that people should have a hearing in order to test whether a rule has been accurately applied. Thus, for example, the Supreme Court has held that

someone who is deprived of welfare benefits has a right to a hearing to contest the deprivation.[20] This understanding of due process fits well with a system of rules. The whole point of the hearing is to see whether the rule has been accurately applied. The hearing fortifies the rule.

But another conception of due process urges that people should be allowed not merely to test the application of law to fact, but also to urge that their case is different from those that have gone before, and that someone in a position of authority ought to pay heed to the particulars of their situation. On this view, people affected by the law should be permitted to participate in the formulation of the very principle to be applied to their case. This is an idea with strong democratic foundations, reflecting the democratic norms of participation and responsiveness. If people are to be permitted to participate in the creation of the legal provision to be applied to their case, rules cannot be set down in advance.

7. *Rules and rule-following have unfortunate psychological effects on public officials.* A long-standing function of equity is to make exceptions to rules that are senseless or too harsh in individual cases. Rules can eliminate the equitable spirit, making officials unwilling to exercise the discretion that they do or should have, and allowing them to be indifferent to or even to take pride in their refusal to counteract error or injustice. This consequence of rules is vividly explored in Robert Cover's work on judging in the era of slavery, when a spirit of ruleness stopped the judges from acting within their authority to work against some of the consequences of slavery.[21]

The harmful psychological effects of rules played a large role in Bentham's critique of rule-following: "Familiarized with the prospect of all those miseries which are attendant on poverty, disappointment, and disgrace, accustomed even to heap those miseries on the heads of those by whom he knows them to be unmerited, he eases himself by habit of the concern which the prospect of them would produce in an unexperienced mind." In this way the rule-bound judge resembles "a man whose trade is in blood," who "becomes insensible to the sufferings which accompany the stroke of death."[22] Hence Bentham favored an "anxious sensibility" incompatible with simple rule-following. Anyone who participates in a legal culture can see the lawyer's special pride in adhering to rules even though the result is absurdity or gross injustice. This pride should be viewed with a combination of respect and alarm.

8. *Good judging outstrips good rules.* These points can be summarized with the suggestion that in many cases, an ideal judge is alert to a range of particulars that cannot be fully captured in rules. In deciding who should have custody in a disputed case or whether a convicted criminal deserves a

long sentence or a short one, rules will be quite crude. Just as good friends, good writers, good tennis players, and good comedians do not entirely rely on a rulebook, so too a good judge is able to see what matters, and how to weigh what matters, in particular cases. To say this is not to say that what the judge "sees" is unguided by considerations at higher levels of abstraction. To know what counts, a judge has to work from an account of some kind. But ideal justice outstrips rules; it adapts the account to the particulars of the case.

Consider the suggestion that "it is just not possible to capture, in a set of explicit imperative sentences or rules, more than a small part of the practical wisdom possessed by a mature moral individual. . . . The sheer amount of information stored in a well-trained network the size of the human brain, and the massively distributed and exquisitely context-sensitive ways in which it is stored therein, preclude its complete expression in a handful of sentences, or even a large bookful. Statable rules are not the basis of one's moral character. They are merely its pale and partial reflection at the comparatively impotent level of language."[23] For a good judge, the same is true in law.

From all this, it cannot be said that rules are always inferior to case-by-case judgments; this would be an absurdly general claim. That very claim—a claimed rule—would be obtuse for the same reason that rules are obtuse. But rules often go wrong because they diverge from the arguments that justify them, producing outcomes that make no sense. When legal systems refuse to make rules, it is because people understand that any rules would misfire too frequently. The largest lesson is no less important for its roots in antiquity: If human frailties and institutional needs are put to one side, particularized judgments, based on the relevant features of the single case, represent the highest form of justice.

6

Without Reasons, Without Rules

We have seen serious problems with rule-bound judgments; it is time to turn to a different way of deciding cases. Problems with rules can push participants in law in the direction of standards, analogies, or some combination of the two. Such problems may even lead in the direction of entirely case-specific judgments, and it is here—with what we might call wholly untheorized outcomes—that I shall begin.

Full Particularity

Reason-giving is prized in law, as of course it should be. Without reasons, there is no assurance that decisions are not arbitrary or invidious, and people will be less able to plan their affairs.

In some areas of both life and law, however, institutions are permitted to operate with full particularity: People converge on the result, but they need offer no reasons for their decisions.[1] Each decision applies to the case at hand and to that case alone. People avoid grand theories, but they avoid low-level justifications too. In refusing to hear a case, for example, the Supreme Court is silent, and its refusal has no precedential force. In issuing verdicts, juries usually do not give reasons. College admissions offices produce results but rarely justifications. Many teachers do not offer reasons for grades, at least not in law school. Outcomes are not merely incompletely theorized; they are not theorized at all. They are based on a special form of casuistry—judgments unaccompanied by reasons uniting or distinguishing cases.

Full particularity has diverse sources. A judge may actually have reasons but fail to give them publicly; people may lack reasons in the sense that they know *what* they think should happen without knowing *why* it should happen; or people on a multimember institution may be unable to agree with one another about relevant reasons and hence leave an outcome officially unexplained. In any of these cases, this approach offers full particularity because by their very nature, reasons are more abstract than the outcomes they justify. Reasons may therefore apply to cases that the court, in justifying a particular decision, does not have before it.

In American law, perhaps the most famous (or infamous) illustration comes from Justice Potter Stewart: "I shall not today attempt further to define the kind of material I understand to be embraced within that shorthand definition [of hard-core pornography] and perhaps I could never succeed in intelligibly doing so. But I know it when I see it, and the motion picture involved in this case is not that."[2] Consider also John Dewey's rendition of "the old story of the layman who was appointed to a position in India where he would have to pass in his official capacity on various matters in controversies between natives. Upon consulting a legal friend, he was told to use his common-sense and announce his decisions firmly; in the majority of cases his natural decision as to what was fair and reasonable would suffice. But, his friend added: 'Never try to give reasons, for they will usually be wrong.'"[3]

We have seen that well-functioning legal systems prize the enterprise of reason-giving, and for good reasons. But there is a good reason to be wary of reason-giving; like rules, reasons may be both over- and underinclusive. Whenever you offer reasons for what you have done, there is a risk that you will regret it—because the reasons offered may turn out, on reflection, to collide with your considered judgment about how a later case should come out. A reason offered in case 1 may generate a bad outcome in case 2. In this way reasons have the disadvantages of rules. And if judges try to ensure that the original statement of reasons is right, they may have to decide all cases in the context of deciding one, and this would impose an intolerable burden. It can be much easier to decide on results than to offer reasons for results; consider college admissions, grading, the denial of certiorari, or a jury verdict.

As we have seen, the distinction between holding and dictum helps reduce this problem. To recapitulate: If we understand the holding to be the narrowest possible basis for the decision, a subsequent court is always in a good position to offer sufficiently narrow reasons for the outcome in case 1—that is, reasons that ensure that the outcome in case 1 does not produce a wrong result in a case that is genuinely different. In initially giving a reason, court 1 may be unaware of possible future cases that will draw that reason into doubt because of its imprecision and excessive generality. But court 2, able to offer some narrower and better-fitting explanation for the outcome, can eliminate the difficulty. It can label the excessive generality "dicta." The subsequent court's power to do this can also endanger the rule of law, since the decision in the earlier case may turn out to be much narrower than it appeared to be, indeed much narrower than the opinion originally suggested. But this disadvantage may be outweighed by the need for flexibility in new circumstances.

The process of recharacterizing holdings may seem mysterious, but it has many parallels in ordinary life. As any parent knows, children often make arguments based on precedents. When parents respond to those arguments, they treat the precedents as filled with dicta. A child says: "But you let me stay up late last night." Parents respond: "That was different because it wasn't a school night." Or: "That was a special occasion; it was your sister's birthday." In short, parents say: That was not what the precedent really stands for. They say that children should respect the holding, as now characterized, rather than the dicta. Parents have to be casuists. Of course discussions between friends and spouses have similar features.

Thus far I have emphasized that reasons offered in one case may turn out to be too crude, but there is another difficulty with reason-giving. It is possible to know something without entirely having, or being able to offer, an explanation for your knowledge. For example, you may know that this is Martin's face, and no other face, without knowing quite why you know that fact.[4] Or you might know that a certain act would be wrong, without knowing quite why it would be wrong. People often know something without being able to give an account of why it is true.

Is there an analogy in law? No simple answer would make sense. A special quality of most legal systems is a requirement of reasons for outcomes, and this requirement makes it hard to prize a capacity to know what the law is without knowing why it is as it is, or how a case should come out without knowing why it should come out that way. Conceivably, however, there is an aspect of socialization into law that enables people to see that case A is "like" case B, and not at all "like" case C, without necessarily having, or being able to offer, much of an account of why this is so.

It is possible that experienced judges, like experienced lawyers, develop a faculty best described as wisdom, perception, or judgment, one that allows them to reach decisions very well and very quickly. This is a faculty quite different from creativity, intelligence, or analytic capacity. It seems to be associated with the ready and sympathetic apprehension of a wide range of diverse particulars, with an appreciation of the appropriate weight to be given to each. Certainly we can imagine a class of people who have a wonderful capacity to tell whether one case is relevantly like another or to decide who should win cases, but who lack much of a capacity to explain what underlies their ultimate judgments or their convictions about relevant similarity and difference. They have a "good ear," unlike some others, who have a "tin ear" for law.

This is an important and familiar phenomenon in private life, public life, and law. We know that a certain friend is a good judge of character; that someone else knows what to do in hard situations; that someone else knows just what sorts of arguments will work in court. At the very least, we can say that some people have a capacity for judgment that outruns their explanatory powers. Compare this striking description of President Franklin Delano Roosevelt:

> Frances Perkins later described the President's idea . . . as a "flash of almost clairvoyant knowledge and understanding." He would have one of these flashes every now and then, she observed, much like those that musicians get when "they see or hear the structure of an entire symphony or opera." He couldn't always hold on to it or verbalize it, but when it came, he suddenly understood how all kinds of disparate things fit together. . . . Roosevelt made up for the defects of an undisciplined mind with a profound ability to integrate a vast multitude of details into a larger pattern that gave shape and direction to the stream of events.[5]

Perhaps it would ultimately be possible for such people (or at least outside observers) to explain what underlies these good apprehensions, but this may not be so. Of course it is important not to mystify these issues. Probably the faculty of wisdom, perception, or judgment amounts to a capacity to think very quickly of a resolution that takes account of everything that matters, including a wide array of competing considerations, and that coheres well with the rest of our particular and general judgments. When someone is thought to be wise about particulars in law, it is because he is able to see how to resolve a case without doing violence to our other judgments at the horizontal and vertical levels. He is thus able to decide cases and to decide who wins and who loses, while minimally endangering other valued goods and goals. A person who has this capacity is a good judge, in the sense that he knows how to resolve legal disputes. But he would be a better judge if he were also able to offer some sort of explanation for his choice.

Factors

Often judges and others who reject rules do offer reasons, but they rely on a set of factors. We can use judgments based on factors as a good way to approach and evaluate rule-free decisions. Like analogies and standards, factors reveal some of the vices and virtues of rulelessness; in their opposition to rules, they much overlap with judgments based on standards or analogies. But judgments based on factors have some distinctive features as well, and these are of considerable independent interest.

Judgments based on factors are not a matter of untrammeled discretion, and legal systems rarely fail to constrain discretion even when the category of relevant factors is wide. Almost every legal system imposes some limits on what may be counted, even if the constraints are only tacit. And in the real world of law, the line between rules and factors is one of degree rather than of kind. We can be clearer about decision by factors after exploring a few examples and also after seeing why a system of factors is often thought to be a good method of decision—required, sometimes, by the Constitution itself. The law governing the death penalty is the best place to start.

Examples

In *Furman v. Georgia*,[6] the Supreme Court, following *Papachristou*, held that a rule-free death penalty violated the due process clause—not because it was excessively barbaric for the state to take life, but because the states allowed too much discretion in the infliction of the penalty of death. The problem with the pre-1970 death penalty was therefore procedural. States did not limit the discretion of juries deciding who deserved to die. Thus Justice Stewart wrote,

> These death sentences are cruel and unusual in the same way that being struck by lightning is cruel and unusual. For, of all the people convicted of rapes and murders in 1967 and 1968, many just as reprehensible as these, the petitioners are among a capriciously selected random handful upon whom the sentence of death has in fact been imposed. . . . [T]he [Constitution] cannot tolerate the infliction of a sentence of death under legal systems that permit this unique penalty to be so wantonly and so freakishly imposed.

North Carolina responded to *Furman* by enacting a "mandatory" death penalty, eliminating judge and jury discretion. Under North Carolina law, a mandatory death penalty was to be imposed for a specified category of homicide offenses. No judge and no jury would have discretion to substitute life imprisonment in cases falling within that category. No judge and no jury would have discretion to decide who would live and who would die. In this way, North Carolina attempted to apply sharp rule of law constraints to the area of death sentencing.

In *Woodson v. North Carolina*,[7] the Supreme Court held, strikingly, that a mandatory death sentence was unconstitutional *because it was a rule*. Invoking the need for individualized consideration, the Court said that "the belief no longer prevails that every offense in a like legal category calls for an identical punishment without regard to the past life and habits of a particular offender." According to the Supreme Court, a serious constitutional shortcoming of the mandatory death sentence

> is its failure to allow the **particularized consideration of relevant aspects of the character and record of each convicted defendant** before the imposition upon him of a sentence of death. . . . A process that accords no significance to relevant facets of the character and record of the individual offender or the circumstances of the particular offense excludes from consideration in fixing the ultimate punishment of death the possibility of compassionate or mitigating factors stemming from the diverse frailties of humankind. **It treats all persons convicted of a designated offense not as uniquely individual human beings, but as members of a faceless, undifferentiated mass to be subjected to the blind infliction of the penalty of death**.

On this view, justice is emphatically not blindfolded. It is attuned to the fact that human beings are "uniquely individual." It sees "diverse frailties" and makes them relevant. It ensures "particularized consideration."

What ultimately emerged from *Woodson* is a system in which the death penalty is generally decided through considering a set of specified factors, in the form of aggravating and mitigating circumstances. It is this system of capital sentencing that, in the current Court's view, walks the constitutionally tolerable line between unacceptably mandatory rules and unacceptably broad discretion. Of course some justices, most recently Justice Blackmun, have contended that the line is too thin—that there is no possible system of capital sentencing that adequately combines the virtues of individualized consideration, required by *Woodson*, with the virtues of nonarbitrary decision, required by *Furman*.

Woodson arose in an especially dramatic setting, but the Court's preferred method—factors rather than rules—can be found in many areas of both life and law. For example, the Court offers no rules for deciding how much in the way of procedure is required before the state may take liberty or property.[8] Any "rules," the Court suggests, would be too inaccurate and too insensitive to individual circumstance. Instead the Court requires an assessment of three factors: the nature and weight of the individual interest at stake; the likelihood of an erroneous determination and the probable value of additional safeguards; and the nature and strength of the government's interest. This somewhat open-ended multifactor test is quite different from what is anticipated in *Papachristou*. It sacrifices predictability for the sake of accuracy in individual cases. Rule of law values might seem to be jeopardized by such a test, but those values have been promoted by analogical reasoning, which has built up, over time, a relatively predictable set of principles.

Or consider the Second Restatement of the Conflict of Laws, which says that in cases having multistate features, the applicable law will be chosen after an assessment of a complex set of factors: "the needs of the interstate and international systems; the relevant policies of the forum; the relevant policies of other interested states and the relative interests of those states in the determination of the particular issue; the protection of justified expectations; the basic policies underlying the particular field of law; certainty, predictability and uniformity of result, and ease in the determination and application of the law to be applied." Similarly, the practice of many college, graduate school, law school, and medical school admissions committees is to rely on a set of factors not reduced to a rule or even a formula. We might refer as well to the practice of criminal sentencing, which sometimes depends on factors rather than rules, even as it is disciplined by the recent sentencing guidelines.

It is useful to compare the short-lived "irrebuttable presumption" doctrine, founded on similar ideas. The key case was brought by Jo Carol Lafleur, a junior high school teacher in Cleveland.[9] The school board required every pregnant schoolteacher to take maternity leave without pay, starting five months before the birth of the child. Lafleur argued that her pregnancy did not adversely affect her ability to teach. The Supreme Court held that the Cleveland rule violated the due process clause simply because it was a rule. "There is no individualized determination by the teacher's doctor—or the school board's—as to any particular teacher's ability to continue at her job. The rules contain an irrebuttable presumption of physical incompetency, and that presumption applies even when the medical evidence as to an individual woman's physical status might be wholly to the contrary." The Court said that the due process clause disfavors "permanent irrebuttable presumptions."

Justice Rehnquist, writing in dissent, was quite mystified by this idea.

> Hundreds of years ago in England, before Parliament came to be thought of as a body having general lawmaking power, controversies were determined on an individualized basis without benefit of any general law. Most students of government consider the shift from this sort of determination, made on an ad hoc basis by the King's representative, to a relatively uniform body of rules enacted by a body exercising legislative authority, to have been a significant step forward in the achievement of a civilized political society.

For Justice Rehnquist, every law is an irrebuttable presumption. In the end the Court's approach is "nothing less than an attack upon the very notion of lawmaking itself." Justice Rehnquist's argument has prevailed in the sense that the Court no longer invokes the irrebuttable presumption doctrine. But the *Lafleur* case reflects a pervasive conception of procedural fairness—one that calls for individualized consideration, based on factors, in lieu of rules.

Factors Without Rules

What are the features of a system based on factors?

1. *Multiple and diverse relevant criteria.* It is obvious that in a system of factors, decisions emerge from multiple and diverse criteria. No simple rule or principle can be applied to the case.

2. *Difficulty of describing relevant factors exhaustively in advance.* In a system of factors, it is often impossible to describe exactly what is relevant in advance. People know too little to say. The relevant terms may be too general and abstract to contain sharp limits on what can be considered. The legal terms are incompletely specified—*exhaustive but vague*. It is in the specification that a more complete account of the factors will be provided. Or the relevant factors may be specified, but there will be some proviso at the end, allowing, for example, consideration of "such other factors as are deemed relevant"—to show that new factors may come up. The legal terms are *specific but nonexhaustive*. Both of these strategies are pervasive.

3. *Absence of a clear, a priori sense of the weight of the criteria.* It is typical of this procedure that the relevant criteria cannot be assigned weights in advance. In deciding how much of a hearing is required before someone may be deprived of something, for example, we do not know how much

weight to give to the government interest in efficiency, or how much weight to assign to the individual interest in ensuring against mistaken deprivations. Answers are offered in the context of concrete controversies.

4. *Attentiveness to (much of) the whole situation.* Rule-governed justice is abstract in the sense that it attends to only a small part of a complex situation. A system of factors looks at a range of particulars. In the college admission setting, for example, officers might examine not just test scores, but also grades, extracurricular activities, family background, geography, race, gender, and much more. In the area of capital sentencing, juries and judges look to a wide range of variables relating to the offender and the offense. In voting rights cases, courts sometimes explore many aspects of the context in order to test for discrimination. Judges frequently say that they are looking to "the totality of the circumstances"; tests of this sort imply a wide and close look at individual circumstances.

On this view, justice is far from blind. It tries to see a great deal. On the other hand, it would be a mistake to say that a system of factors is attentive to all aspects of the situation. There is no such thing as attention to "all" particulars. Human and legal perception are inevitably selective. Every legal system based on factors excludes a wide range of variables, treating them as irrelevant or illegitimate. Even in a discretionary admissions program, for example, the authority is not expected to care about an applicant's initials or foot size.

These points suggest that a system based on factors attends to much of the whole situation but certainly not to all of it. And because decision by factors entails attention to much of the whole situation, and thus to a range of particulars, it is familiar to see people arguing that their case is relevantly different from those that have come before. A litigant in case A can always say that in some particular way, his case is relevantly different from case B. And in the subsequent cases, litigants who invoke relevant particulars can show that the "real" argument on behalf of case A is much narrower than had been thought.

5. *Attentiveness to particulars; avoidance of abstractions.* In decisions by reference to factors, decisions do not necessarily govern other situations; they are often said to be "fact-bound." A special fear is that abstractions will be not only too contentious and sectarian, but also both overinclusive and underinclusive. Suppose, for example, that it is urged that the law of state x applies whenever the dispute arises between two residents of that state. We can readily imagine cases in which this outcome may be wrong because, for example, all the relevant evidence and witnesses are in state y. A prime goal of decision by reference to factors is the avoidance of error through insufficiently considered rules or principles—insufficiently con-

sidered in the sense of insufficiently attuned to the full range of particular cases.

6. *Attention to precedent; analogical reasoning.* Rules provide consistency; a system based on factors aspires to do the same. Such a system aspires to ensure that all similarly situated people are treated similarly. A must be treated the same as B, unless there is a principled reason to treat them differently.

In a system of factors, the relevant consistency is sought through comparison with previous cases. Suppose, for example, that a full trial-type hearing has been required before someone may be deprived of welfare benefits. The question then arises whether a similiar hearing is required before someone may be deprived of Social Security disability benefits. Perhaps this case is different because many Social Security recipients are not poor or because disability determinations do not turn heavily on issues of credibility. Hence a full trial-type hearing may not be required, but the Social Security recipient is entitled at least to some opportunity to counter the government's claims in writing. Then the question arises about what kind of hearing is required before a grade-school student may be suspended from school for misconduct. Here the individual interest seems weaker still, and here the government can invoke the distinctive interest in avoiding excessive formality in student–teacher relations. Through routes of this sort, a system based on factors can generate a complex set of outcomes, all rationalized with each other.

7. *Diversely valued goods and problems of commensurability.* Usually the factors at work are valued in qualitatively different ways. Moreover, those factors cannot be placed on a single metric; they are not commensurable. To understand these claims, something must be said about diverse kinds of valuation and about the difficult problem of incommensurability.

The factors involved in legal decisions are often qualitatively different from one another. Human beings value goods, things, relationships, and states of affairs in diverse ways; all goodness is goodness-of-a-kind.[10] There is of course a distinction between instrumental and intrinsic goods. We value some things, like money, purely or principally for use. Other things, like knowledge or friendship, have intrinsic value. But the distinction between intrinsic and instrumental goods captures only a part of the picture. Intrinsically valued things produce a range of diverse responses. Some bring about wonder and awe; consider a mountain or certain artistic works. Toward some people, we feel respect; toward others, affection; toward others, love. People worship their deity. Negative valuations are similarly diverse. To lose money is to lose an instrumental good (though one that might be used for intrinsic goods, like the preservation of human life). To lose a friend is a qualitatively different matter. So too our responses to intrinsic bads are diverse. Many of these distinctions play a role in law, as when beaches must be compared with dollars, protection of racial equality measured against associational freedom, or when law has to decide whether to subject certain items—body parts, the right to vote, sexual or reproductive capacities—to the market.

Human goods cannot without significant loss be reduced to a single "superconcept," such as happiness, utility, or pleasure.[11] Any such reduction produces significant loss because it yields an inadequate description of our actual valuations when things are going well.

The relevant factors to be assessed by the legal system may not be commensurable. Return, for example, to the idea that the Constitution requires courts to decide on the extent of procedural protection by assessing three factors: the individual interest at stake; the likelihood of error and the probable value of additional safeguards; and the government's interest in avoiding complex procedures. It would be odd to say that this assessment can be made through lining up the relevant variables along any single metric. There is no scale by which it makes sense to weigh these matters. If we devise a scale, we will have to recharacterize the relevant goods in a way that changes their character and effaces qualitative differences.

As I understand the notion here, incommensurability exists when the relevant goods cannot be aligned along a single metric without doing violence to our considered judgments about how these goods are best characterized. By our considered judgments, I mean our reflective assessments of how certain relationships and events should be understood, evaluated, and experienced. The notion of a single metric should be understood quite literally. By this I mean a standard of valuation that (1) operates at a workable level of specificity, (2) fails to make qualitative distinctions, and (3) allows comparison along the same dimension. When courts decide cases according to factors, they lack any unitary metric. Decisions nonetheless are made, and they can be justified or criticized on the basis of reasons. But those reasons do not amount to a single scale of value. Rules too are often developed after an assessment of incommensurable goods.

These are brisk remarks about a complex subject.[12] For the moment my claim is simple: The factors that are typically at stake in law are valued in different ways, and these factors are not commensurable along any scale. Trade-offs and choices are necessary, but not through ranking along a scale.

8. *Absence of a full theory to account for foundations of decision.* When

participants in a legal system are deciding on the basis of factors, they usually do not have a deep theory to account for their convictions. They refer to ideas that operate at a low or intermediate level of generality. Judges may know that an AFDC recipient is entitled to a hearing before being deprived of benefits, and that a social security recipient is not, without having developed a large-scale theory to explain their judgments.

To return to our familiar theme: It is this feature of the procedure that permits the emergence of agreement on particular outcomes. People may agree that a defendant x does or does not deserve the death penalty without agreeing on anything like a theory about the appropriate aims of punishment. People may agree that a full hearing is not required before a student is suspended from elementary school without having reached agreement about the basic purposes of hearings. People may believe that when a contract is made and performed in New York, New York's law applies, even if they do not have anything like a theory of sovereignty.

These, then, are the features of judgments based on factors. Certainly such judgments are casuistical, even if they offer far more guidance than full particularity. We have seen that case-by-case judgments, based on factors, have many virtues. But it would be wrong to deny that some settings call for more ruleness than factors are likely to provide. It is now time to see how a legal system might choose between rules and ruleless-ness and try to overcome the problems associated with each.

7

Adapting Rules, Privately and Publicly

How can a legal system minimize the risks of unreasonable generality on the one hand and potentially abusive rulelessness on the other? There are three good answers.

The first answer calls for a species of casuistry. In deciding between rules and rulelessness, officials should examine the context and inquire into the likelihood of error and abuse with either rules or rulelessness—and hence make an "on balance" judgment about risk. A good deal of progress can be made through this route. We can see, for example, that clear rules are generally required for the criminal law, and that for college admissions, casuistical judgments may well be best. We can allow casuistry in contexts in which casuistry makes sense and move in the direction of rules when the context suggests that rules are better.

The second answer involves a presumption in favor of a particular kind of rule, that is, the *privately adaptable rule* that allocates initial entitlements and does not specify outcomes. Many of the pathologies of modern law, and especially modern regulation, stem from the fact that rules are too rigid and do not allow ordinary people to adapt them to suit individual situations and ends. Reforms could produce privately adaptable rules that overcome the senselessly mechanical quality of much of what modern government does.

The third answer involves a recognition that both citizens and officials can make *legitimate departures from rules*. Juries are allowed to say that in some cases, the rules should not be applied because they make no sense. Police and prosecutors have similar authority. Ordinary citizens can be permitted to deviate from rules when compliance would produce more harm than good. Citizens may also be permitted to deviate from the rules when the particular application has no support in public convictions. When a legal system recognizes—even if quietly—a power to deviate from rules, it chooses between rules and rulelessness through a complex strategy, one that insists on rules, but that makes space for exceptions. As we will see, this strategy has powerful democratic foundations.

In General

Under what circumstances is it appropriate to rely on something other than rules? And under what circumstances might a legal system be expected to choose rules or rulelessness?

It is unlikely that we will be able to generate a reliable and general predictive theory on this topic, at least in thinking about what lawmakers do. Legislation is a complex product of the legislators' self-interest, private influence, and public-spirited motivations on the part of both legislators and those who influence them. Judicial choices between rules and factors are even more difficult to attribute to a single behavioral influence or a set of behavioral influences. It is hard to imagine a simple testable hypothesis that would not be falsified by many results in the world.

We are likely to do far better by identifying mechanisms through which certain choices might be made, rather than lawlike generalizations by which choices are usually made.[1] Moreover, the occasional role of public spirit in legislative deliberations—from legislators themselves or from people who influence them—means that theories of what ought to be done cannot be separated so sharply from theories of what will be done. People's views about what makes best sense will undoubtedly affect outcomes; certainly this is true of those faced with the choice between rules and rulelessness, including judges and bureaucrats.

It is nonetheless possible to offer some rough-and-ready generalizations. Most broadly, rules will be avoided (1) when the lawmaker lacks information and expertise, so that the information costs are too high to produce reliable rules; (2) when it is difficult to choose rules because of political disagreement within the relevant institution, so that the political costs of rules are too high to justify them; (3) when people in a position to decide whether to have rules do not fear the bias, interest, or corruption of those who decide particular cases; (4) when those who make the law do not disagree much with those who will interpret the law, and hence when the lawmakers do not need rules to discipline administrators, judges, or others; and (5) when the applications of the legal provision are few in number or relevantly different from one another. Most simply, rules might thus be chosen when the error rate with the particular rules is relatively low, when the error rate for rulelessness is high, and when the number of cases is large.

Of course it can be costly to make rules, at least if we seek rules that have some degree of accuracy. Any legislature faces a serious problem if it tries to design rules: It may lack information to make rules that are good, and political disagreement may mean that a lot of time and effort is necessary to come up with satisfactory rules. Often this problem leads legislatures to avoid rules in favor of standards, factors, or guidelines. Consider the fact that constitutional provisions and international agreements often take the form of incompletely specified standards rather than rules.

On the other hand, the absence of rules may impose significant costs at the stage when particular decisions have to made. People deciding on the particular applications must find not only the facts but also the law. Consider, for example, the problem of deciding whether airline pilots over the age of sixty are still able to do their jobs competently. Such decisions will be time-consuming, may produce unequal treatment, and may create a lot of error under the pressure of the moment (errors founded in mistaken stereotypes about people over sixty, or perhaps in misplaced sympathy for discharged employees). Rule-free decisions may also impair predictability and thus create high costs for people trying to order their affairs under law. An important question is who bears these costs, and how much power they have to minimize them, by asking the legislature for rules instead.

If the people who make the law are not the same as those who interpret and enforce it, there will be complex pressures. On the one hand, the lawmakers may distrust the interpreters and enforcers and may therefore seek to impose rules. On the other hand, the split between lawmaking and law-interpretation/enforcement means that many of the costs of producing clarity before the fact will be faced by lawmakers themselves, whereas many of the costs of producing clarity after the fact will be faced by others. A lawmaking body that does not enforce law can thus "export" the costs of rulelessness to those who must enforce whatever provisions have been enacted. There may be political and other advantages in doing this.

In this way a system of separated powers imposes pressure toward avoiding rules. A system of unified powers does not impose similar pressure, since in such a system people who refuse to make rules before the fact will face the costs of rulelessness after the fact. Of course the benefits for lawmakers of refusing to make rules may be countered by other factors. The failure to make rules may be punished by the interests that fear bad outcomes within another branch of government, or it may fit poorly with the representatives' own political commitments or electoral self-interest. Perhaps voters will refuse to reelect legislators who refuse to make rules.

A decentralized, hierarchical judiciary can be analyzed similarly. In such a system, there will be some incentive for the Supreme Court to avoid making rules and to export the costs of rulelessness to others. The Court may call for standards or factors because it does not itself face the costs of making decisions under those tests. But this incentive can be overcome by other considerations. As we will soon see, some of these speculations are borne out by comparing the legal system in England with that in the United States.

Bentham and Acoustic Separation

Jeremy Bentham favored clear rules, laid down in advance and broadly communicated. In at least some of his writings, he also favored adjudicative flexibility, allowing judges to adapt the rules to the complexities of individual cases. Bentham was well aware that rules could badly misfire as they encountered particular controversies. In courts of law, he concluded, rules would not be fully binding, and judges could decide cases on their merits, free from the constraints of law laid down in advance.

This prescription suggests a paradox: How could someone advocate clear rules without asking judges to follow them? Bentham's ingenious answer involved *different audiences for law*. The public would "hear" general rules; the judges would hear individual cases.[2] This is the important idea of an "acoustic separation" for legal terms, a separation justified on utilitarian grounds. Rules governing *conduct* would be broadcast to the public; rules governing *decision* would be communicated to judges. The public would not be informed of the decision rules. As odd as it may seem, there is a separation of this very sort in many areas of law, including the law relating to excuses for criminality. Ordinary people think that ignorance of the law is no excuse, but in the courtroom things are far more complex, for ignorance of the law may well be an excuse.

Following Bentham's idea, we might suggest that legislatures should lay down rules, but that interpreters should feel free to ignore them where they produce mistakes. Of course it is important to develop principles to discipline the idea of "mistakes" and to give it concrete meaning. Modern administrative agencies, more than courts, might be entrusted with the job of adapting general rules to particular circumstances.

There are, however, two difficulties with the Benthamite strategy. The first involves the right to democratic publicity—more particularly, the people's right to know what the law is. The Benthamite strategy severely compromises that right. The rule of law and democratic values are jeopardized if the law is not what the statute books say that it is. Benthamite approaches seem unacceptable to the extent that utilitarian judgments about acoustic separation run into liberal principles of publicity. A gap between rules of conduct and rules of decision is also damaging to democratic deliberation. If citizens do not know what the law is, they are in a terrible position to evaluate the law and to say whether and how it should be changed. It is also an insult to the individual autonomy of the citizen not to inform him of the actual content of the law.

The second problem is that the Benthamite strategy fails to take account of the fact that general rules can be unacceptable precisely because general rules can create *bad private incentives* as compared with more fine-grained approaches. The secrecy of the Benthamite approach—the distinction between the law as it is known and the law as it operates in courts of law—will do nothing at all about the problem of poor incentives produced by crude rules. Indeed, publicizing the exceptions, and telling everyone about the possibility of close judicial attention to the particulars of your case, may well be a good idea if we seek optimal incentives. At least this is so if people would not react to the presence of exceptions by believing that they can do whatever they want and that the rule does not exist at all.

The Benthamite strategy is neither democratic nor efficient. But there is still a place for a version of it. A legal system might provide that in exceptional cases, interpreters can soften rules, by exploring whether they create absurdity or injustice in the particular case. We might even see a judicial (or administrative) power of this kind as part of the legitimate authority to interpret rules, not as an authority to change rules. This power should be publicly known—a fully disclosed aspect of administration and interpretation. In some contexts, of course, the possibility of changing rules, or of interpreting them with close reference to whether they make sense in particular circumstances, might be too damaging to the project of having rules. But this contextual judgment cannot be made in the abstract. Let us now elaborate on this idea.

Legitimate Rule Revision

Many legal systems allow people to deviate from rules. Indeed, many public officials have at least a tacit power to revise the rules when rule-following would be senseless. Citizens as a whole are often given the same power.[3] Legitimate rule revisions make rules "on the books" something other than what they appear to be. And legitimate rule revisions can help promote the democratic character of the law, by allowing exceptions to rules where they no longer fit with reflective public convictions.

Officials

The class of legitimate official revisions is exceptionally large; it helps supplement the process of legislation with a set of postenactment, or extraenactment, constraints on what government may do through law. Juries sometimes "nullify" outcomes that the law, interpreted in a rule-bound way, appears to mandate. The practice of jury nullification is widely understood as legitimate, so long as it does not occur very often. There is even a democratic justification for the practice. It allows a salutary public check on rules, or applications of rules, that produce unjust or irrational outcomes.

So too police have a widely acknowledged authority to revise rules, by deciding which crimes really warrant arrest, and criminal prosecutors have a widely acknowledged authority to revise rules, by refusing to initiate proceedings against certain rule violations. Thus officials might refuse to punish conduct that, while technically violative of rules on the book, is not widely perceived as deserving criminal punishment. Prosecutions are almost never brought for sodomy or adultery, in part because such behavior, even if condemned, is no longer condemned in such a way as to call for jail sentences or criminal fines. We might also understand judicial "softening" or "moderation" of rules—sometimes under the guise of interpretation (discussed in Chapters 6 and 8)—as an exercise of a tacitly legitimated authority to reject rules when they make no sense.

Administrative agencies exercise this power too. In fact they do so nearly every day. In some cases, for example, enforcement of statutes protecting the environment would cost a lot of money and do the environment little good; in such cases administrators refuse to enforce them. In deciding when to enforce rules, administrators can use their discretion and common sense to take the harsh edges off the rules. In many contexts, life in the modern regulatory state is possible only because it is well understood that administrators will engage in what is, by common understanding, legitimate rule revision.

Of course many people question these various exercises of discretion to depart from rules. Some rule revisions might be unjust and hence illegitimate. Suppose, for example, that police officers refuse to stop domestic violence because they think that spousal abuse is not so bad or because many people think that government should not "intervene in the family." We might conclude that the refusal to enforce the law is nonetheless unacceptable because it produces injustice and indeed contributes to inequality on the basis of sex. Or suppose that administrators of a statute protecting endangered species take little or no enforcement action, perhaps because public opinion is, at the relevant time, indifferent to the protection of endangered species. This may be nothing to celebrate. The judgments that underlie rule revisions might be unjust or otherwise wrong. I am suggesting only that rule revisions, if democratically grounded and not otherwise objectionable, can be a good response to the problems posed by rule-bounded law.

The existence of enforcement discretion raises some doubts about certain understandings of the rule of law. If what I am saying is right, there will often be a gap between law on the books and law in the world, and for good democratic reasons. We might conclude that officials in certain social roles—jurors, prosecutors, police—should believe that rules are generally binding, but that they have authority to depart from the rules in compelling circumstances. I have said that this authority has democratic foundations; it might promote liberty as well.

Citizens

Now let us turn to the situation of the citizen. Ordinarily we think that people must obey the law or face the consequences of violating it. If you are a conscientious objector—consider Martin Luther King, Jr., or abortion protestors—your violation of the law may be a product of deeply felt moral judgments and your acts may be heroic. But you must face the consequences. This picture has much truth in it, but it is too simple. Often citizens, like officials, are allowed to depart from the rules.

Citizens who object to the constitutionality of rules might violate the rules and seek a judicial judgment on the constitutional issue. That judgment may relieve them of the duty to comply with rules. Since there is an overlap between moral argument and constitutional argument, the power to test rules against constitutional standards might well be seen as a power to ask rules to be revised when they are especially bad.

Perhaps this power should not be treated as a genuine power to revise rules, since the Constitution provides rules too. In fact it provides the fundamental rules of the American legal system. But citizens have other powers as well, and these powers amount to an authority to change or to soften rules. People are allowed to depart from the rules in cases of "necessity," and they are also permitted to depart from the rules in a more controversial category of cases, in which the rules are anachronistic and no longer can claim public support.

We should start with the necessity defense. We have seen that if someone violates a speed limit law in order to escape from a terrorist, a criminal conviction is highly unlikely. In all probability, the driver will be held to have acted out of necessity or to have created a "lesser evil." The same result will be reached if Jones trespasses on property in order to prevent someone's death or if Smith steals a weapon from a third-party in order to prevent bodily harm to Young. Of course citizens are not permitted to decide freely and for themselves whether compliance with the rule is justified in the particular case. But in many legal systems, a citizen will have a legally sufficient excuse for violating the rule if the violation was necessary to avert a greater harm, and the excuse will exist whether or not any statute or any past legal decision has previously recognized it as such.

There is a more controversial category of legally permissible law violations by citizens. It involves the old notion (recognized in England though not always in the United States) of *desuetude*, which forbids the invocation of old, unenforced rules to ban conduct in cases in which people have come to rely on governmental nonenforcement.[4] If a rule lies dormant on the books, citizens are permitted to violate it. The idea has a powerful democratic dimension. Why and when might a law not be enforced? In a democratic society, the answer has to do with political checks on enforcement practices. If a rule, or a particular application of a rule, is founded on a social judgment that no longer has support, we might expect it to be enforced not at all, or only on rare occasions. It is therefore a nullity, or perhaps a tool for harassment, and not an ordinary law at all. The rare occasions of enforcement might well involve arbitrary or discriminatory factors. They might result from a police officer's mood, personal animus, or bias of some kind. A criminal prosecution for fornication or adultery, brought in 1997, might well have such features. In the United States, hundreds of laws are obsolete and understood as such. As a general rule, efforts to enforce them should be viewed as unacceptable.

Consider in this regard the controversial case of *Griswold v. Connecticut*,[5] involving Connecticut's ban on the use of contraceptives by a married couple. The ban was not directly enforced by prosecutors. No such prosecution could receive public support; it would have been an outrage. The real function of the ban was principally to deter clinics from dispensing contraceptives to poor people. The problem with the ban was not that it was unsupported by old traditions, but that it had no basis in modern convictions. Few people—certainly much fewer than a majority—believed that sex within marriage was acceptable only if engaged in for purposes of procreation, and those people could not possibly have commanded a legislative majority, or even made it possible to bring actual prosecutions against married couples.

In *Griswold*, the Supreme Court invalidated the Connecticut law on the ground that it invaded the abstract "right of privacy." But instead of speaking of a broad right of "privacy," the Supreme Court should have struck down the law on the narrower ground that citizens need not comply with laws, or applications of laws, that lack real enforcement and that find no support in anything like common democratic conviction. A judgment of this kind would have had the large advantage of producing a narrow and incompletely theorized outcome. It might have obtained a range of agreement from people who reject any "right of privacy" or are uncertain about its foundations and limits.

Turn now to another controversial case, *Bowers v. Hardwick*,[6] where the Supreme Court upheld Georgia's ban on homosexual sodomy against constitutional attack. *Hardwick* was a repeat of *Griswold*. The ban on homosexual sodomy is almost never enforced against consenting adults. Prosecutors simply do not initiate proceedings, since prevailing social convictions would not permit prosecutions of this kind. Realistically speaking, the ban on consensual homosexual sodomy is a weapon by which police officers and others harass people on invidious grounds. The existence of unenforced and unenforceable sodomy laws, used for purposes of harassment, is objectionable under the due process clause for that reason. Citizens legitimately revise rules, or applications of rules, that lack support in popular convictions—unless those convictions are themselves unjust or otherwise unacceptable.

Griswold and *Bowers* involved rules that citizens legitimately disregard. When citizens disregard rules that are not and could not be enforced, they behave properly. They participate, as citizens, in a healthy and continuous process of democratic deliberation.

It is not clear whether American law fully recognizes the citizen's right to revise rules in this way. But the dilemmas posed by rules and ruleless-ness would be less difficult if citizens, like officials, are permitted to depart from rules in the sorts of cases just described. Through this route we might well respond to Bentham's problem in a way that avoids the dangers of Bentham's solution.

Privately Adaptable Rules

An ambitious strategy for overcoming the problems with rules —and a key to a well-functioning legal system—emerges from distinguishing between two sorts of rules.[7] Some rules allocate initial rights and entitlements—they unquestionably count as rules—but at the same time they maximize flexibility and minimize the informational burden on government, by allowing private adaptation. They allow private adaptation because they permit ordinary people, rather than rulemakers, to determine ultimate outcomes. Rules of this kind help overcome many of the problems of rules and rulelessness. Consider, for example, "default rules" in the law of contract. Default rules provide standard terms to solve problems that the parties have not addressed; if the parties have said nothing, the default rules apply. But default rules can be changed by the parties as they choose. A great virtue of the default rule is that it can be tailored by the parties or replaced altogether.

Consider, as broadly analogous, the rules of the road; taxes imposed on dangerous workplaces; rules creating private property and allocating property rights; or rules governing entry into contractual agreements. All these might be described as *privately adaptable rules*. They are privately adaptable because they allow people a great deal of room to maneuver. Once property rights are in place, people can trade (mostly) as they wish. The rules of the road help people to do what they want, which is to drive their cars without risking their lives. If you are faced with a tax when your workplace is dangerous, you can reduce the tax by reducing the danger as you think best.

By contrast, some laws do not merely allocate entitlements, but also minimize private flexibility, by mandating particular end-states or outcomes. Consider price controls, or specified technology for new cars, or flat bans on the presence of carcinogens in the workplace. Rules that specify end-states are common in modern law, in the form of "command and control" regulation that says exactly what people must do and how they must do it. Much debate over the status of law in modern democracies involves complaints about command and control regulation. Many people think, with good reason, that such regulation is unduly rigid and unduly associated with the pathologies of rules, and for that reason too costly and invasive of liberty.

Thus far I have written as if there are two kinds of rules, but the line between the two is really one of degree rather than one of kind. Every law allows some room for private adaptation; you can always go to jail or try to leave the country. Even the most privately adaptable rules impose constraints on end-states. All rules are coercive, including rules creating property rights and rules of the road. What I am describing is a characteristic shared more by some rules than by others, rather than a crisp category of rules. Notably, all rules allocate entitlements, and the allocation may well have an effect on people's preferences and on distributions of wealth, and hence on end-states as well.[8] Government cannot avoid the task of allocating entitlements and of doing so through rules. The idea of "laissez-faire" is a myth, a fraud, a chimera. What is familiarly described as laissez-faire is actually a particular set of legal rules. Our rights, as we live them, do not come from nature. They depend on law.[9]

We own property only because the legal system has allocated property rights to us. Property rights are anything but natural. Freedom of contract is not part of nature. It is a function of legal rules creating and constituting that form of freedom.[10] The rules of private property and freedom of contract are rules, and they are legal in character. Freedom to act is itself in important part a product of the legal system, which says, often, that people can do as they wish without public or private interference and with public or private protection. Legal rules are in this sense pervasive and inevitable, indeed coercive in their own way, even in the most market-oriented of free market systems.[11] (People in Eastern Europe, now undertaking the difficult task of creating markets, have seen this all too well.)

The claim on behalf of privately adaptable rules is not that laissez-faire is a possibility for law. It is instead that law can choose rules with certain characteristics—rules that will reduce the risks of rules, by allowing private adaptation and by harnessing market and private forces in such a way as to minimize the informational and political burden imposed on government. Hence the rules that constitute markets are entirely acceptable insofar as their ruleness usually does not produce the risks that tend to accompany rules.

There is a related point. Markets allow for interactions among people who disagree with one another on fundamental matters, and indeed who could not easily speak with one another about their deepest or most defining commitments.[12] Partners to an exchange need not agree about basic values or ends; they need not share a common conception of the right or the good. In this way, a commitment to markets, and to the rules that underlie them, allows stable cooperation among people who disagree on first principles. Here too there is room for incompletely theorized agreements, though of a distinctive sort.

A key feature of privately adaptable rules is their association with free alienability of rights. As a general rule, ownership rights are freely alienable, and in this way they attend to the fact that owners (and purchasers) know how valuable the relevant rights are to them. The informational burden on government is therefore minimized. The surrounding rules—of contract, property, and tort—do not operate as personal orders. They allow room for individual maneuver. Of course they are coercive. The law of property is coercive insofar as it prevents nonowners (homeless people, for example) from claiming what they would otherwise claim and doing what they would otherwise do. The virtue of privately adaptable rules is not that they are not coercive and not that they are "natural" or in any deep sense "neutral"; it is that they reduce the costs of rulemaking and harness private information and preferences in the service of outcomes that are themselves not identified before the fact.

To be sure, restrictions on the power of private adaptation, and on free alienability, might be justified for many reasons. Some goods should not be treated as commodities at all, and hence should not be traded on markets; consider, as possibilities, the right to vote, reproductive capacities, and body parts. Sometimes private adaptation creates serious collective action problems, as in the environmental context, where restrictions on trades between polluters and victims of pollution might be adopted for this reason. Sometimes parties to a trade inflict harms on third parties, and these harms justify a ban on the trade. In some cases, there will be reason to limit private flexibility.

People who favor privately adaptable rules, and who distrust rules that specify end-states, are often known as critics of the modern regulatory state.[13] Enthusiasm for privately adaptable rules might easily be harnessed in the service of an argument for private property, freedom of contract, simple rules of tort law, and relatively little else. It would be better, however, to use the same insights on behalf of reform strategies that see the goals of regulation as entirely worthy. Many current regulatory rules cause problems not because they promote the goals of the modern state, but because they unnecessarily specify end-states. In so doing, they produce both injustice and inefficiency, in the form of over-inclusiveness and underinclusiveness, replicating all of the problems typically associated with a refusal to make inquiries at the point of application.

As I have noted, a prominent example is command and control regulation, pervasive in the law of environmental protection. This form of regulation has often failed because it embodies the pathologies of rules. It makes no sense to say that all industries must adopt the same control technology, regardless of the costs and benefits of adoption in the particular case. Command-and-control regulation should be replaced by more flexible, incentive-based strategies, using privately adaptable rules. Instead of saying, for example, what technologies companies must use, the law might impose pollution taxes or fees, and then allow private judgments about the best means of achieving desirable social goals. Government might also allow companies to buy and sell pollution "licenses," a system that would create good incentives for pollution reduction without imposing on government the significant informational burden of specifying means of pollution reduction. The conventional economic argument for incentives rather than mandates is a key part of the argument for privately adaptable rules.

Or consider the area of telecommunications, an area that has, in the United States, been burdened by rigid rules. The Federal Communications Commission has been faced with the task of deciding to whom to allocate licenses. In making this decision, it has alternated between rules and factors. When using factors, the FCC has referred to a wide range of considerations: local ownership, minority ownership, participation by owners in public affairs, broadcast experience, the adequacy of technical facilities, the background and qualifications of staff, the character of owners, and more. In this context the problems with both rules and factors are entirely predictable—inaccuracy through excessive rigidity on the one hand, and discretionary, ad hoc, costly, potentially abusive judgments on the other. It is no wonder that both approaches have largely failed.

What alternatives are possible? In a famous early article, Ronald Coase argued that the government should allocate broadcasting licenses through what I am calling privately adaptable rules[14]—based on property rights and market transfers, as we use (for example) for ownership of newspapers and automobiles. The FCC now uses auctions quite successfully. But there is an obvious objection to Coase's proposal. Perhaps broadcasting licenses should not be regarded as ordinary property; perhaps the criterion of private willingness to pay is an inadequate basis for awarding licenses. The objection contains a real point.[15] Broadcasting might protect a range of aspirational values, captured in the social goal of promoting attention to public affairs, diversity of view, and high-quality programming. But the objection is not a justification for command and control regulation. Instead the rules for license auctions might be designed so as to ensure auction credits for those applicants who promise to promote social aspirations. The example shows that privately adaptable rules might well be used not to oppose regulatory goals, but instead to harness market forces in the interest of those very goals.

Notably, this alternative might itself be part of an incompletely theorized agreement, in the sense that it might be chosen by people who disagree on a great deal that is fundamental. Something of this sort has happened in the last decade in many areas of federal regulation, including environmental protection, telecommunications, and occupational safety and health.

Pragmatic Judgments

Often a legal system should make the choice between rules and ruleless-ness on the basis of a contextual inquiry into the aggregate level of likely errors and abuses. I have suggested that when judges or other interpreters are perceived to be ignorant, corrupt, or biased, or in any case when they diverge in their judgments from the people who make rules, a legal system should and will proceed with rules. Even a poor fit, in the form of over- and underinclusive rules, can be tolerated when individual decisions will be inaccurate as well. Thus we might find rulelessness when there is no special reason to distrust those who will make decisions. Rules are likely to be favored when it is possible to come up with rules that fit well.

The choice between rules and rulelessness might be seen as presenting a principal-agent problem. The legislature, as the principal, seeks to con-trol the decisions of its agents. For this task rules might be best. But a problem with rules is that the agents might be able to track the principal's wishes better if they are given the freedom to take account of individual circumstances. Any rule might inadequately capture the legislature's con-sidered judgments about particular cases. Hence the costs of rulelessness might be acceptable if the legislature does not believe that the court or other interpreter is likely to be untrustworthy.

Rules tend to be adopted in the face of social consensus within the law-making body; rule-free decisions are more probable when there is disagree-ment. It is not hard to obtain a ban on racial discrimination when people agree that this form of discrimination is illegitimate; it is much harder to obtain a similar ban on discrimination against the handicapped, where standards and factors are pervasive. The legislature often delegates discre-tionary power to an agency when it is unable to agree on the appropriate rule, because of social disagreement, and therefore it tells the agency to act "reasonably." In the United States, prominent examples include the areas of broadcasting regulation and occupational safety and health.

Sometimes it is impossible to come up with rules in a multimember body. Participants may begin and even end discussion by attempting agreement on "principles" rather than concrete rules, as in Middle East peace negotia-tions. So too people may be able to agree on a set of relevant factors, or perhaps on some but not all particular outcomes, without being able to agree on a rule, or on the general reasons that account for particular outcomes.

Return here to the fact that legislatures that delegate broad discretion can internalize two large benefits of rulelessness: economizing on information costs and avoiding the political costs of specificity. Legislatures can simultaneously externalize the costs of rulelessness, which are faced by other people. Other officials must compile relevant information and face the political heat associated with making hard choices.

It follows that we tend to find rules when one group of interests is well-organized or otherwise powerful, and when its adversaries are not. A well-organized group is unlikely to allow itself to become at risk through rulelessness when it need not do so (unless, perhaps, it believes that it is even more likely to be successful with bureaucrats or judges). Consider, in the United States, laws governing the regulation of agriculture, which are often highly specific in their generosity to farmers, because the farmers' lobby is well-organized and because the opponents of such laws are not.

Standards or factors are more likely to be the basis for decision when opposing interests have roughly equivalent power in the law-making body, and when they are willing to take their chances with a bureaucracy or a judge. This may be so because they are both highly organized or because they are both weak and diffuse. An example is the American Occupational Safety and Health Act, which is quite vague, in part because its opponents and adversaries are both powerful. On the other hand, two well-organized groups might produce rules when compromise is possible and when there are, to both groups, special risks from relying on an agency or a court. This may be the case when, for example, the regulated class needs to know what the rule is, so that it can plan its affairs. Perhaps it is better to have fairly bad rules than no rules at all. When such planning is made possible by clear rules, members of the regulated class may have it within their power to avoid (some of) the costs of inaccurate rules. Perhaps they can alter their conduct so as to avoid triggering the rule in cases in which the rule is overinclusive. On the other hand, this avoidance may itself be an undesirable social cost. Return to the problem of site-level unreasonableness, where application of an overbroad rule forces employers to make workplace changes that produce little gain, and at great expense.

Rules are also more likely to be unacceptable when the costs of error in particular cases are very high. It is one thing to have a flat rule that people under the age of sixteen cannot drive; the costs of the rule—mistaken denials of a license—are relatively low. It is quite another thing to have a flat rule that people falling in a certain class will be put to death. It is for this reason that rule-bound decisions are unacceptable in inflicting capital punishment, and to some extent in criminal sentencing generally. (But here we must believe not only that rules make for error, but also that case-by-case decisions will make for less error.) This point helps explain the dramatic difference between criminal liability, which is generally rule-bound, and criminal sentencing, which is more discretionary. Relative specificity is needed at the liability stage, so that people can plan accordingly, and so that the discretion of the police is sharply cabined. Both interests are far weaker at the sentencing stage. Planning is not so insistently at stake. Moreover, the discretion of the sentencing judge or jury is less prone to abuse than the discretion of the police officer.

Rules are also less acceptable when circumstances are changing rapidly. Consider, for example, a legislative decision to issue a statutory rule containing permissible emissions levels for coal-fired power plants. Surely any such standard will be out of date in a short time because of technological change. If rules will become obsolete very quickly, it may be best to delegate decisions to institutions capable of changing them rapidly, or perhaps to allow case-by-case judgments based on relevant factors.

When numerous decisions of the same general class must be made, the inaccuracy of rules becomes far more tolerable. Consider, for example, the requirement that all drivers must be over the age of sixteen, or the use of the social security grid to decide disability claims. Bureaucratic insistence on "the technicalities" can be infuriating, but it may result simply because individualized inquiry into whether technicalities make sense in particular cases is too time-consuming. It follows that rules can be avoided when few decisions need to be made, or when each case effectively stands on its own.

There is a general conclusion. The choice between rules and rulelessness cannot be made on the basis of rules. That choice is itself a function of factors. It would be obtuse to say that one or another usually makes sense or is justified in most settings. To decide between them, we need to engage in a form of casuistry. We need to know a great deal about the context, and in particular about the likelihood of bias, the location and nature of social disagreement, the stakes, the risk of overinclusiveness, the quality of those who apply the law, the alignment or nonalignment of views between lawmakers and others, and the sheer number of cases.

England and America

These speculations are borne out by comparing the legal system in England with that in the United States.[16] English law is far more rule-bound than American law. The British Parliament is less likely to delegate discretionary authority to judges. For their part, English judges treat statutes as rules, generally refusing to investigate whether the particular application of the rule makes sense as a matter of policy or principle. In England, lawmaking and law-interpretation are far more rigid than in the United States, where lawmaking often takes place in the process of confrontation with particular cases.

How might this be explained? Institutional differences help provide an answer. Laws in England are drafted by the Office of Parliamentary Counsel, a highly professional body that consists of skilled authors of laws. The Parliamentary Counsel brings about a uniform style of drafting. The Counsel is also closely attuned to the methods of English judges. The judges' practice is itself uniform and relatively simple. In a parliamentary system, the government and the legislature are allied, and the high degree of party control means that there is a level of homogeneity in England at the law-making stage. Moreover, and critically, Parliament revisits statutes with some frequency, and it fixes mistakes that are shown as such when particular cases arise.

The situation in the United States is very different. There is no centralized drafting body and hence no uniformity in terminology. There is little professionalization in the production of statutes. In America, the drafters of legislation are multiple and uncoordinated. Except in rare cases, the party system no longer provides a great deal of coherence, and the executive and legislature are hardly aligned. Congress appears only intermittently aware of the judges' interpretive practices, which are themselves not easy to describe in light of the sheer size of the federal judiciary and the existence of sharp splits, on just this point, within the Supreme Court. It would be wrong to say that Congress is oblivious to judicial decisions interpreting statutes.[17] But Congress is not in the business of responding rapidly and regularly to particular cases in which interpretations, literal or otherwise, tend to misfire. Hence both law-making and law-interpreting practice are very different from what they are in England.

This brief description connects well with the pragmatic suggestions offered here. There is more disagreement in America than in England at the law-making stage. The quality of drafting is lower, as is the possibility of legislative correction after the fact. None of this suggests that England or America has the optimal level of rules in light of its own institutional characteristics. But it does suggest that the two legal systems are highly responsive to distinctive contextual features.

Abolition

Sometimes both rules and rulelessness are intolerable; sometimes market forces cannot or should not be harnessed. Having eliminated both rules and rulelessness, the law might use a lottery instead. (Of course, the decision to hold a lottery must be supported by a rule.) This is a characteristic approach to the military draft, where rule-bound judgments seem too crude, and where judgments based on factors or standards are too obviously subject to discrimination and caprice. Of course, lotteries have an arbitrariness of their own, by virtue of their random character, and for this reason, they may be rejected.

Alternatively, the legal system, having found both rules and rulelessness inadequate, might abolish the relevant institution itself. (The abolition must of course be accomplished by rule.) Hence the best argument for abolition of the death penalty takes the following form. Rules are unacceptable because they eliminate the possibility of adaptation and tailoring to individual circumstances. Rule-bound death sentences are too crude and impersonal. But factors are unacceptable too because they allow excessive discretion, and because they create a risk that illegitimate considerations will enter the decision to impose capital punishment. When judgments are to be made about who is to live and who is to die, a high degree of accuracy is necessary, and errors based on confusion, bias, or venality are intolerable. Human institutions cannot devise a system for making capital punishment decisions in a way that sufficiently diminishes the risk of error.

The strongest argument against the death penalty is not that the penalty of death is too brutal, but that it cannot be administered in a sufficiently accurate way. Suppose it could be shown that through individualized consideration in the form of factors, the rate of error is high, at least in the sense that invidious factors play a large role in the ultimate decision of life or death. Suppose that rules are the only way to eliminate the role of such factors, but that rules are objectionable in their own way because they do not allow consideration of mitigating factors. Perhaps evidence to this effect would not be sufficient to convince most people that the death penalty is unacceptable. But if an incompletely theorized agreement is possible in this area, its sources lie in evidence of this sort.

Concluding Remarks

Some of the most difficult issues in law involve the choice between rules and rulelessness in cases in which both seem unacceptable—rules because of their crudeness and their insensitivity to particulars that confound them; rulelessness because of the likelihood of arbitrariness and discrimination in application. The Benthamite strategy calls for rigid rules for the public and flexible, case-by-case particularism for judges. I have questioned this strategy on both economic and democratic grounds. It is far better to allow citizens and officials to engage in legitimate rule revision. This practice is an important part of a well-functioning democratic regime; it suggests that democratic forces operate not just at the stage of lawmaking but at the stage of law-enforcement as well.

More generally, the choice between rules and rulelessness might well be based on a highly pragmatic, casuistical inquiry into the pathologies of the two approaches in the particular area at hand. Privately adaptable rules are a promising effort to minimize the problems of excessive generality, by facilitating private ordering and thus reducing the informational demands placed on government. Some people who favor privately adaptable rules intend their arguments to be a critique of government regulation and a basis for approval of unrestricted (though rule-governed) free markets. But rules are a precondition for free markets, and there is no simple opposition between regulation and markets. In fact, privately adaptable rules may enjoy an important rebirth in the context of modern regulation—in the creation of rules that accomplish regulatory goals by specifying initial entitlements rather than by fixing outcomes, and that harness market forces in the interest of democratically chosen ends.

8

Interpretation

We have seen that interpretation is a pervasive part of legal thinking. The Constitution says that "Congress shall make no law abridging the freedom of speech"; what does this mean? What strategies should we use in deciding what it means? A statute authorizes the Environmental Protection Agency to issue regulations governing hazardous waste "as may be necessary to protect human health." What, then, are the legal limits on the agency's power?

Such questions are pervasive, and they have immense practical importance. They must be asked not only by judges but also by legislators, administrators, and citizens trying to understand what the law is. In this chapter, I seek to show that many debates over interpretation are disguised debates over whether rules are possible and, if possible, desirable. I also argue that we are unlikely to find a good *general* theory of interpretation. Interpretive practices are highly dependent on context and on role, and by abstracting from context and role, any theory is likely to prove uninformatively broad or to go badly wrong in particular cases. For similar reasons, there is no such thing as a good general theory of legal interpretation, though some general claims about interpretation in law can clarify matters and guide inquiry.

I offer one such general claim here: Interpretive debates in law involve different views about what approach to interpretation will make for the

167

best system of law, all things considered. Of course this is an impossibly large and abstract matter, and hence participants in law seek, here as elsewhere, to achieve agreements on particular outcomes amid their disagreements on fundamental issues, including issues about appropriate interpretation. Thus we can find efforts to agree on particular cases despite disagreement about interpretive method, and also efforts to agree on interpretive method despite disagreements about fundamental issues of (for example) justice and democracy. There is a search as well for incompletely specified agreements—agreements on certain abstractions about interpretation in the midst of uncertainty about what, specifically, those abstractions entail.

As we can see, the subject of interpretation unites the two principal subjects of this book—the incompletely theorized agreement and the choice between rules and casuistry. In exploring the resulting debates, I will describe some long-standing disputes over interpretation in American law and also set out my own preferred solutions, though I will not attempt to defend them in detail here.

Rules and Interpretation

Interpretation would be simple if it could proceed through rules. But often there are no rules for the interpretation of legal texts. And even when legislatures, administrators, and courts have offered rules to govern interpretation, there are no rules for interpreting those rules (and so on). Texts inevitably require interpretation, and interpretation inevitably requires discretionary judgments, if only about the appropriate method of interpretation. This fact raises some of the most important questions in all of legal theory. No approach to interpretation is self-justifying; any particular approach requires an argument. If a judge says that texts should be interpreted by looking at dictionary definitions, by looking at the intentions of those who enacted them, or by inquiring into questions of distributive justice or economic efficiency, it is always necessary to ask: Why should that approach to interpretation be accepted? On what account is it superior to other possibilities? Perhaps people could converge on a particular answer from disparate foundations, so that incompletely theorized judgments could be reached in favor of an interpretive method; and in any case it is notable that participants in the legal culture usually interpret texts without converging on a full account of the appropriate interpretive method.

In law, approaches to interpretation face distinctive constraints. People trying to choose an interpretive method must decide how to allocate power among various groups and institutions—indeed, allocating power is what the choice of an interpretive method *does*. They must also try to generate interpretive practices that minimize the discretion of the institutions they trust least. These are common issues in debates about interpretation. Many methods are best defended on the ground that they allocate power in the right way. If courts insist on following the "ordinary meaning" of legal terms, for example, they may be trying to limit judicial discretion, to make law more like a system of rules, and to give good incentives to legislatures, by encouraging them to speak clearly and in ordinary ways.

Theories and Interpretation

In any field, interpretive practices should be chosen because of the setting in which interpretation occurs; such practices have particular purposes and particular effects. For this reason no general account of appropriate interpretive practice would make much sense. The best approach to interpretation of a literary text may well differ from the best approach to a legal text, and interpreters of a legal text may well take an approach quite different from that of interpreters of the Bible or of a manual for operating electric cars. There is no good general theory of how to interpret texts (except perhaps if we describe it at a very high level of abstraction). Interpretive practices are a function of the role in which interpreters find themselves.

In law, debates over interpretation are insistently *institutional*, in the sense that they raise issues about who should make what sorts of decisions. An account of legal interpretation will therefore have a lot to do with issues of authority; a good understanding of the foundations of authority would help us develop a view of interpretation.[1] Such an approach may or may not be based on democratic considerations; in any case courts might develop interpretive practices that promote a well-functioning system of deliberative democracy. Or interpretive practices might be rooted in economic thinking and try to minimize aggregate rates of error. Or we might try to identify a certain set of rights and connect interpretive practices to the protection of those rights.

In any of these cases, the question of interpretation would be likely to reflect, at least in part, a debate over the virtues and vices of rules. Thus, for example, some people search for interpretive practices that limit judicial discretion at the point of application, by holding judges to principles that come close to rules. Other people believe that rulelike interpretation is not feasible, or not desirable, for reasons very much like those discussed in Chapter 5. For such people, it is worthwhile to allow judges and others a high degree of discretion in the interpretation of legal texts. There are also questions about whether interpreters or instead law-making bodies should be entrusted with the authority to change the law when circumstances so require, or whether from the courts' point of view, a high degree of fixity is important across time.

I have said that even in law, a general theory of interpretation is unlikely to make sense. The appropriate approach to administrative regulations differs from the appropriate approach to statutes, and American courts do not interpret statutes in the way they interpret the Constitution. Hence my most general claim here is close to a tautology: Any approach to interpretation must be defended on the ground that it will produce the best system of law, all things considered. The tautology is far from a theory of interpretation. But the claim is also more useful and contentious than it seems, because many observers of (and participants in) the legal culture act as if their preferred approach is self-justifying, or as if it follows from the very concept of interpretation. It is often thought, for example, that efforts to interpret texts by reference to their "original meaning" need not be defended at all, and that such efforts follow from the notion of interpretation itself. This is a species of bad formalism. The use of original meaning, in the interpretation of texts, is a choice—the selection of a particular interpretive strategy—and the choice needs to be defended with reasons.

In so saying I endorse the view (associated with such diverse figures as Benjamin Cardozo, Ronald Dworkin, and Richard Posner[2]) that any approach to interpretation requires a justification of some kind. That justification must be independent of any texts that are being interpreted. Any understanding of the "meaning" of texts depends on judgments and commitments that are independent of the texts themselves.

This claim leaves many crucial questions open. It does not tell us how rule-bound interpretation ought to be. It does not say whether we should look pragmatically at social consequences, as Judge Posner would have it, or pay close attention to the intentions of enacting bodies, as many American judges argue. My basic claim does not require acceptance of Dworkin's conception of law as integrity (see Chapter 2). The idea of "producing the best system of law, all things considered" is agnostic on the choice between what Dworkin calls integrity and the more forward-looking, policy-oriented approach to interpretation that he labels pragmatism. These points are difficult to discuss in the abstract; they can be explored more fruitfully if we examine the concrete subjects of constitutional and statutory interpretation.

First, however, a cautionary note. As I have said, members of legal cultures frequently interpret texts without reaching closure on the appropriate approach to interpretation. In American constitutional law, particular cases are decided every day, but revealingly and perhaps astonishingly the Supreme Court has not, over two hundred years after ratification of the Constitution, made a final choice among several possible interpretive strategies (just as it has not chosen a "theory" of free expression or racial equality, see Chapter 2). Some options have been ruled out, but several remain. So too for statutory interpretation; members of the judiciary remain uncertain or publicly undecided about some deep underlying questions about the interpretation of statutes, and they attempt, to the extent they can, to decide questions of statutory meaning without answering those questions.

Of course if a particular approach is really right, and if diverse judges could be persuaded to accept it, nothing would be amiss, even if that approach is highly theorized (see Chapter 2). I will be outlining my preferred approach to these issues, and I would not be unhappy if that approach were adopted. But it is notable that in American law, judges have neither accepted nor rejected an approach of the sort I defend. They have reached incompletely theorized agreements on particular outcomes amid disagreements on many general questions of interpretive method.

Interpreting Constitutions

Most constitutions contain rules as well as standards. The American Constitution, for example, says that people under the age of thirty-five cannot be president, and that laws can be enacted only with the concurrence of both the House and the Senate. These and many other constitutional provisions operate as rules. But in the most famous cases, the American Constitution—like many other constitutions—is generally taken to establish standards rather than rules. The right to "freedom of speech," to "equal protection of the laws," the right to be free from "unreasonable searches and seizures," the prohibition on "cruel or unusual punishments"—all these are understood to establish standards to be specified in the context of actual cases. The same is true of many constitutional provisions not involving rights, such as the grant of "executive" power to the president, or the judicial power to decide "cases and controversies."

These provisions exemplify incompletely theorized agreements of a distinctive sort: incompletely theorized convergence on an abstraction. As we have seen, this is a common phenomenon with constitutional provisions, which are designed to last for a long time, and which are often possible only because people are able to agree on an abstraction when they cannot agree on how to specify it. We have also seen that the American Constitution is a common law constitution, in which key decisions are often reached via analogical thinking. As a result, constitutionalism in the United States is far from entirely rule-bound, and many of its key rules are stated in cases, not in the text of the Constitution. Consider, for example, the *Miranda* rules, outlining the warnings that police officers must give to suspects in custody; the rules governing permissible restraints on the right to choose abortion; or the elaborate body of rules protecting the right to free speech, rules that contain a dazzling number of categories and subcategories.

Many people are alarmed that constitutional law consists of many such rules. How—it is asked—can the Court insist on rules that are not in the Constitution? But the alarm is misplaced. Constitutional abstractions inevitably leave gaps and ambiguities, and they have to be specified through implementing doctrines that do not appear in the Constitution itself. For example, the right to free speech bears ambiguously on many issues; consider commercial advertising, obscenity, libel, and flagburning, none of which can be resolved simply as a matter of history or basic principle. It is inevitable that in deciding what kinds of speech can be regulated, the Court will come up with "tests" in the form of principles, rules, and categories that cannot be found in the Constitution itself. These "tests" are the stuff of legal doctrine. Of course a number of doctrines could plausibly do a good job of implementation; many disagreements in constitutional law are about the best implementing doctrine.

Some of the largest debates in American law involve the appropriate interpretive stance toward constitutional provisions that are incompletely specified and for that very reason, threaten to produce grave uncertainty, judicial tyranny, or both. Perhaps judges will take open-ended provisions to mean whatever the judges want them to mean? Perhaps judges will take a provision guaranteeing "equal protection of the laws" as the basis for imposing the judges' own preferred conception of equality?

Such questions have prompted a variety of approaches to constitutional interpretation. In exploring that issue, we should emphasize once again that no system of interpretation is self-justifying and that any system of interpretation requires a defense in terms of recognizable human values, including, for example, the limitation of judicial discretion through rules, the promotion of democratic self-government, the preservation of liberty. Of course—our usual suggestion—judges might be able to reach an incompletely theorized agreement on particular cases amid disagreements on interpretive strategies, or, more ambitiously, agreement on a system of interpretation from diverse foundations, and amid disagreement on much else. Let us now turn to some particular approaches.

Originalism, Hard and Soft

Inspired by the hope of reaching agreements not merely on cases but on interpretive practices despite divergence on fundamental issues, some people think that the meaning of the American Constitution should be settled by the original understanding of those who ratified the relevant provision. On this "originalist" view, associated most closely with Justice Antonin Scalia and former Judge Robert Bork, constitutional provisions might turn out to be quite rulelike even if they look like standards.[3] If courts can discern an original understanding that is clear, perhaps the relevant provision is highly determinate or rulelike after all, and perhaps it settles many, most, or all the cases before they actually arise. This is a large part of the appeal of originalism in constitutional law. (It provides part of the case for originalism in statutory interpretation as well.)

We should distinguish here between two forms of originalism, which might be called "hard" and "soft." For the hard originalist, the meaning of the Constitution is settled by asking how those who ratified the relevant provision would have answered very specific questions. Does the free speech principle include commercial advertising, a particular kind of libelous statement, or sexually explicit movies? Does the equal protection clause allow states to segregate schools on the basis of race or sex? For soft originalists, things are different. For them, the historical inquiry is necessary not to obtain specific answers to specific questions, but instead to get a more general sense of goals and purposes; it is these more general goals and purposes that matter in constitutional interpretation. For the hard originalist, the goal of originalism is to discover rules; for the soft originalist, the goal is to discover constraining but nonetheless flexible standards.

Many originalists, both hard and soft, write as if their preferred method is not a choice at all, but a necessary way of understanding human communication. This is false. We do not have to interpret words by looking at their original meaning. Originalism, like any system of interpretation, needs a defense of some kind. It must be defended as making things better rather than worse. (Certainly, we can have many different ideas about how to figure out whether a system of interpretation does this.) In this particular way, no system of interpretation can avoid personal judgments, and hence a system of legal interpretation is inevitably a function of decisions that are, broadly speaking, political in character. But of course, this does not mean that particular outcomes in constitutional cases are simply a matter of politics. Once courts have chosen an interpretive method, particular judgments will be constrained, and perhaps very much constrained. Indeed, courts may have settled on a particular interpretive method in the hope of constraining discretion at the point of application.

The impulse toward originalism in constitutional law is best understood as an effort to make constitutional law into, or closer to, a system of rules, in which judges are disciplined by provisions that are far from open-ended standards, that limit in advance, that do not threaten predictability, and that have a kind of democratic pedigree by virtue of their connection to past judgments of those who have ratified constitutional provisions—"we the people." Thus the argument for hard originalism, to be made convincing, would have to stress that judicial discretion will otherwise be badly exercised; that great uncertainty is introduced by the alternatives to originalism; that original understandings are generally sound or just, and in any case democratically grounded and subject to democratic correction; and that majoritarian government has many virtues. These points attempt to defend hard originalism partly on the ground that it promotes a system of rules, and partly on the ground that it is the most democratic approach to interpretation.

In the abstract, the argument may seem reasonable, but it does not make a convincing case for hard originalism, which has played at most a sporadic role in American constitutional law. If hard originalism is defended as a way of yielding rules, it is a failure, since concrete questions do not always have concrete historical answers. The search for original understandings leads to many indeterminacies, and hence rule-bound constitutionalism will not result from hard originalism. Sometimes the ratifiers of a constitutional provision did not agree on how to answer particular questions. Sometimes they had no clear understanding of its meaning. Sometimes they intended to establish a standard with varying content over time.

A particular problem with hard originalism is that new and unanticipated circumstances can much complicate the attempt to find clear answers in history.[4] In asking the ratifiers a hypothetical question—about free speech, racial discrimination, sex equality—might we not have to give the ratifiers some of the information that we now have? This question cannot itself be answered by mastering the historical record. The problem of understanding meaning in new circumstances raises serious difficulties for the originalist project, whether hard or soft.[5]

Thus far we have seen that hard originalism is unlikely to generate rules and thus unlikely to do what its proponents want it to do. There are other reasons why hard originalism would produce a bad system of constitutional law. The democratic arguments for originalism are far less plausible than they seem. When many generations have passed between a current problem and ratification of a constitutional provision, the democratic case for following the (narrowly conceived) original understanding weakens substantially. The case for following the Constitution itself is very strong, but why should current citizens be bound by the particular historical judgments made by its drafters generations ago? The American system of rights, including rights that are a precondition for democratic governance, would be inexcusably modest if we followed hard originalism. Free speech, freedom of religion, race equality, sex equality—all these and more would be narrow indeed if the United States Supreme Court confined itself to the original understanding of the ratifiers. In fact hard originalism would produce a worse—less just—society than the one America now has, even or perhaps especially if we attend to democratic considerations.

These claims are of course relevant to the case for originalism, since the view that the original understanding is binding cannot be justified by reference to the original understanding. The claim for originalism requires a defense that is not itself historical in character. Many people believe, and I think rightly, that a wide range of Supreme Court decisions protecting basic rights should be taken as fixed points against which any method of interpretation must be tested; hard originalism cannot account for these fixed points. For this reason hard originalism is unacceptable. And whether or not this is so, we have uncovered the grounds on which the debate over interpretive method must be fought: the question whether, all things considered, a particular method will lead to a good system of constitutional law. To the claim that this view makes the choice of interpretive method turn on people's judgments, it should be responded: On what else could the choice of interpretive method possibly turn?

Judicial Restraint

Having rejected originalist approaches on grounds very much like these, many people think that in constitutional cases, judges should take constitutional provisions to set out broad "concepts"—standards rather than rules. If judges proceed in this way, should they be reluctant to invalidate statutes? Should they give democratic processes the benefit of the doubt? Some people do not think so. Many Americans have been enthusiastic about the practices of the Warren Court, which, among other things, reformed the criminal justice system, vigorously protected political dissent, and launched an attack on practices of racial exclusion. Reflecting that enthusiasm, some people firmly reject judicial restraint. In support of this conclusion it is said that there is no evidence that "over the long run legislatures are more likely to develop a sounder theory of what rights justice does require than courts trying to interpret the vague language of abstract constitutional provisions."[6] On the contrary, it is said, the majority should not be allowed to decide what rights the minority has. And because the legislature is vulnerable to political pressure and in particular to the political pressure of the majority, it seems less likely to reach good decisions about rights than judicial officials, who are not vulnerable in that way.

These are the building-blocks for a theory of interpretation that rejects judicial restraint and that gives the Supreme Court a large role in American government. An argument of this kind is being heard in many other nations as well. For present purposes, the nature of the argument is as important as its substance. Notice that the argument derives an approach to constitutional interpretation from a set of claims about what would, all things considered, make the constitutional system better rather than worse. In this way the antirestraint position takes on the burden that originalists must shoulder as well. But the argument rests on questionable empirical and theoretical claims; let us now explore them.

I have suggested that judges are usually not effective in producing social reform. In fact the Court's effort to desegregate the South was mostly a failure. Consider, for example, the astonishing fact that a decade after the Supreme Court announced that school segregation was unconstitutional, less than 2 percent of black children in the South were attending desegregated schools. Real desegregation began only after the democratic branches—Congress and the president—became involved. Perhaps the involvement of the democratic branches was a result of *Brown*, but there is little evidence that this is so.[7] These simple empirical points do not mean that *Brown*, one of the cornerstones of American constitutional law, was wrongly decided; but they do count against judge-led efforts to change social practices in a dramatic way. Even when judges recognize rights that deserve to be recognized, and even when judges rule that those rights must be protected, society may stand firm or rebel, and the rights may not come to fruition in the real world. Indeed, judge-led protection of rights may disserve those very rights. This may well have happened in the United States with judicial efforts to protect abortion—efforts that may well have undermined the movement for sex equality.[8]

By itself this point is not decisive; it is speculative and general, and in some circumstances judges can do a lot of good, especially when their decrees do not require large-scale social reform. But there are further considerations. The context of litigation means that judges will see only small parts of complex wholes. If someone claims that there is a constitutional right to welfare, to environmental protection, to bear arms, or to compensation for any governmentally induced diminution in the value of property, the particular case may seem very insistent; but judges are unlikely to be able to have a grasp on the systemic effects or collateral consequences of any changes that they require. The point is not simply that judges are not experts in areas that often require expertise, though this is both true and important. The point is that legislatures and bureaucracies are in a far better position to get a sense of the complex systemic effects of small-scale changes. Usually ignorant of those effects, judges may not see where the litigated issue fits in a social pattern, or what sorts of problems are created by a judicial solution. This too is a reason for caution, even in constitutional cases.

In most nations, moreover, judges are drawn from a narrow segment of society. In England and America, for example, judges tend to be lawyers, mostly male, white, wealthy, and while some of them are undoubtedly superb deliberators about rights, or expert in particular areas of law, they are not trained in philosophy, political theory, or empirical analysis. Of course, we can point to judicial virtues stemming from legal education and political independence. But there is no convincing reason to think that judges are better at moral and political deliberation than are members of other branches of government. In the face of uncertainty on that question, and legitimate disagreement on many of the underlying moral issues, the democratic judgment should prevail, at least in most cases where there is real doubt about whether the constitutional provision really forbids it.

The fact that judges are not subject to electoral pressure in some ways supports a more aggressive judicial role, since judges do not have to worry about reelection and majority will. But actually the point cuts both ways, since people with claims of right, even minorities, often make moral arguments in front of legislatures or use political pressure to make their moral views count. Electoral accountability means vulnerability to moral judgments as well as vulnerability to pressure and self-interest.

It is correct to say that the majority should not decide on the rights of the minority, but almost any claim of right is made by a group that is in the minority—property owners resisting environmental regulation, rich people resisting progressive taxation, people seeking to eliminate endangered species, and much more. From the fact that majorities should not decide on the rights of the minority, nothing at all follows for the role of the courts in constitutional interpretation.

In any case, any system of constitutional interpretation must be closely attuned to the risks of judicial discretion. Rules of interpretation should be designed to minimize those risks. A view that treats the Constitution as setting out very abstract standards, to be given content by judges thinking deeply about political philosophy, is unacceptable because of the power it confers on judges. The requirement of "fit" with precedents is important in reducing judicial power, but then we need to specify how much weight judges should give to "fit," and how much weight they should give to their own political judgments. Advocates of limited judicial discretion insist that much weight should be given to the former. The most general point is that the right to democratic governance is an important part of the rights that people have, and this point suggests that judges, especially judges interested in protecting rights, should be cautious before invalidating democratic outcomes. Thus the case for judicial restraint in constitutional law is quite strong. This is why people from diverse theoretical positions may converge on it.

From these points we might suggest that within the judiciary, constitutional norms are often "underenforced" and properly so.[9] As it operates in courts, constitutional law is a mixture of substantive principle and institutional constraint. Any judicial pronouncement about the meaning of the Constitution is partly a product of the courts' weak institutional position. Judicial caution is a function of distinctly judicial incapacities. Hence Congress or the president might urge a broader understanding of the Constitution—because the meaning of the Constitution is a function of the institution that is interpreting it, and because Congress and the president, with their greater democratic pedigree and fact-finding capacity, do not labor under the disabilities faced by courts. In a deliberative democracy, there is nothing wrong with a situation in which democratic branches interpret the Constitution more expansively than courts, and indeed this has happened on many occasions in American history, with rights of property, sex equality, and freedom of speech.

Ingredients of an Approach

Of course general propositions of this sort do not resolve hard cases. Any choice of method will depend not on a demonstration of some kind, but on somewhat speculative claims about likely institutional practices and about where there is most to fear. Moreover, there are times when the Court appropriately intervenes in democratic processes in order to vindicate large-scale aspirations, as we will soon see. A degree of casuistry is desirable here as elsewhere in law. No approach to constitutional law will look like an algorithm.

In any event it is now clear that any approach to interpretation should develop constraints on judges interpreting the Constitution. To supply such constraints, it makes sense to look in three principal places. First, the case for soft originalism is very strong. The text of the Constitution is often quite open-ended, and an inquiry into general goals or purposes can help discipline interpretation. What emerges from soft originalism is a standard rather than a rule, but it is constraining nonetheless, at least compared with the text itself. The resulting constraints do not have the problems associated with hard originalism, since they would not lead to an inferior system of constitutional law. Thus, for example, democratic aspirations can help give content to the free speech principle, and the opposition to the system of racial caste can help in the specification of the equal protection clause.

Second, the process of case-by-case judgment and analogical thinking supplies many of the rules of American constitutionalism, and that process also helps limit the exercise of judicial discretion where no rules can be found. This is a large part of the answer to those who fear that without hard originalism, judges are basically at sea.[10] Most of the real constraint on judicial discretion in constitutional law comes from precedent. In Chapter 3 we saw that analogies play a key role in constitutional interpretation. We should now say that analogical reasoning is an alternative not only to deep philosophical arguments but also to originalism. A claim of analogy does require a reason, but as constitutional law typically operates, people can converge on the relevant reason from many different foundations.

Third, judges interpreting constitutional rights should move to a certain level of theoretical ambition, seeing the judicial role as most firm where democratic processes in an existing government are most likely to break down or least likely to be reliable.[11] This is of course an incompletely theorized abstraction, leaving room for a great deal of specification in individual cases. Thus the most promising approaches to constitutional interpretation call for an aggressive judicial role when there are defects in purportedly democratic processes. If the right to vote is at stake, or the right to political speech, courts are more properly intrusive. So too when courts are asked to protect people who are at a systematic disadvantage in the democratic process. In such cases considerations of democracy argue for rather than against a judicial role. A well-functioning system of deliberative democracy—the basic aspiration of Anglo-American political systems—should not be confused with simple majoritarian politics.

Majority rule is not itself democracy; if majorities intrude on political rights or exclude despised groups, they violate democratic norms. If the majoritarian process is defective from the standpoint of deliberative democracy itself, the case for judicial control becomes stronger. And if an agreement—completely or incompletely theorized—is to be possible on a general approach, an interpretive method centered on democratic considerations is probably the most promising alternative.

To the complaint that this view requires its own justification it must be emphasized yet again that this is true for any theory of interpretation. No theory of interpretation justifies itself. The question is whether the justification is convincing, not whether it is a justification.

We might use these thoughts to build toward a particular understanding of constitutional interpretation. Much of the discipline on judges comes not from constitutional text and history, but from past cases. Past cases produce rules, in the form of precedents, as well as analogies. Most constitutional problems have easy answers for this reason. Where no clear answer exists, judges do best to work analogically; to inquire into history, conceived broadly rather than narrowly; and to adopt a presumption in favor of democratic outcomes. But the presumption is weaker when democratic rights are at stake or when politically vulnerable groups are at risk. In this way the judicial role might be derived in large part by reference to democratic considerations.

Consider, as illustrations, two controversial issues: the right to abortion and the legal treatment of homosexuality. It would not be especially hard to reach the conclusion that laws forbidding abortion are constitutionally troublesome because they discriminate against women, a politically vulnerable group. To summarize a complex argument: Women are the special target of such laws; men are nowhere required to devote their bodies to the protection of vulnerable people; prohibitions on abortion often grow out of stereotypical conceptions of women's proper role; and in the real world, such prohibitions may well contribute to second-class citizenship for women and are unlikely to protect fetuses very much.[12] But—and this is an important qualification—it does not follow that the Supreme Court was correct to invalidate such laws in 1973 in *Roe v. Wade.* The Court would have done far better to proceed slowly and incrementally, and on grounds that could have gathered wider social agreement and thus fractured society much less severely. The Court might have ruled that abortions could not be prohibited in cases of rape or incest, or that the law at issue in *Roe* was invalid even if some abortion restrictions might be acceptable. Such narrow grounds would have allowed democratic processes to proceed with a degree of independence—and perhaps to find their own creative solutions acceptable to many sides. In this way a narrow, incompletely theorized agreement could have been possible in the Court, in a way that would have been much healthier for democratic processes in the United States. And in this fashion other branches of govenment might have participated in the evolving interpretation of the Constitution, with a possible conclusion, from democratic sources, that the right to sex equality is broader than the Court (properly in light of its institutional position) understands it.

The case of homosexuality is similar. Suppose that one believes (as I do) that homosexuals are a politically vulnerable group, and that laws discriminating against homosexuals are inconsistent with the equal protection clause of the United States Constitution. Suppose one concludes (as I would) that the equal protection clause, rightly interpreted, forbids laws against same-sex marriages or preventing homosexuals from serving in the military. It does not at all follow that the Supreme Court should announce this fact now or as soon as it can. Instead the Court ought to proceed cautiously, narrowly, and with the easiest cases. Understanding that a broad and immediate judicial ruling would be inconsistent with democratic deliberation, it might say, for example, that states may not adopt laws that forbid localities from enacting antidiscrimination ordinances. Or the Court might conclude that government may not discharge homosexuals from ordinary jobs, at least without a demonstration that homosexuality actually impairs job performance.

With incremental steps of this kind, the Court might be able to forge and to participate in incompletely theorized judgments on particular outcomes—while allowing democratic processes to come to terms with the broader and more fundamental issues. The Court might wait a long time before generally banning discrimination on the basis of sexual orientation, even if it believes, early on, that this is the best view. Attention to particulars, and reluctance to embrace abstractions, would be a good way for the Court to avoid hubris and to allow constitutional judgments to be reached by other branches as well. These branches might appropriately understand the antidiscrimination right more broadly than the Court does.

An elaboration of this general approach would require a book or perhaps several books. Of course, the category of democratic rights is not self-defining; so too for the notion of politically vulnerable groups. As I have said, these are incompletely theorized abstractions, and in specifying them, courts will participate in incompletely theorized judgments on particular cases. Something of this sort has happened in American law, as judges have agreed that discrimination on the basis of sex and race call for special judicial skepticism, while concluding that this is not true for discrimination on the basis of age and disability, without coming up with a full theory to account for these conclusions. If we believe in incompletely theorized agreements, we will insist that judges deciding particular constitutional cases need not commit themselves to a complete theory of interpretation, and they should not resolve the more high-level issues unless they must. But I hope that I have said enough to show that debates over the best approach to constitutional interpretation depend on claims—often tacit—about what approach is most promising in terms of recognizable human values. To evaluate competing claims, we need to look at both theoretical issues about democratic government and empirical issues about actual governmental institutions—their composition, competence, biases, and skills.

Here again we see the extent to which debates over interpretation are tied up with debates about which institutions should have what powers. Here again we see the extent to which debates over interpretation are debates about the possibility and value of rules and rulelike constraints—and the choice, at least in American law, for a form of casuistry.

On Interpretation of Statutes

The legislature enacts statutes, and sometimes those statutes raise serious interpretive difficulties. What should judges do in the face of interpretive doubt? Should they rely on the "ordinary meaning" of the text? On legislative intentions? On their own views about the best justifications for the statutes, or about justice and efficiency? What role is there for the so-called "canons" of interpretation, which involve syntactic, procedural, or substantive principles that are brought to bear on the interpretive enterprise? These are the enduring questions of statutory interpretation.

My basic claim here is a simple and familiar one: Such questions actually involve debates over what would make for the best system of statutory law, all things considered. Sometimes the ingredients of the underlying debates—which very much involve the virtues and vices of rules—are obscured. It would be good to bring them out into the open and to attempt to obtain an incompletely theorized agreement on cases amid disagreements on interpretive approach, or more ambitiously, an incompletely theorized agreement on a particular interpretive approach.

Literalism

Let us approach these issues by exploring a narrower but also enduring question in law: Ought statutes to be interpreted "literally" or instead in accordance with their purpose, which typically takes the form of a standard? To make the question vivid, assume that the words of a statute do have a literal meaning, in the sense that the ordinary understanding of the terms, in the dictionary sense, leads in one direction. (Often, of course, this assumption cannot be sustained, but let us begin with the simplest case.) Thus a law might say that no dogs are allowed in restaurants, that smoking is banned on airplanes, or that it is a crime to go over 65 miles per hour. Return to our now-familiar questions: Does the prohibition on dogs apply to the case of a police officer accompanied by a German shepherd trained to smell bombs, when the restaurant owner has received a call to the effect that a bomb is about to go off somewhere in the building? Does the speed limit law apply to a driver fleeing from an armed terrorist? As we have seen, most judges would say that statutes should not be construed so as to produce absurdity, and that the literal language will not be controlling in such cases. A key part of the argument is that the underlying purpose of the statute does not apply, much or at all, to the case at hand, and that a reasonable legislature could not possibly have wanted the statutes to apply to that case. If there is no considered legislative judgment that the rules should extend to these situations, why should the court produce absurdity or injustice?

Some people think that judges who reject literal meaning are proceeding illegitimately. Perhaps such judges are engaging in "policymaking" that should be reserved to legislatures. On this view, any exceptions should be made by the legislature, not by the courts. This claim—that literal interpretation is best—often purports to stem from democratic considerations, but the democratic arguments are very weak. By hypothesis, there is no considered democratic judgment that the rule should apply in the cases at hand. The judges are not acting inconsistently with any such judgment. On the contrary, purposive interpretation, attending to legislative goals and to context, seems far more likely to fit with actual democratic judgments, if we are entitled to imagine what they would likely be.

The real argument for literalism rests not on democratic considerations at all, but instead on two things: a set of arguments for rules rather than standards, and a set of judgments about which institutions should do what things. If courts ask whether an application of a rule is absurd, and if they do so by asking what the rule's purposes are, they will convert the rule into something more like a standard. The rule may then start to unravel.

In addition, statutes do not come clothed with purposes, ready to proclaim themselves. Any conception of a statute's purpose involves an element of evaluation and construction. What is the purpose of a law that forbids "racial discrimination," in a context in which an employer is adopting an affirmative action program (see Chapter 3)? What is the purpose of a law that forbids "baby selling," in the context of an arrangement for surrogate motherhood? The effort to identify and to work with purposes rather than literal text may be bad because it makes planning harder; because it weakens the legislature's incentives to come up with a clear, good rule in the first instance; because the judge's judgments about purposes and absurdity may be unreliable; because it is costly and time-consuming for litigants and courts to inquire into purpose and absurdity; and because the legislature can correct the absurdity in any event. These are the considerations—highly pragmatic in character—that support literal interpretation of statutes.

The argument for literal interpretation, made in this way, is really an argument about what system of interpretation will make things better rather than worse. But exposed as a set of (broadly speaking) pragmatic claims, the argument is unconvincing. A legislature's failure to anticipate an absurd application of a statutory term, and to make a correction before the fact, is usually not a result of sloppiness or negligence. Sometimes it is impossible for good lawmakers to foresee odd applications; as we have seen, life outruns even the most well-considered law. The legislature's power to correct absurd or unjust outcomes after the fact is an unreliable safeguard, since the legislature has many things to worry over, and a particular absurd outcome may not seem sufficiently pressing to claim its attention after the fact. The legislature as a whole may never even know about it. In any case it is unclear how much is gained by forcing the legislature to amend a statute to avoid an absurd outcome when courts could prevent an outcome that is absurd by general agreement. And if courts will depart from literal meaning only when the absurdity is clear, the resort to purpose ought not to impede planning or to raise the costs of decision significantly; and we are unlikely to have to worry that judges will exercise their judgments in an unreliable or biased way.

The courts' institutional position, allowing judges to see particular applications that legislatures cannot anticipate in advance, puts them in an especially good place to correct absurd applications. For this reason a degree of casuistical interpretation, adapting the general rule to the particular situation, is probably going to be a desirable part of statutory interpretation. Of course there can be legitimate dispute about how absurd the outcome has to be in order to qualify as such. (See the remarks about England and America in Chapter 7.)

Benzene

Consider in this regard an important and controversial case in American law, *Industrial Union Department, AFL-CIO v. American Petroleum Institute*.[13] The case involved a regulation of a carcinogenic substance, benzene; the regulation would have cost many hundreds of millions of dollars, in return for an uncertain benefit to employees. Some evidence in the case suggested that the regulation might save as few as two lives every six years. The agency did not specify the level of health gains, saying that it was unnecessary to show that the risk was significant or to balance costs against benefits.

The text of the relevant law seemed to support the agency. The Occupational Safety and Health Act says that the Secretary of Labor

> in promulgating standards dealing with toxic materials or harmful physical agents . . . shall set the standard which most adequately ensures, to the extent feasible, on the basis of the best available evidence, that *no employee will suffer material impairment of health or functional capacity even if such employee has regular exposure to the hazard dealt with by such standard for the period of his working life.* (emphasis added)

These words appear to set out a rule, requiring the Secretary to issue regulations even if only one employee is at risk. Writing in dissent, Justice Marshall invoked the need for rule-bound interpretation to urge that the statute should be read literally. In Justice Marshall's view, the agency had done what it was plainly required to do. (No one argued that the regulation was not "feasible," since it was agreed that the industry could bear the expense.)

The plurality of the Court refused to engage in literal interpretation. Instead it suggested that despite the words of the law, Congress could not possibly have intended to allow the result that the agency sought. "In the absence of a clear mandate in the Act, it is unreasonable to assume that Congress intended to give the Secretary the unprecedented power over American industry that would result from the Government's view. . . . [T]he Government theory would give OSHA power to impose enormous costs that might produce little, if any, discernible benefit." Hence the plurality said that OSHA could not regulate unless it could show that a risk was "significant." Thus the statutory rule was interpreted, or rewritten, so as to require a demonstration that a risk was "significant" before regulation could go forward.

Did the plurality of the Court abuse its interpretive authority? It did not. A literal interpretation would have been feasible, but it would have made little sense. A degree of purposive interpretation gave reasonableness the benefit of the doubt. Despite the words of the statute, there was absolutely no indication that Congress had arrived at a considered judgment to the effect that OSHA should impose hundreds of millions of dollars in expense for a trivial health benefit. In the absence of such evidence, in the text or history, the plurality was right. With this conclusion, we are well on our way to an appreciation of the virtues of casuistry in law, even in the interpretation of apparently clear statutory terms.

If this conclusion is to be resisted, it is for the pragmatic reasons considered above. Perhaps the outcome in the benzene case reduces incentives for Congress to legislate clearly; perhaps it reflects a misunderstanding of the problem of regulating carcinogens; perhaps it increases the cost and uncertainty associated with the interpretation of rules; perhaps it will lead to other cases in which courts abuse their interpretive authority by rejecting actual legislative judgments. What is most important here is that the debate over literalism is really a debate over such concerns.

Ingredients of Interpretation

To endorse the outcome in the benzene case is not to support any particular approach to statutory interpretation. People with widely divergent views on that topic could accept the plurality's approach. Even if we agree that statutory terms should be interpreted to avoid absurdity or injustice, many questions remain. When the text is ambiguous, should the court venture its own account of what arguments lie behind statutes or should it pay close attention to the legislature's own account? Should judges rely on the ordinary meaning of the text or instead on the legislatively intended meaning, as revealed by legislative history? And what role should be played by the so-called canons of interpretation?

Whose Account?

Let us begin with the first question. Judges are not specialists in the many subjects that call for interpretive judgments, and they have little electoral legitimacy. It follows that in general, courts should attend closely to the legislature's views, so as to recognize the law-making primacy of the legislature and simultaneously to discipline their own decisions. This argument is based on a set of judgments about where errors are most likely to lie. The complexity of modern statutory regimes, and the controversial character of the values that underlie them, ought to lead judges to be attentive to the arguments of elected officials about what made the statutes necessary or desirable. Judges' accounts of what best justifies statutes are too likely to be confused or sectarian.

Of course the development of an account behind legislation will not be pure description. Typically there will be conflicting elements, and what the interpreter does will have a constructive or evaluative dimension, making sense rather than nonsense out of what can be found. But the emphasis on the legislature's own views has the advantage of disciplining the inquiry and promoting democratic accountability.

Text, Intentions, History

These considerations provide a good start toward sorting out the relationships among text, legislative intentions, and legislative history. It seems reasonable to say that judges should rely on the ordinary meaning of statutory language, taken in the context of the statute as a whole and the period in which it was enacted. This approach to interpretation calls for the use of common understandings of language ("background knowledge" or "background lawyers' knowledge"); it does not depend on dictionary definitions. As Learned Hand warned, judges should not make "a fortress out of the dictionary."[14] Dictionary definitions can be too numerous or too crude to capture contextual meaning. (Consider the words "bat," "equal," and "motor vehicle.") But courts should use the ordinary understandings of speakers of the relevant language. This approach promotes planning and imposes good incentives on legislators, by encouraging them to write in the way that people read. It also serves an important coordinating function, by allowing judges, who are not specialists, to start from common ground.[15]

The ordinary meaning of words, however, can produce gaps or ambiguities, and the particular context can suggest reason for interpretive doubt. When this is so, courts should examine the particular setting and try to identify legislative *purposes*, understood as general goals, and legislative *intentions*, understood as particular judgments. Of course there are serious problems in discerning the "intentions" of a large law-making body, and the identification of intentions, here as elsewhere, will not be a matter of uncovering a simple fact. But this point should not be exaggerated. We do and can speak of the intentions of a team, a corporate body, or a public institution, and the underlying complexities do not justify eliminating the concept entirely.

In searching for purposes and intentions, courts should feel free to take the legislative history as relevant.[16] It is true that the history has not been enacted and that it may be a product of legislative staff or powerful private groups. The history certainly does not have the same status as the text. But an investigation of the history can be helpful in showing what the legislature was concerned about, whether in general or in particular. Interpreters should be interested in obtaining that knowledge. Of course it is possible to imagine a legal system in which legislative history is not kept at all, is kept poorly, or is entirely unreliable. If so, it makes no sense to rely on legislative history, and interpreters should use any other contextual clues.

What is the relationship, on these counts, between constitutional and statutory interpretation? The case for reliance on general purposes is similar and similarly strong in both areas, but in the statutory context, there is a better argument for holding interpreters to particular intentions. The two major differences between constitutions and statutes are that the former can be changed only with difficulty and that the former tend to be old. Recall in this connection that the case against hard originalism in constitutional interpretation is based on the claim that it would result in an inferior system of constitutional law—a claim founded partly on the fact that democratic ideals are not well-promoted by requiring courts to adhere to the unenacted judgments of constitutional ratifiers in the distant past.

In the context of statutory interpretation, things are quite different. Statutes are more readily amended and usually more recently enacted. Hence something approaching hard originalism makes far more sense for statutes. This does not mean that hard originalism offers a complete approach to statutory interpretation. Sometimes it will leave gaps or ambiguities; sometimes changed circumstances or the passage of time will make statutory interpretation more like constitutional interpretation. And as we will soon see, courts properly invoke background principles to push statutes in particular directions.

Principles and Canons

The inquiry I have suggested itself may reveal gaps or ambiguities, and when this is so, courts should look elsewhere. In most legal systems, courts rely on "principles" or "canons" of interpretation.[17] And in most legal systems, there are many such principles and canons on which to draw. In a famous article, Karl Llewellyn cast great doubt on this practice.[18] In Llewellyn's view, every canon has a countercanon—a principle pointing in the opposite direction. In Llewellyn's view, there are dozens of different canons, counseling wildly varied results, and courts can pick out canons as they see fit. Thus Llewellyn argued that the canons are useless, after-the-fact explanations for decisions reached on other grounds.

There is some truth in Llewellyn's influential critique, but it is greatly overdrawn. Interpretation is simply not possible without both *syntactic* and *substantive* canons or principles (see Chapter 5). Syntactic principles are part of the background knowledge of readers, including legal readers. Such principles give meaning to words, which would be (at best) odd ink formations without them. Substantive principles are omnipresent as well, and they too usually need not be articulated. Consider, for example, the idea that courts should not do whatever they think best, or that Congress should not be taken to be joking. Texts are readable in virtue of such principles. Every legal system is pervaded by them.

Easy cases are easy only because of shared agreement on syntactic and substantive principles. When judges rely on the ordinary meaning of the words in context, interpretive principles of various sorts are certainly present. Interpreters are usually not self-conscious about them, but this is so only because the principles are so obvious that they appear invisible, operating as part of the uncontested background for interpretive work. (If the words in day-to-day conversation, or in this very paragraph, are clear, it is for the same reason.) The legal culture—what lawyers know—consists largely of this uncontested background. An important task of legal theory is to identify its content. And when statutes are unclear, every legal system relies on principles that allocate burdens of doubt and inertia. These principles are based on procedural and substantive policies. They are designed to make the legal system better rather than worse.

The American legal system contains many such principles. Courts say, for example, that ambiguous statutes will not be construed to raise serious constitutional questions; to apply retroactively; to preempt state law; to apply outside the borders of the United States; to invade presidential authority; or to eliminate judicial review of administrative action.[19] Some of these principles tell courts what to do when the interpretive enterprise otherwise leaves judges in equipoise. Some of them are not just tie-breakers, but impose a presumption, one that can be overcome only through a "clear statement" from the legislature. These "clear statement" principles are designed to push statutes in a particular direction, where they stay unless there is firm evidence of a legislative judgment to the contrary.

When things are working well, the relevant principles are easy to defend and indeed defensible from multiple competing foundations. Thus an incompletely theorized agreement might well be possible on the idea that federal statutes should not lightly be taken to preempt state law, that courts should presume that Congress has not intended to apply statutes retroactively, or that judicial review should be available unless Congress has spoken unambiguously.

To explain and justify particular principles, much more would have to be said.[20] A legal system may well shift from one set of principles to another over time; the Supreme Court of the United States now uses principles that are quite different from those prevailing in 1968, and the principles used in 1968 were quite different from those prevailing in 1931. Undoubtedly some current principles are outmoded or counterproductive. Undoubtedly some of them lead to injustice.

For the present we can reach a simpler conclusion, one that returns us to the central themes of this chapter. Any approach to interpretation requires a defense. Debates over interpretive practices are really debates over which practices will lead to a better system of law. Debates over the value and possibility of rules are a large part of those debates. A system of law tries to achieve an incompletely theorized agreement on appropriate constraints on judicial discretion, on particular cases amid disagreement about interpretive method, and if possible, on interpretive method amid disagreement on much else. There is no general theory of interpretation. But any legal system reflects, at any given time, a particular set of interpretive judgments and commitments. It is important to lay bare those judgments and commitments. We can begin to make progress once the underlying questions are revealed.

Conclusion:
Law and Politics

Participants in any legal system disagree on basic principles. Sometimes they have no convictions about large-scale issues of the right and the good. Sometimes they find these issues deeply confusing. They must nonetheless make a wide range of particular decisions. They have to do this in a short time. In accomplishing this task, they seek to achieve incompletely theorized agreements on particular outcomes. This is a key to legal reasoning. It is also the law's distinctive approach to the problem of social pluralism.

Legal Reasoning, Rule of Law

Rules are often the mechanism by which legal actors reach agreement; a central virtue of (many) rules is that people can converge on them from diverse foundations. Rules sharply discipline the territory over which argument can occur. The rule of law, if understood as a law of rules, allows people to form expectations, to make plans, and to conduct their affairs without fear of governmental malice, arbitrariness, or surprise. It allows cases to be decided without requiring participants in the legal system to assess large-scale principles or to develop general theories. Participants in law create and reason from rules precisely because of the advantages of rules on these scores.

191

But rules are blunt and crude instruments, and case-by-case judgments can allow a greater degree of fairness and precision. The highest form of justice requires official attention to a range of contextual features, and it avoids rules, which are often made necessary only because of the failings of human beings and of human institutions. When participants in law reject rules, they tend to reason analogically, and in a way that is fine-tuned, that involves low-level principles, that brackets large claims about the right or the good, and that leaves many cases to be decided on another day. We have seen that analogical reasoning plays a key role not only in common law but also in constitutional law, which results largely from casuistical judgments rather than from constitutional text and history. We have also seen that analogical reasoning has a place in the interpretation of rules themselves. Rules are often defined by reference to prototypical or exemplary cases, and the meaning of rules becomes obscure because cases arise that seem relevantly different from the exemplary ones.

These various ways of proceeding—the characteristic lawyer's methods—might appear inferior to more ambitious alternatives, such as the careful investigation of the consequences of legal rules, the search for reflective equilibrium, or the development and application of some large theory. Certainly it is good to know the consequences of legal rules, and lawyers do not yet have adequate tools to make that assessment. More and better social science would be helpful. Sometimes greater abstraction is necessary or otherwise desirable, even in courts. But incompletely theorized agreements are well-suited to a system of adjudication, containing diverse people who disagree on first principles; who have limited time and capacities; who cannot be expected to invent the system of law from the ground up; who are not sure what they think about the largest problems; and who want to avoid hubris.

With these various points, we have come far from some familiar understandings of the rule of law. This ideal does not require full specification of legal rules before actual cases arise. For human beings, this is an impossibly ambitious goal. Instead it requires, more modestly, a degree of conformity with past decisions, and for intensely pragmatic reasons: minimization of the burdens of decision, equal treatment, and judicial modesty in the face of limited wisdom and experience at the time of decision. Exactly what degree and kind of conformity with the past—and exactly what degree of ruleness—depends on the context. Sometimes a legal system minimizes the pathologies of rule-bound justice by allowing rule revisions by public officials and ordinary citizens. Sometimes a legal system takes advantage of privately adaptable rules, which offer people a great deal of flexibility to make their own way.

In many areas a system committed to the rule of law allows for casuistical, particularistic forms of reasoning, in which much of the content of law is made at the point of application. There are many constraints on this process. A full understanding of those constraints would amount to a (nearly) full understanding of the relevant legal system. The choice among the various items found in law's toolbox—rules, factors, guidelines, standards, principles, analogies, and more—cannot be made in the abstract. We can identify characteristic problems and characteristic responses to those problems. We can point to legitimate rule revisions and privately adaptable rules as especially promising approaches to the crudeness of rules. But to know whether the problems will be severe, and whether and which responses will work, we need to know the details.

Rules, Analogies, Justice

What is the relation between rules and justice? Between analogies and justice? It cannot be said that a system complying with the rule of law must be just, or that analogical thinking produces just outcomes. Many genuine rules are unjust. To take one example, the fundamental problem with the system of apartheid in South Africa was emphatically not that it violated the rule of law. On the contrary, the basic features of apartheid could be made entirely consistent with the rule of law. Rules do not guarantee justice.

Similarly, a great deal of injustice has been brought about through analogical thinking. When analogies produce injustice, we have to insist that the principles or policies that undergird analogies are wrong. But nothing internal to analogical thinking will support the claim of wrongness—just like nothing internal to the rule of law will support a claim that a rule has been drawn up too narrowly or otherwise unjustly.

From this it emerges that the virtues of both rules and analogies are partial. But they are considerable. It is obvious but worth emphasizing that rules operate to constrain the exercise of arbitrary power. Rules also create a space in which people can act free from fear of the state. Recall that the ancient Goddess Justice is blindfolded; she does not and indeed cannot play favorites. By subsuming people under a single umbrella, rules make irrelevant differences that might otherwise reflect prejudice, ignorance, or invidious discrimination. While a rule is on the books, everyone subject to state power may invoke its protections and disabilities. The requirements of consistency and of a form of neutrality are vital social goods.

Like rules, analogies and case-by-case judgments force people in positions of authority to be consistent. But they allow for particularity as well as generality. In analogical thinking, many possible similarities and differences are in play. Of course analogies allow people to ask: If you have treated x that way, must you not treat me that way as well? But they also allow people to say: You treated x that way, to be sure, but my case is different; should you not treat me differently? Rules are impartial because they are blind. A comparative advantage of analogies is that they characteristically see a great deal.

When a case operates as an analogy, it has many features of a novel or a poem. It is subject to frequent revisiting, in which new or unexpected features may emerge. Great events in the past—a revolution, an assassination, a death, a marriage, the birth of a child, a war—frequently have this characteristic. Novel discoveries occur through creative rereadings in each generation. The meaning of an analogous case may be inexhaustible; in America alone, consider the lawyers' (and the public's) disputes over not just the legitimacy but also the real meaning of *Brown v. Board of Education, Roe v. Wade, Lochner v. New York*. The true lesson of the analogy is never given in advance. And in a system based on analogy, each participant in the legal system is entitled to say that when his case is investigated, it will appear that previous cases mean something quite different from what had been thought before. This is one of the most distinctive features of the common law.

We can connect this idea to an important understanding of procedural justice. That understanding entails an opportunity for each person to argue that his case should be treated differently from those already decided—that if we investigate his situation in all its detail, we will see that special treatment is warranted. If this is an ambiguous and partial virtue, it is nonetheless a familiar part of all legal systems that aspire to do justice, and no well-functioning legal system should dispense with it.

Is it better to be faced with the benefits and burdens of rules or instead to proceed with analogies? No general answer could make sense. Most tyrannical systems are tyrannical because officials are not constrained by rules. But some systems are tyrannical because citizens are not allowed to insist that officials look at the particulars of their situation and investigate whether they are relevantly different. Undoubtedly excessive rulelessness poses the more severe risks. But if what I have said here is right, excessively rule-bound judgments pose risks in more subtle and more revealing ways.

The Limits of Theory

General theories do not decide concrete cases, and case-by-case particularism has advantages over the creation and application of broad rules.

But for participants in a legal system, there are importantly common strengths to rule-bound justice and case-by-case judgments. As I have emphasized, both of them allow people who disagree on first principles to converge in their own ways on outcomes in particular cases. To decide what a rule means, it is ordinarily unnecessary to take a stand on large issues of the right or the good. To decide whether one case is analogous to another, we need not, much of the time, attempt to say much about large-scale social controversies.

The impulse to theory should hardly be disparaged. In some areas of law, we cannot think very well without embarking on a kind of conceptual ascent from the analogical process, and the conceptual ascent will require us to say broader and deeper things. Sometimes it is desirable to think about an issue both completely and deeply. Sometimes courts do think ambitiously, and their ambition can produce some of the most stirring moments in a nation's history. But judges are far from the whole of government; they are usually unelected; they face sharp time constraints; and they lack much in the way of specialized competence. They must decide many cases quickly. They must also work with each other, and contests over fundamental values—over the right and the good—can make it hard for them to do this. Like ordinary people, judges should obey a norm of mutual respect, or of reciprocity, and this norm can incline judges to avoid large-scale contests, at least when they involve people's deepest or most defining commitments.

I have suggested that how people reason is a function of the particular social role in which they find themselves, and I have tried to develop a role-specific account of public reason—an account of reasoning identifying the usual practices of participants in law. Legal reasoning—with its elaborate system of analogy, precedent-following, specification of abstract terms, rule-creation, and incompletely theorized agreement—reflects an understanding that courts are far from preeminent actors in the system of democratic deliberation. As I have emphasized throughout, it is in democratic processes, not in courtrooms, that large-scale issues are usually, and best, debated and identified. This allocation of authority embodies a time-honored understanding of political freedom; it also leads to a particular conception of legal reasoning.

Of course incompletely theorized agreements have an honored place in politics. But in democratic arenas, there is no taboo, presumptive or otherwise, on the broadest and most ambitious claims. We may thus conclude our account of legal reasoning by referring to the American Constitution itself, with its glorious opening words, "We the People"; by reflecting on the extraordinary extent to which large-scale social transformations, in America and elsewhere, have had their foundations in popular rather than judicial convictions; and by insisting that in a well-functioning deliberative democracy, the most important social commitments emerge not from courtrooms, but from the reflective judgments of a nation's citizenry.

Notes

Introduction

1. John Rawls, *Political Liberalism* (New York: Columbia University Press, 1993), pp. 133–72.

2. Joshua Cohen, A More Democratic Liberalism, 92 Mich. L. Rev. 1503, 1546 (1994).

3. See Richard A. Posner, *Economic Analysis of Law*, 4th ed. (Boston: Little, Brown, 1992). See also Ronald M. Dworkin, *Law's Empire* (Cambridge: Harvard University Press, 1986).

4. 410 U.S. 113 (1973). On the refusal to overrule Roe, see Planned Parenthood v. Casey, 112 S. Ct. 2791 (1992).

5. Breyer, The Federal Sentencing Guidelines and the Key Compromises Upon Which They Rest, 17 Hofstra L. Rev. 1, 14–19 (1988).

6. As quoted in The New Republic, June 6, 1994, p. 12.

7. Bentham was, however, quite ambiguous on the point. See Gerald J. Postema, *Bentham and the Common Law Tradition* (Oxford: Oxford University Press, 1986).

8. See Sullivan, Foreword: The Justices of Rules and Standards, 105 Harv. L. Rev. 22 (1993).

Chapter 1

1. See Posner, An Economic Theory of Criminal Law, 85 Colum. L. Rev. 1193, 1198–99 (1985).

2. Robert H. Bork, *The Tempting of America: The Political Seduction of the Law* (New York: Free Press, 1990).

3. Jeremy Bentham, *Collected Works of Jeremy Bentham*, J. H. Burns ed. (London: Clarendon Press, 1968), p. 206.

4. See John Rawls, *A Theory of Justice* (Cambridge: Harvard University Press, 1971), pp. 19–22, 46–51; Rawls, The Independence of Moral Theory, 47 Proceedings and Addresses of the American Philosophical Association 5 (1974–75). See also Henry S. Richardson, *Practical Reasoning About Final Ends* (Cambridge: Cambridge University Press, 1994).

5. Wechsler, Toward Neutral Principles of Constitutional Law, 73 Harv. L. Rev. 1 (1959), is the most notable example. The search for reflective equilibrium is criticized as unacceptably dependent on existing intuitions in, among other places, Richard B. Brandt, *A Theory of the Good and the Right* (New York: Oxford University Press, 1979), ch. 1; P. Singer, Sidgwick and Reflective Equilibrium, 58 The Monist 490 (1974); R. M. Hare, Rawls's Theory of Justice, 23 Phil. Q. (1973). Related criticisms are made in Raz, The Claims of Reflective Equilibrium, 25 Inquiry 307 (1982).

6. 347 U.S. 483 (1954).

7. 410 U.S. 113 (1973).

8. See Joseph Raz, *Practical Reasons and Norms* (Princeton: Princeton University Press, 1990), pp. 59–62; Frederick Schauer, *Playing by the Rules: A Philosophical Examination of Rule-Based Decision Making in Law and in Life* (New York: Oxford University Press, 1991), pp. 4–5.

9. Heckler v. Campbell, 461 U.S. 458 (1983).

10. See Lochner v. New York, 198 U.S. 5 (1905).

11. I take the examples in this paragraph from Schauer, Formalism, 97 Yale L.J. 509 (1988).

12. Terminiello v. Chicago, 337 U.S. 1, 16 (1949) (Jackson, J., dissenting).

13. See, e.g., Kaplow, Rules and Standards: An Economic Analysis, 42 Duke L.J. 189 (1992); Sullivan, Foreword: The Justices of Rules and Standards, 105 Harv. L. Rev. 22 (1993).

14. Act Nov. 27, 1973, P.L. 93–159, at 1, 87 Stat. 627 (1973).

15. See Ronald Dworkin, *Taking Rights Seriously* (Cambridge: Harvard University Press, 1976).

Chapter 2

1. Lochner v. New York, 198 U.S. 48, 69 (1908) (Holmes, J., dissenting).

2. See, e.g., Charles Fried, *Contract as Promise: A Theory of Contractual Obligation* (Cambridge: Harvard University Press, 1981); Ronald M. Dworkin, *Law's Empire* (Cambridge: Harvard University Press, 1986).

3. Of course concurring opinions are common, sometimes because an incompletely theorized agreement is possible on a result without being possible on a rationale, and sometimes because one judge wants to theorize an issue more (or less) deeply than do others. Sometimes the existence of a concurring opinion can compromise rule of law values by making it hard to form expectations; sometimes concurring opinions raise issues of collegiality, since authors of majority opinions are not thrilled to find separate concurrences.

4. See John Rawls, *Political Liberalism* (New York: Columbia University Press, 1993), pp. 16–17, 50.

5. This is the goal of the equal protection argument. See Cass R. Sunstein, *The Partial Constitution* (Cambridge: Harvard University Press, 1993), ch. 9.

6. See Planned Parenthood v. Casey, 112 S. Ct. 2791 (1992). Arrow's Impossibility Theorem, see Kenneth Arrow, *Social Choice and Individual Values*, 2d ed. (New York: Wiley, 1962), raises important problems for coherence theories in law. I cannot discuss those problems in detail here, but it is worthwhile to note that on a multimember judicial body, there may be serious cycling problems, in which, paradoxically, result A is favored over result B, which is favored over result C, which is (and here is the paradox) favored over result A; this may happen because coalitions can be mustered for the inconsistent outcomes. Alternatively, decisions may turn, arbitrarily, on the order in which issues happen to arise ("path dependence"). A strong theory of stare decisis, combined with a commitment to analogical thinking, may alleviate some of the cycling problems and thus produce greater stability in law, but it will simultaneously aggravate the problems of path dependence. The point suggests that it will be difficult to achieve real coherence through decentralized, multimember courts. A system built on analogical reasoning aspires to less and can diminish cycling; but the problem of path dependence can result in a degree of arbitrariness. Much more work remains to be done on this subject.

7. I borrow here from Joseph Raz, "The Relevance of Coherence," in *Ethics in the Public Domain: Essays in the Morality of Law and Politics* (Oxford: Oxford University Press, 1994), p. 261.

8. See Amartya K. Sen, *Commodities and Capabilities* (Amsterdam: North-Holland, 1985).

9. I am putting to one side the questions raised by "comprehensive views," see Rawls, supra note 4.

10. See Gerald N. Rosenberg, *The Hollow Hope: Can Courts Bring About Social Change?* (Chicago: University of Chicago Press, 1991).

11. Examples are offered in R. Shep Melnick, *Regulation and the Courts: The Case of the Clean Air Act* (Washington, D.C.: Brookings Institution, 1983), and Donald Horowitz, *The Courts and Social Policy* (Washington, D.C.: Brookings Institution, 1977). The point is described from the theoretical point of view in Lon Fuller, The Forms and Limits of Adjudication, 92 Harv. L. Rev. 353 (1978), and Joseph Raz, The Inner Logic of the Law, in *Ethics in the Public Domain*, supra note 7, at 224.

12. This is the vision of judicial review in Bruce A. Ackerman, *We the People, vol. 1: Foundations* (Cambridge: Harvard University Press, 1991). Note that it differs dramatically from the understanding in Ronald Dworkin, *Law's Empire*, in the sense that Ackerman insists that large-scale principles have sources in actual judgments of "we the people." There is, however, a commonality between Ackerman and Dworkin in the sense that both see the use of such principles as a large part of the Court's work. It is along that dimension that I am doubting both of their accounts.

13. Rawls, supra note 4, at 133–72. See also John Rawls, Reply to Habermas, 92 J. Phil. 132 (1995).

14. See Rawls, supra note 4, at 43–45.

15. Id. at 46.

16. Rawls, Reply to Habermas, supra note 13, at 134.

17. Dworkin, supra note 2, at 224.

18. Dworkin is not entirely clear on the relationship between fit and good moral theory. Hercules will not insist on what he sees as the best moral theory if it cannot fit the cases at all, and certainly he will exclude an outlier case if, in so doing, he can knit all other cases together into a morally compelling whole. But it is not clear to what extent fit is sacrificed for the sake of theory, and vice versa. For present purposes I put these complexities to one side and simply note that the supreme lawyerly virtue of integrity is connected with achievement of principled consistency among similar and dissimilar cases.

19. Thus Dworkin writes about constitutional interpretation: "The Constitution is foundational of other law, so Hercules' interpretation of the document as a whole, and of its abstract clauses, must be foundational as well. . . . [I]t must be a justification drawn from the most philosophical reaches of political theory. . . . In constitutional theory philosophy is closer to the surface of the argument and, if the theory is good, explicit in it." Supra note 2, at 380. These are points that I deny here. In fact Dworkin's account of the judicial role says very little about the various fact-finding, theory-building, and electoral weaknesses of judges, and about judges' own knowledge of their weaknesses, even though much of judge-made law is based on that knowledge. This seems to me a major gap in Dworkin's view. I should say, however, that I am not sure to what extent an appreciation of incompletely theorized agreements counts as a criticism of Dworkin, since Dworkin presents Hercules as a thought experiment, and it is unclear to what extent Hercules' approach is supposed to be an ideal for real-world judges. To my knowledge, Dworkin has not discussed the question of appropriate levels of abstraction in legal justification, though he does urge, as I would not, a kind of merger of constitutional law and political philosophy.

20. See Alexander M. Bickel, *The Least Dangerous Branch: The Supreme Court at the Bar of Politics* (New Haven: Yale University Press, 1986).

21. Dworkin, supra note 2, at 265.

22. See Henry Sidgwick, *The Methods of Ethics*, 7th ed. (New York: Dover, 1966), pp. 96–104.

23. "[T]he resulting code seems an accidental aggregate of precepts, which stands in need of some rational synthesis." Sidgwick, supra note 22, at 102.

24. See Richard A. Posner, *Economic Analysis of Law*, 4th ed. (Boston: Little, Brown, 1992); see also the discussion of the law of tort in Dworkin, supra note 2.

25. In Rawls's understanding of the search for reflective equilibrium, we consult "our considered convictions at all levels of generality; no one level, say that of abstract principle or that of particular judgments in particular cases, is viewed as foundational. They all may have an initial credibility." Supra note 4, at 8.

26. "One's ability to recognize instances of cruelty, patience, meanness, and courage, for example, far outstrips one's capacity for verbal definition of those notions." Paul M. Churchland, *The Engine of Reason, the Seat of the Soul* (Cambridge: MIT Press, 1995), p. 145; see also id. at 144, 293.

27. See, e.g., Continental TV v. GTE Sylvania, 433 U.S. 36, 56–59 (1977).

28. The best example is the law of free speech. See Whitney v. California, 274 U.S. 357, 372, 375–78 (1927) (Brandeis, J., dissenting); Abrams v. U.S., 250 U.S. 616, 624, 630–31 (Holmes, J., dissenting). Note, however, that even here, no

unitary theory of free speech is offered, and nothing very much like a philosophical account appears in the relevant opinions.

29. See Gordon S. Wood, *The Radicalism of the American Revolution* (New York: Knopf, 1991), p. 27.

30. See Cass R. Sunstein, *The Partial Constitution* (Cambridge: Harvard University Press, 1993), ch. 2.

31. See Geoffrey R. Stone, Louis M. Seidman, Cass R. Sunstein, and Mark V. Tushnet, *Constitutional Law* (Boston: Little, Brown, 1991), ch. 6.

32. Thus Jefferson said that turbulence is "productive of good. It prevents the degeneracy of government, and nourishes a general attention to . . . public affairs. I hold . . . that a little rebellion now and then is a good thing." Letter to Madison (Jan. 30, 1798), reprinted in *The Portable Thomas Jefferson*, Merrill D. Peterson ed. (New York: Viking Press, 1975).

33. See Henry Hart and Albert Sacks, *The Legal Process* (New York: Foundation Press, 1994).

34. "The Forum of Principle," in Ronald Dworkin, *A Matter of Principle* (Cambrige: Harvard University Press, 1986).

35. Note, however, that the grounds for such agreements are diverse and that it is possible to accept some while rejecting others; in that sense an incompletely theorized judgment in support of incompletely theorized agreements is certainly imaginable.

Chapter 3

1. Paul M. Churchland, *The Engine of Reason, the Seat of the Soul* (Cambridge: MIT Press, 1995), p. 278.

2. See Keith James Holyoak and Paul Thagaard, *Mental Leaps: Analogy in Creative Thought* (Cambridge: MIT Press, 1995).

3. What I am describing in the text is a form of inductive analogy, in the sense that it depends on predictive conjectures about an unknown case that are based on but go beyond stated premises. Inductive analogy is different from the usual case of induction, which occurs by enumeration. An example of nonanalogical inductive reasoning is: I have seen 100 German shepherds, and they are all gentle with children. From this I infer that the latest German shepherd is also gentle with children.

For the most part I deal here with analogical reasoning that is roughly propositional in the sense that should emerge from the text. I do not discuss the growing work dealing with analogy and metaphor at nonpropositional levels. See George Lakoff, *Women, Fire and Dangerous Things: What Categories Reveal About the Mind* (Chicago: University of Chicago Press, 1987); Mark Johnson, "Some Constraints on Embodied Analogical Reasoning," in *Analogical Reasoning*, David H. Helman ed. (Boston: Kluwer, 1988), pp. 25, 39: "[A]nalogies cannot be understood as propositional or conceptual mechanisms for reflecting on already-determinate experiences; rather, we can actually speak of them as *constitutive* of our experience, because they are partially constitutive of our understanding, our mode of experiencing our world. Analogy is a basic means by which form, pattern, and connection emerge in our understanding and are then articulated in our reflective cognition and in our language."

4. See Brandenburg v. Ohio, 395 U.S. 444 (1969).

5. See Dandridge v. Williams, 397 U.S. 471 (1970).

6. Brandenburg v. Ohio, 395 U.S. 444 (1969).

7. I am not speaking here of the use of analogy in creative leaps in science, where a different process is at work. See Churchland, supra note 1, at 271–86.

8. See id.; Douglas R. Hofstadter, *Fluid Concepts and Creative Analogies: Computer Models and the Fundamental Mechanisms of Thought* (New York: Basic Books, 1995).

9. Holmes, Codes and the Arrangements of Law, 44 Harv. L. Rev. 725 (1931) (reprinted from 5 Am. L. Rev. 11 (1870)).

10. See Posner, Legal Reasoning from the Top Down and from the Bottom Up: The Question of Unenumerated Constitutional Rights, 59 U. Chi. L. Rev. 433 (1992); see also Jon Elster, *Local Justice: How Institutions Allocate Scarce Goods and Necessary Burdens* (New York: Russell Sage Foundation, 1992), pp. 189–94 (distinguishing between "hard" and "soft" theories in a similar way). A valuable discussion is Henry S. Richardson, *Practical Reasoning About Final Ends* (Cambridge: Cambridge University Press, 1994), pp. 165–90.

11. See Churchland, supra note 1, at 286–94, describing moral argument and cognition as founded on prototypical cases. (See also Gilboa and Schmeidler, Case-based Decision Theory, 110 Q.J. Economics 605 (1995).

Interesting issues of collective choice lurk in the background here. Important problems of cycling, strategic behavior, and path dependence may arise in multi-member bodies containing people with divergent rationales, each of whom wants to make her own rationale part of law. See Kenneth Arrow, *Social Choice and Individual Values*, 2d ed. (New York: Wiley, 1962). There may also be complex bargaining issues as some officials or judges seek to implement a broad theory as part of the outcome, while others seek a narrow theory, and still others are undecided between the two. Cf. Douglas Baird et al., *Game Theory and the Law* (Cambridge: Harvard University Press, 1994), ch. 1. These important issues are beyond the scope of the present discussion, though it would be most illuminating to have a better grasp, theoretical and empirical, on the sorts of bargaining games that occur as officials and judges decide on the scope of the theory to accompany an outcome.

12. See, e.g., *On Metaphor*, Sheldon Sacks ed. (Chicago: University of Chicago Press, 1988).

13. See Davidson, "What Metaphors Mean," in id. (challenging this conception of metaphor); Johnson, supra note 3, at 25 (claiming that metaphor is a kind of analogical process); Gentner, Falkenhainer, and Sokrstad, "Viewing Metaphor as Analogy," in id. at 171.

14. William James, "The Meaning of Truth," in *Pragmatism and the Meaning of Truth*, A. J. Ayer ed. (Cambridge: Harvard University Press, 1978), pp. 136, 302.

15. 274 U.S. 200 (1927).

16. See Edward Levi, *An Introduction to Legal Reasoning* (Chicago: University of Chicago Press, 1947).

17. Id. at 4–6.

18. Richard Posner, *Overcoming Law* (Cambridge: Harvard University Press, 1995).

19. Petermann v. Local 396, 344 P.2d 25, 26 (Cal. 1959).

20. Svenko v. Kroger, 245 NW2d 151, 153–54 (Mich. 1976).

21. Palmateer v. Kroger Co., 245 NW2d 151 (Ill. 1976); Monge v. Beebe Rubber Co., 316 A.2d 589 (NH 1974).

22. See Richard A. Posner, *Economic Analysis of Law*, 4th ed. (Boston: Little, Brown, 1992); Ronald Dworkin, *Law's Empire* Cambridge: Harvard University Press, 1986).

23. See Strauss, Common Law Constitutionalism, University of Chicago Law Review (1996).

24. United States v. O'Brien, 391 U.S. 367 (1968).

25. The best discussion is Strauss, supra note 23; see also Wellington, Common Law Rules and Constitutional Double Standards, 83 Yale L.J. 221 (1973).

26. Hart makes the same point in his discussion of the distinction between law via examples and law via rules. See H. L. A. Hart, *The Concept of Law*, 2d ed. (New York: Oxford University Press, 1994), pp. 127–29. Consider especially the suggestion that "the authoritative general language in which a rule is expressed may guide only in an uncertain way much as an authoritative example does. The sense that the language of a rule will enable us simply to pick out easily recognizable instances, at this point gives way; subsumption and the drawing of a syllogistic conclusion no longer characterize the nerve of the reasoning involved in determining what is the right thing to do. Instead, the language of the rule seems now only to mark out an authoritative example, namely that constituted by the plain case. This may be used in much the same way as a precedent. . . . [A]ll that the person called upon to answer can do is to consider (as does one who makes use of a precedent) whether the present case resembles the plain case "sufficiently" in "relevant" respects." Id. at 127.

27. Cf. Ludwig Wittgenstein, *Philosophical Investigations* (New York: Macmillan, 1953), p. 83: "But if a person has not yet got the concepts, I shall teach him to use the words by means of examples and by practice.—And when I do this I do not communicate less to him than I know myself." See also Churchland, supra note 1, which uses cognitive science to suggest the same result.

28. McBoyle v. U.S., 283 U.S. 25, 28 (1931).

29. See Churchland, supra note 1; Massimo Piattelli-Palmarini, *Inevitable Illusions: How Mistakes of Reason Rule Our Minds* (New York: Wiley, 1994).

30. See Piattelli-Palmarini, supra note 29, at 152.

31. Surrogate Parenting Assn. v. Kentucky, 704 SW2d 209 (1986).

32. Smith v. U.S., 113 S. Ct. 2050 (1993).

33. United Steelworkers v. Kaiser Aluminum, 443 U.S. 193 (1979).

34. This is Dworkin's suggestion. See supra note 22, at ch. 7.

35. On this score reasoning in science is no different from reasoning elsewhere. Both depend on a certain degree of consensus. The perceived differences between scientific and other thought may stem partly from the fact that we tend to compare ethical or legal issues where judgments are contested (affirmative action, the death penalty) with scientific issues where matters are settled (the earth goes around the sun, dropped objects will fall). This is probably misleading; we might do better to compare the settled scientific judgments with the settled ethical ones (slavery is wrong, purposeless human suffering cannot be justified).

36. This sort of attack on analogy is traceable to Plato and to ancient attacks on "casuistry." See Albert Jonson and Stephen Toulmin, *The Abuse of Casuistry* (Berkeley: University of California Press, 1991).

37. See Koppelman, Why Discrimination Against Lesbians and Gay Men Is Sex Discrimination, 69 NYU L. Rev. 197 (1994); Law, Homosexuality and the Social Meaning of Gender, 1988 Wisc. L. Rev. 187.

38. Joseph Raz, in *The Authority of Law: Essays on Law and Morality* (Oxford: Oxford University Press, 1979), defends analogical thinking as a response to the problem of "partial reform," that is, the risk that piecemeal reforms will fail to serve their own purposes because public or private actors will adapt (as in the idea that the minimum wage decreases employment). In Raz's view, analogical thinking responds to this risk by ensuring that any "new rule is a conservative one, that it does not introduce new discordant and conflicting purposes or value into the law, that its purpose and the values it promotes are already served by existing rules." Id. at 204. There is truth in this claim, but if the purpose or values are described in certain ways, the analogical process may lead in highly nonconservative directions, with no abuse to analogies themselves.

39. Jonathan Swift, *Gulliver's Travels*, IV, 5, in *The Writings of Jonathan Swift* (New York: Norton, 1973), p. 216.

40. See, e.g., Posner, supra note 22.

41. Richard A. Posner, *Overcoming Law* (Cambridge: Harvard University Press, 1995).

42. See Charles Taylor, "The Diversity of Goods," in *Philosophy and the Human Sciences*, Charles Taylor ed. (New York: Cambridge University Press, 1985), pp. 230, 243; Sen, Plural Utility, 81 Proc. Aristotelian Soc. 193 (1981); Richardson, supra note 10.

43. This is of course an Aristotelian point. See Aristotle, Nicomachean Ethics, D. Ross trans. (J. L. Ackrill and J. O. Urmson revision, 1980), pp. 149–53; see also Oliver Wendell Holmes, *The Essential Holmes*, Richard A. Posner ed. (Chicago: University of Chicago Press, 1992), p. 58: "After a sociological riot I read Aristotle's Ethics with some pleasure. The eternal, universal, wise, good man. He is much in advance of ordinary Christian morality with its slapdash universals (Never tell a lie. Sell all thou hast and give to the poor etc.) He has the ideals of altruism, and yet understands that life is painting a picture not doing a sum, that specific cases can't be decided by general rules, and that everything is a question of degree."

44. See Scanlon, A Theory of Free Expression, 1 Phil. & Pub. Aff. 204 (1962); Alexander Meiklejohn, *Free Speech and Its Relation to Self-Government* (New York: Vintage, 1948); Bork, Neutral Principles and Some First Amendment Problems, 47 Ind. L.J. 1 (1971). I try to defend this view in Cass R. Sunstein, *Democracy and the Problem of Free Speech* (New York: Free Press, 1993).

45. Scanlon, Freedom of Speech and Categories of Expression, 40 U. Pitt. L. Rev. 519 (1979).

Chapter 4

1. I oversimplify. See Kahan, Lenity and Federal Common Law Crimes, 1994 S. Ct. Rev. 345.

2. 405 U.S. 156 (1972).

3. See Jon Elster, *Solomonic Judgments: Studies in the Limitations of Rationality*

(Cambridge: Cambridge University Press, 1989), citing an unpublished paper by Hungdad Chiu. England too had analogical crimes. This tradition was of course rejected in the United States, or at least this is the official story. It is illuminatingly questioned in Kahan, supra note 1.

4. I claim little originality here. See Lon L. Fuller, *The Morality of Law* (New Haven: Yale University Press, 1964), and Joseph Raz, *The Authority of Law: Essays on Law and Morality* (New York: Oxford University Press, 1979), pp. 213–24.

5. Bowen v. Georgetown Univ. Hosp., 488 U.S. 204 (1988).

6. Letter to Thomas Jefferson, October 24, 1787.

7. See Joseph Raz, *Practical Reason and Norms*, 2d ed. (Princeton: Princeton University Press, 1990).

8. Cf. John Searle, *The Construction of Social Reality* (New York: Free Press, 1995); Rawls, Two Concepts of Rules, 45 Phil. Rev. 3 (1955). The idea is illuminatingly criticized in Raz, supra note 7, at 108–11.

9. See Searle, supra note 8.

10. See Stephen Holmes, *Passions and Constraint: Essays on the Theory of Liberal Democracy* (Chicago: University of Chicago Press, 1995).

11. Consider as well evidence that American courts tend, in the social welfare area, to insist on individualized assessments of claimants, and thus to invalidate regulations that make categorical judgments about when income is actually available to recipients. Perhaps those who issued the regulations were insufficiently attuned to the rigidity and inaccuracy of rules. But perhaps the courts, encountering a particular case that confounded the rules, are insufficiently attuned to the costs of individuation and hence to the aggregate benefits of ruleness despite the existence of errors in particular cases. R. Shep Melnick, *Between the Lines: Interpreting Welfare Rights* (Washington, D.C.: Brookings Institution, 1994).

12. Dennis v. U.S., 341 U.S. 494 (1951).

13. See Frederick Schauer, *Playing by the Rules: A Philosophical Examination of Rule-Based Decision Making in Law and in Life* (New York: Oxford University Press, 1991), pp. 136–37.

14. See Scalia, The Rule of Law Is a Law of Rules, 56 U. Chi. L. Rev. 1175, 1185 (1989).

15. 336 U.S. 106, 116 (1941) (Jackson, J., concurring).

16. See also Raz, supra note 4, at 219–23.

17. Friedrich A. von Hayek, *The Constitution of Liberty* (Chicago: University of Chicago Press, 1960), pp. 220–35.

18. Horwitz, The Rule of Law: An Unqualified Human Good? 86 Yale L.J. 561 (1977).

Chapter 5

1. This is a version of an argument fueled by legal realism. For a good discussion, see Kennedy, Legal Formality, 2 J. Legal Stud. 335 (1973).

2. Cabell v. Markham, 148 F2d 737, 739 (2d Cir. 1945).

3. See Waismann, "Verifiability," in *Essays on Logic and Language: First Series*, Antony Flew ed. (Oxford: Blackwell, 1951), pp. 117–44.

4. See *Interpreting Statutes: A Comparative Study*, D. Neil McCormick and Robert S. Summers eds. (Aldershot, Eng.; Brookfield, Vt.: Dartmouth, 1991).

5. 143 U.S. 457 (1892).

6. Frederick Schauer, *Playing by the Rules: A Philosophical Examination of Rule-Based Decision Making in Law and in Life* (New York: Oxford University Press, 1991), pp. 196–208.

7. See H.L.A. Hart, "Postscript," *The Concept of Law*, 2d ed. (New York: Oxford University Press, 1994).

8. See Schauer, supra note 6, at 94, distinguishing between substantive justifications and rule-generating justifications.

9. See Katherine Montgomery Hunter, *Doctors' Stories: The Narrative Structure of Medical Knowledge* (Princeton: Princeton University Press, 1991).

10. 428 U.S. 280 (1976).

11. Thus J. S. Mill: "But in the complicated affairs of life, and still more in those of states and societies, rules cannot be relied on. . . . By a wise practitioner, therefore, rules of conduct will only be considered as provisional. Being made for the most numerous cases, or for those of most ordinary occurrence, they point out the manner in which it will be least perilous to act, where time or means do not exist for analysing the actual circumstances of the case, or where we cannot trust our judgement in evaluating them. But they do not at all supersede the necessity of going through (when circumstances permit) the scientific process requisite for framing a rule from the data of the particular case before us." *The Logic of the Social Sciences*, A. J. Ayer, ed. (London: Duckworth, 1987), p. 137.

Thus Dewey, Logical Method and Law, 10 Cornell L. Q. 17 (1924): "I should not hesitate to assert that the sanctification of ready-made antecedent universal principles as methods of thinking is the chief obstacle to the kind of thinking which is the indispensable prerequisite of steady, secure and intelligent social reforms in general and social advance in particular."

Thus Aristotle's famous discussion of the problem: "[T]here are some things about which it is not possible to pronounce rightly in general terms; therefore in cases where it is necessary to make a general pronouncement, but impossible to do so rightly, the law takes account of the majority of cases, though not unaware that in this way errors are made. . . . This is the essential nature of equity; it is a rectification of law in so far as law is defective on account of its generality. This in fact is also the reason why everything is not regulated by law: it is because there are some cases that no law can be framed to cover, so that they require a special ordinance. An irregular object has a rule of irregular shape, like the leaden rule of Lesbian architecture: just as this rule is not rigid but is adapted to the shape of the stone, so the ordinance is framed to fit the circumstances." *The Ethics of Aristotle*, J.A.K. Thomson, trans. (New York: Penguin, 1976), p. 200. See also Martha C. Nussbaum, *The Fragility of Goodness* (Cambridge: Cambridge University Press, 1986), pp. 290–317.

12. Eugene Bardach and Robert Kagan, *Going by the Book: The Problem of Regulatory Unreasonableness* (New York: Brookings Institution, 1982).

13. Pound, The Scope and Purpose of Sociological Jurisprudence, 25 Harv. L. Rev. 489, 515 (1912).

14. John Dewey, supra note 11, at 17.

15. Anatole France, *The Red Lilly* (New York: Modern Library, 1917), p. 75.

16. 428 U.S. 280 (1976).

17. David Schoenbrod, *Power Without Responsibility: How Congress Abuses the People* (New Haven: Yale University Press, 1993), p. 111.

18. Charles Lund Black, Jr., "Law as an Art," in *The Humane Imagination* (Woodbridge Conn.: Oxbow Press, 1986). See also Kahan, Lenity and Federal Common Law Crimes, 1994 S. Ct. Rev. 345.

19. See Cass R. Sunstein, *After the Rights Revolution: Reinventing the Regulatory State* (Cambridge: Harvard University Press, 1990), ch. 4.

20. Goldberg v. Kelly, 397 U.S. 254 (1970).

21. See Robert M. Cover, *Justice Accused: Antislavery and the Judicial Process* (New Haven: Yale University Press, 1970).

22. Jeremy Bentham, On Laws in General XV, H.L.A. Hart ed. (Oxford: Oxford University Press, 1970), p. 12 n. 1. See the discussion in Gerald Postema, *Bentham and the Common Law Tradition* (Oxford: Oxford University Press, 1986), pp. 280–85.

23. Paul M. Churchland, *The Engine of Reason, the Seat of the Soul* (Cambridge: MIT Press, 1995), p. 293.

Chapter 6

1. See Schauer, Giving Reasons, 47 Stan. L. Rev. 633 (1995), on which I draw thoughout this section.

2. Jacobellis v. Ohio, 378 U.S. 184, 197 (1964) (Stewart, J., concurring).

3. Logical Method and Law, 10 Cornell L.Q. 17, 17 (1924).

4. See the discussion of how the capacity for verbal description is outstripped by sensory analysis in Paul M. Churchland, *The Engine of Reason, the Seat of the Soul* (Cambridge: MIT Press, 1995), pp. 21, 29. See also the remarks on moral judgment in id. at 144–45.

5. Doris Kearns Goodwin, *No Ordinary Time: Franklin and Eleanor Roosevelt: The Home Front in World War II* (New York: Simon and Schuster, 1994), p. 193.

6. 408 U.S. 238 (1972).

7. 428 U.S. 280 (1976).

8. Matthews v. Eldridge, 424 U.S. 319 (1976).

9. See Cleveland Board of Educ. v. Lafleur, 414 U.S. 632 (1974).

10. See Elizabeth Anderson, *Value in Ethics and Economics* (Cambridge: Harvard University Press, 1993); Michael M. Stocker, *Plural and Conflicting Values* (Oxford: Clarendon Press; New York: Oxford University Press, 1990).

11. Consider John Dewey's complaint that utilitarianism "never questioned the idea of a fixed, final and supreme end. . . . Such a point of view treats concrete activities and specific interests not as worth while in themselves, or as constituents of happiness, but as mere external means to getting pleasures. The upholders of the old tradition could therefore easily accuse utilitarianism of making not only virtue but art, poetry, religion and the state into mere servile means of attaining sensuous enjoyment. . . . The idea of a fixed and single end lying beyond the diversity of human needs and acts rendered utilitarianism incapable of being

an adequate representation of the modern spirit." *Reconstruction in Philosophy* (New York: Holt, 1920), pp. 143–45.

12. More detailed discussion can be found in Cass R. Sunstein, *Free Markets and Social Justice* (New York: Oxford University Press, forthcoming); Sunstein, Incommensurability and Valuation in Law, 92 Mich. L. Rev. 779 (1993).

Chapter 7

1. See Jon Elster, *Nuts and Bolts for the Social Sciences* (New York: Cambridge University Press, 1989), making this claim much more generally.

2. See Gerald Postema, *Bentham and the Common Law Tradition* (Oxford: Oxford University Press, 1986). An excellent discussion is Dan-Cohen, Decision Rules and Conduct Rules: Acoustic Separation in the Criminal Law, 97 Harv. L. Rev. 625 (1984).

3. I borrow in this section from the instructive discussion in Mortimer R. Kadish and Sanford H. Kadish, *Discretion to Disobey: A Study of Lawful Departures from Legal Rules* (Stanford: Stanford University Press, 1973).

4. See Alexander Bickel, *The Least Dangerous Branch: The Supreme Court at the Bar of Politics* (New Haven: Yale University Press, 1986). I am grateful to Michael McConnell for helpful discussion of this point.

5. 381 U.S. 479 (1965).

6. 478 U.S. 186 (1986).

7. Related discussion can be found in Friedrich A. von Hayek, *The Constitution of Liberty* (Chicago: University of Chicago Press, 1960), pp. 220–35, distinguishing between "laws" and "commands." This is a highly illuminating but also confused discussion; I have drawn on some of Hayek's ideas but tried to reduce the level of confusion.

8. Hence the Coase theorem will sometimes be wrong insofar as it predicts the initial allocation of the entitlement will not affect outcomes. See Sunstein, Endogenous Preferences, Environmental Law, 22 J. Legal Stud. 217 (1993); Cass R. Sunstein, *Free Markets and Social Justice* (New York: Oxford University Press, forthcoming).

9. See the instructive discussion of how cooperation must precede competition in Jules L. Coleman, *Risks and Wrongs* (New York: Cambridge University Press, 1992), pp. 60–62. This was an important theme in the New Deal era. For general discussion, see Cass R. Sunstein, *The Partial Constitution* (Cambridge: Harvard University Press, 1993), pp. 45–62.

10. Some qualifications emerge from Robert C. Ellickson, *Order Without Law* (Cambridge: Harvard University Press, 1992).

11. See Friedrich A. von Hayek, *The Road to Serfdom* (London: Routledge, 1944), pp. 38–39: "The functioning of a competition . . . depends, above all, on the existence of an appropriate legal system. . . . In no system that could be rationally defended would the state just do nothing. An effective competitive system needs an intelligently designed and continuously adjusted legal framework as much as any other." See also Amartya Sen, *Poverty and Famines: An Essay on Entitlement and Deprivation* (New York: Oxford University Press, 1981), pp. 165–66: "Finally, the focus on entitlement has the effect of emphasizing legal

rights. Other relevant factors, for example market forces, can be seen as operating *through* a system of legal relations (ownership rights, contractual obligations, legal exchanges, etc.). The law stands between food availability and food entitlement. Starvation deaths can reflect legality with a vengeance."

12. See Coleman, supra note 9, at 62.

13. See Hayek, supra note 11; Richard Epstein, *Simple Rules for a Complex World* (Cambridge: Harvard University Press, 1995).

14. See Coase, The Federal Communications Commission, 2 J. Law & Econ. 1 (1959).

15. I try to support this view in Cass R. Sunstein, *Democracy and the Problem of Free Speech* (New York: Free Press, 1993).

16. I draw in this section on the extremely illuminating discussion in P. S. Atiyah and Robert S. Summers, *Form and Substance in Anglo-American Law: A Comparative Study of Legal Reasoning, Legal Theory and Legal Institutions* (New York: Oxford University Press, 1987).

17. See William N. Eskridge, Jr., *Dynamic Statutory Interpretation* (Cambridge: Harvard University Press, 1994).

Chapter 8

1. See Andrei Marmor, *Interpretation and Legal Theory* (Oxford: Oxford University Press, 1991), drawing on the work of Joseph Raz, especially *The Authority of Law: Essays on Law and Morality* (Oxford: Oxford University Press, 1979). In this chapter, however, I largely bracket the precise relationship between authority and lawmaker intention, a topic taken up by Marmor and in ongoing work by Raz.

2. See Benjamin Cardozo, *The Nature of the Judicial Process* (New Haven: Yale University Press, 1960); Ronald Dworkin, *Law's Empire* (Cambridge: Harvard University Press, 1986); Richard Posner, *The Problems of Jurisprudence* (Cambridge: Harvard University Press, 1991).

3. See Robert Bork, *The Tempting of America* (New York: Free Press, 1990).

4. See Lessig, Understanding Changed Readings: Fidelity and Theory, 47 Stan. L. Rev. 395 (1995); Lessig, Fidelity in Translation, 71 Tex. L. Rev. 1165 (1993).

5. Some hard originalists try to handle this problem by claiming that unless the original view unambiguously condemns an existing law, the law should be upheld. This claim would indeed lead to more rule-bound constitutional law, but it depends on a political argument, not a historical one, and once it is evaluated as such, it seem unacceptable, for reasons that are explored below.

6. Dworkin, supra note 2, at 375.

7. See Gerald N. Rosenberg, *The Hollow Hope: Can Courts Bring About Social Change?* (Chicago: University of Chicago Press, 1991).

8. Id. at ch. 6.

9. See Sager, Fair Measure: The Status of Underenforced Constitutional Norms, 91 Harv. L. Rev. 1212 (1978).

10. See Strauss, Common Law Constitutionalism (forthcoming).

11. See John Hart Ely, *Democracy and Distrust: A Theory of Judicial Review*

(Cambridge: Harvard University Press, 1981); Cass R. Sunstein, *The Partial Constitution* (Cambridge: Harvard University Press, 1993), pp. 142–61.

12. See Sunstein, supra note 11, at 270–85.

13. 448 U.S. 607 (1980).

14. Cabell v. Markham, 148 F2d 737, 739 (2d Cir. 1945).

15. See Schauer, The Coordinating Function of Plain Meaning, 1994 Supreme Court Rev. 231.

16. See Breyer, On the Uses of Legislative History in Interpreting Statutes, 65 S. Calif. L. Rev. 845 (1992).

17. See *Interpreting Statutes: A Comparative Study*, D. Neil McCormick and Robert S. Summers, eds. (Aldershot, Eng.; Brookfield, Vt.: Dartmouth, 1991).

18. See Llewellyn, Remarks on the Theory of Appellate Decisions and the Rules or Canons About How Statutes Are To Be Construed, 3 Vand. L. Rev. 395 (1950).

19. See, for an illuminating catalogue, William N. Eskridge, Jr., *Dynamic Statutory Interpretation* (Cambridge: Harvard University Press, 1994), Appendix 3, at 323–33.

20. I try to do this in Cass R. Sunstein, *After the Rights Revolution: Reinventing the Regulatory State* (Cambridge: Harvard University Press, 1990), and Sunstein, Interpreting Statutes in the Regulatory State, 103 Harv. L. Rev. 405 (1989).

Index

Printed in the United States
745500003B

9 780195 118049